Language, Ideology and

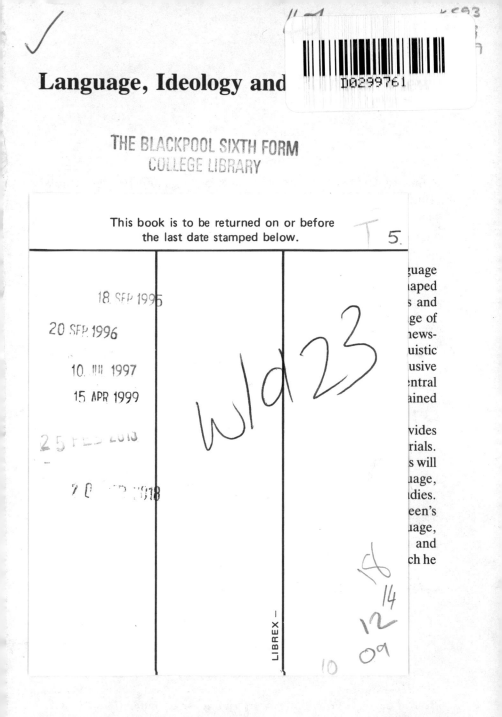

This book is to be returned on or before
the last date stamped below.

18. SEP 1995

20 SEP 1996

10. JUL 1997

15 APR 1999

25 FEB 2013

7 0 ... 918

juage
maped
s and
ge of
news-
uistic
usive
entral
ained

vides
rials.
s will
uage,
dies.
een's
uage,
and
ch he

LIBREX —

The INTERFACE Series

A linguist deaf to the poetic function of language and a literary scholar indifferent to linguistic problems and unconversant with linguistic methods, are equally flagrant anachronisms. – Roman Jakobson

This statement, made over twenty-five years ago, is no less relevant today, and 'flagrant anachronisms' still abound. The aim of the INTERFACE series is to examine topics at the 'interface' of language studies and literary criticism and in so doing to build bridges between these traditionally divided disciplines.

Already published in the series:

The Series Editor
Ronald Carter is Professor of Modern English Language at the University of Nottingham and was National Coordinator of the 'Language in the National Curriculum' Project (LINC) from 1989 to 1992.

Language, Ideology and Point of View

Paul Simpson

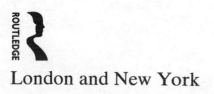

London and New York

First published 1993
by Routledge
11 New Fetter Lane, London EC4P 4EE

Simultaneously published in the USA and Canada
by Routledge
29 West 35th Street, New York, NY 10001

Printed in Great Britain by T. J. Press (Padstow) Ltd,
Padstow, Cornwall

British Library Cataloguing in Publication Data
Simpson, Paul
    Language, Ideology and Point of View. –
    (Interface Series)
    I. Title II. Series
    410

Library of Congress Cataloging in Publication Data
Simpson, Paul
    Language, ideology, and point of view / Paul Simpson.
        p. cm. – (Interface)
    Includes bibliographical references and index.
    1. Language and languages – Style. 2. Point of view
(Literature). 3. Ideology. 4. Grammar, Comparative and
general – Transitivity. 5. Pragmatics. 6. Sexism in language.
I. Title. II. Series: Interface (London, England)
P301.5.P65S56   1993
415–dc20   92-27422 CIP

ISBN 0-415-07106-2
      0-415-07107-0 pbk

To my Dad, Bill Simpson,
for teaching me the art of fly fishing.

Contents

Series editor's introduction to the Interface series

There have been many books published this century which have been devoted to the interface of language and literary studies. This is the first series of books devoted to this area commissioned by a major international publisher; it is the first time a group of writers have addressed themselves to issues at the interface of language and literature; and it is the first time an international professional association has worked closely with a publisher to establish such a venture. It is the purpose of this general introduction to the series to outline some of the main guiding principles underlying the books in the series.

The first principle adopted is one of not foreclosing on the many possibilities for the integration of language and literature studies. There are many ways in which the study of language and literature can be combined and many different theoretical, practical and curricular objects to be realized. Obviously, a close relationship with the aims and methods of descriptive linguistics will play a prominent part, so readers will encounter some detailed analysis of language in places. In keeping with a goal of much work in this field, writers will try to make their analysis sufficiently replicable for other analysts to see how they have arrived at the interpretative decisions they have reached and to allow others to reproduce their methods on the same or on other texts. But linguistic science does not have a monopoly in methodology and description any more than linguists can have sole possession of insights into language and its workings. Some contributors to the series adopt quite rigorous linguistic procedures; others proceed less rigorously but no less revealingly. All are, however, united by a belief that detailed scrutiny of the role of language in literary texts can be mutually enriching to language and literary studies.

Series of books are usually written to an overall formula or design. In the case of the Interface series this was considered to be not entirely appropriate. This is for the reasons given above, but also because, as the first series of its kind, it would be wrong to suggest that there are formulaic modes by which integration can be achieved. The fact that all the books address themselves to the integration of language and literature in any case imparts a natural and organic unity to the series.

Thus, some of the books in this series will provide descriptive overviews, others will offer detailed case studies of a particular topic, others will involve single author studies, and some will be more pedagogically oriented.

This range of design and procedure means that a wide variety of audiences is envisaged for the series as a whole, though, of course, individual books are necessarily quite specifically targeted. The general level of exposition presumes quite advanced students of language and literature. Approximately, this level covers students of English language and literature (though not exclusively English) at senior high-school/upper sixth-form level to university students in their first or second year of study. Many of the books in the series are designed to be used by students. Some may serve as course books – these will normally contain exercises and suggestions for further work as well as glossaries and graded bibliographies which point the student towards further reading. Some books are also designed to be used by teachers for their own reading and updating, and to supplement courses; in some cases, specific questions of pedagogic theory, teaching procedure and methodology at the interface of language and literature are addressed.

From a pedagogic point of view it is the case in many parts of the world that students focus on literary texts, especially in the mother tongue, before undertaking any formal study of the language. With this fact in mind, contributors to the series have attempted to gloss all new technical terms and to assume on the part of their readers little or no previous knowledge of linguistics or formal language studies. They see no merit in not being detailed and explicit about what they describe in the linguistic properties of texts; but they recognize that formal language study can seem forbidding if it is not properly introduced.

A further characteristic of the series is that the authors engage in a direct relationship with their readers. The overall style of writing is informal and there is above all an attempt to lighten the usual style of academic discourse. In some cases this extends to the way in which notes and guidance for further work are presented. In all cases, the style adopted by authors is judged to be that most appropriate to the mediation of their chosen subject matter.

We now come to two major points of principle which underlie the conceptual scheme for the series. One is that the term 'literature' cannot be defined in isolation from an expression of ideology. In fact, no academic study, and certainly no description of the language of texts, can be neutral and objective, for the sociocultural positioning of the analyst will mean that the description is unavoidably political.

Contributors to the series recognize and, in so far as this accords with the aims of each book, attempt to explore the role of ideology at the interface of language and literature. Second, most writers also prefer the term 'literatures' to a singular notion of literature. Some replace 'literature' altogether with the neutral term 'text'. It is for this reason that readers will not find exclusive discussions of the literary language of canonical literary texts; instead the linguistic heterogeneity of literature and the permeation of many discourses with what is conventionally thought of as poetic or literary language will be a focus. This means that in places as much space can be devoted to examples of word play in jokes, newspaper editorials, advertisements, historical writing, or a popular thriller as to a sonnet by Shakespeare or a passage from Jane Austen. It is also important to stress how the term 'literature' itself is historically variable and how different social and cultural assumptions can condition what is regarded as literature. In this respect the role of linguistic and literary theory is vital. It is an aim of the series to be constantly alert to new developments in the description and theory of texts.

Finally, as series editor, I have to underline the partnership and co-operation of the whole enterprise of the Interface series and acknowledge the advice and assistance received at many stages from the PALA Committee and from Routledge. In turn, we are all fortunate to have the benefit of three associate editors with considerable collective depth of experience in this field in different parts of the world: Professor Roger Fowler, Professor Mary Louise Pratt, Professor Michael Halliday. In spite of their own individual orientations, I am sure that all concerned with the series would want to endorse the statement by Roman Jakobson made over twenty-five years ago but which is no less relevant today:

> A linguist deaf to the poetic function of language and a literary scholar indifferent to linguistic problems and unconversant with linguistic methods, are equally flagrant anachronisms.

Paul Simpson's contribution to the Interface series is in an area which is central to literary criticism. It has long been an aim of literary criticism to account for point of view in fiction. *Language, Ideology and Point of View* provides precise and systematic frameworks for taking this account further with particular reference to the significance of linguistic choices in representation. At the same time, Dr Simpson does not describe these linguistic choices as if they were neutral; instead he relates language and point of view to the particular social, cultural and ideological positioning of the various narrative voices within a text.

The whole study is enlightened and enlivened by comparison of the relationship between literary and non-literary texts, underlining how studies of literary language are always more revealing if they do not presume that all discourses are discontinuous but that they are part of the same linguistic, textual and ideological fabric.

Acknowledgements

Acknowledging all those whose ideas have helped shape this book was never going to be easy. The greatest peril posed by selective acknowledgement is not deciding whom to include, but trying to decide whom to leave out. So, to the many colleagues and friends whose work in stylistics, linguistics and literary theory has in some way influenced and shaped the material presented here, I would like to express my deepest gratitude. Without this background of high-quality research, this book could never have been written.

If selective I must be, then it is best to start at the beginning. I'd like to thank Ron Carter not only for commissioning the book for Routledge's *Interface* series, but for his continued support and loyalty over the years. Others whose suggestions have fed directly into this project are: Bill Nash, Emma Williams, Peter Stockwell, David Seed, Linda Williams, Margaret Polomska, and Jenny Potts. Less direct, though none the less invaluable, has been the work of co-members of the Poetics and Linguistics Association with whom I have liaised regularly for well over a decade now. A special mention must also be made of my colleagues in Venezuela who, in a series of workshops on stylistics, provided much appreciated feedback on many of the pedagogical implications of the book – feedback made all the more stimulating when offered against a backdrop infinitely more exotic than that of a British university campus in winter. For permission to use their advertising copy in chapter 5, I am also grateful to Newton's 'Herbal Remedies'.

The bulk of this book was written during my time as a lecturer at the University of Liverpool. From that institution, Cathy Rees and, especially, Barbara Smith deserve special credit for their word-processing wizardry. I'd also like to thank my Liverpool friends for their patience during the 'gestation' period of the project, particularly those at the Oxford pub who on more than one occasion had to stifle a yawn over a pint while being treated to exuberant resumés of that day's progress on the book. And all this at a time when the threatened demise of a struggling Everton FC formed the real agenda for late evening debate!

My greatest debt of all, however, must go to Janice Hoadley, not only for her stoic support over the course of the book's development, but for her insightful critique of the manuscript itself. It was her sense of stylistic clarity which led to the substantial re-writing of a number of passages; her academic level-headedness which prompted the removal of much of the 'vitriol' from parts of the argument. And while the flaws that remain in the book are to be attributed entirely to the author, they would have numbered many more had it not been for her patience, incisiveness and clarity of thought.

1 Introduction: analysing point of view in language

Saying what happened is an angle of saying – the angle of saying is what is important.
Seamus Heaney on *The South Bank Show*, ITV, 27 October 1991.

1.1 INTRODUCTION

The Mexican film director Alejandro Jodorowsky, perpetrator of cult classics like *El topo* and *Santa sangre*, tells a germane if characteristically grisly parable to explain his film technique. The parable is about a one-eyed, one-legged, hunch-backed king who commissions a portrait of himself from his court artist. Faced with the obvious dilemma, the artist, trying not to insult the king, decides to paint out any of the deformities which might cause offence. However, the king is appalled by the untruthfulness and inaccuracy of the portrait and, in a course of action consistent with the narrative genre, summarily sentences the artist to death. A second artist is commissioned who, aware of the fate of the first, decides that a straightforward, honest and accurate representation is the best tactic. Yet the grotesque realism of this portrait makes the king furious, and the predictable execution ensues. The third artist does not have an easy task: on the face of it, the two obvious strategies have been tried and both have resulted in death. After a great deal of thought, he decides to paint the king in the role of a huntsman. By getting him to strike the pose of drawing a bow and arrow, the artist is able to paint the king with one leg resting on a log, with one eye closed and with one shoulder raised above the other. This representation of the king ingeniously disguises the disfigurements which led to the demise of the second artist, while avoiding the fabrications which resulted in the demise of the first. The king is delighted, of course, with the 'likeness' and rewards the artist with time-honoured commodities like riches, residences and sexual partners. It is the technique of this third artist which, Jodorowsky claims, characterizes his own *œuvre*.

Transposed to the domain of language, the technique of the third artist will also be the primary concern of this book. The chapters which follow share the common aim of exploring the ways in which things are 'made to look' in language. They focus on language as representation, as a projection of positions and perspectives, as a way of communicating attitudes and assumptions. The elusive question of the 'truth' of what a text says is not an issue here; rather, it is the 'angle of telling' adopted in a text, whether this be an advertisement, a novel or a newspaper report. In short, this book is all about *point of view* in language.

Over the next five chapters, a package of linguistic materials will be developed to account for this aspect of textual meaning. A 'toolkit' will be assembled progressively throughout the book and will draw on an extensive range of research on the structures and functions of the English language. To this extent, the book can be regarded, first and foremost, as a book about language. It provides a broad-based programme of language-study, a programme for textual analysis that concentrates on the ways in which the resources of language are exploited in a variety of texts. Throughout the programme, theory and analysis will be united by the common theme of point of view in language.

Before we embark on this programme, however, we will need to locate the present study within the broader traditions of textual analysis from which it derives. A clearer picture of the theoretical background which informs it and the critical assumptions which underpin it will need to be provided. The following section addresses precisely this issue.

1.2 STYLISTICS AND CRITICAL LINGUISTICS

Two interrelated branches of linguistic enquiry which have flourished over the last two decades are *stylistics* and *critical linguistics*. Both disciplines are compatible theoretically in so far as their practitioners use linguistic analysis as a basis for their interpretations of texts. Indeed, this interrelationship has been consolidated further by the recent appearance of textbooks, monographs and collections of articles which bring together the interests and concerns of both disciplines under a single cover.[1]

Stylistics, first of all, normally refers to the practice of using linguistics for the study of literature. Exponents of stylistics are quick to point out, however, that stylistic techniques can be applied to texts other than those included in the established literary canon. Indeed, a central axiom of much modern stylistic analysis is that there is no such thing as an exclusively 'literary language'. While literary communication may be privileged as a site for much experimentation and inventiveness in language, the same type of linguistic innovation can occur in many other discourse contexts. This axiom is what sets stylistics apart from more traditional literary-critical approaches which view 'literary language' as a special, ontologically stable language form which is the exclusive property of literary texts. Such approaches thus embrace a rigorous distinction between literary language and the more prosaic, ordinary language which characterizes everyday interaction. Thus, in the literary-critical tradition of F. R. Leavis and his followers, 'literary language' is simply what makes up literature and so if a text is to be regarded as a work of literature, then it must be, *ipso facto*, comprised of 'literary language'. A typical stylistic approach to this question would, by contrast, prefer to invoke the term 'literariness' to account for the linguistic innovation which often occurs in the context of literary communication, but recognizing also that 'literariness' is a property of many texts other than those conventionally designated by the label 'literature'.[2]

Of course, what also sets stylistics apart from other types of critical practice is its emphasis, first and foremost, on the *language* of the text. This does not invalidate those other approaches to textual analysis – indeed, many stylisticians have sought to enrich their linguistic analyses by importing ideas from psychoanalysis, structuralism and deconstruction. But what captures the essence of the stylistic method is the *primacy* which it assigns to language. A text is a linguistic construct and we process it as a linguistic construct before anything else. And, the argument runs, if there is to be any serious attempt to engage with the meaning of a particular text, then there must be some concomitant engagement with the language of that text.

Because of this reliance on the 'science' of linguistics, it is often assumed that stylistics claims to be a purely 'objective' method of textual analysis. The analyst stands by disinterestedly while the linguistic machine squeezes out of a text whatever meanings have been put there by the writer. Yet few stylisticians claim such objectivity. They prefer to recognize instead that all interpretations are in some sense context-bound and are contingent on the position of the analyst relative to the text. As Toolan suggests, stylistics offers a 'way' of reading, a way which is 'a confessedly partial or oriented act of intervention, a reading which is strategic, as all readings necessarily are' (1990: 11). Where the benefit of linguistics does lie is in the way it offers an established metalanguage which can account systematically for what the analyst feels are significant features of language in a text. When employed in stylistic criticism, linguistic terms have standardized reference; they are not what Fowler calls 'chameleon adaptations' which are invoked to suit the needs of the critic (1986: 3). Thus, terms like 'modality', 'transitivity' and 'deixis' all have commonly accepted designations. This terminological agreement contrasts markedly with a common literary-critical habit of using terms in a semi-technical, pseudo-descriptive fashion. One of the consequences of more traditional critical practices which employ no shared metalanguage is the tendency to conflate ill-defined grammatical terms with impressionistic value judgements. Here is an example of the type of critical 'squish' which I have in mind:

> In the fabulous linguistics of the quatrain in question, ablaut is not morphological but moral, the soft fruit of forbearance shrivelling into its own pit.[3]

This type of explanation, where linguistic terms are merged with affective commentary, renders communication with other critics fortuitous.

The rigour which the use of linguistics brings to textual analysis has another pay-off. Literary texts offer an exciting testing ground for linguistic theories and constructs, often forming a path to clearer formalizations of linguistic knowledge. There is a kind of bivalent heuristic here: linguistic models offer a 'way in' to a text, while the text itself allows for a challenging application for those models. It is no surprise, then, that this potential for increased awareness of language structure and function has resulted in stylistics occupying an increasingly prominent place in both undergraduate English-language courses and English-language teaching courses. This increase in interest is also reflected by the publication of textbooks and manuals on language which incorporate substantial stylistics components.[4]

The dependency of stylistics on linguistics means that as techniques in linguistics become more sophisticated, so stylistic models become enriched and revitalized. Stylisticians are thus continually re-assessing their methods in the light of new developments in linguistics. One topic of investigation in stylistics which has been subject to this type of progressive revision is the concept of *point of view*. In the context of narrative fiction, point of view refers generally to the psychological perspective through which a story is told. It encompasses the narrative framework which a writer employs, whether this be first person or third person, restricted perspective or omniscient perspective, and accounts for the basic viewing position which is adopted in a story. Narrative point of view is arguably the very essence of a story's style, what gives it its 'feel' and 'colour'. Justification for this stance will be provided shortly when, in chapter 2, clearer definitions along with a detailed review of stylistic approaches to point of view will be provided. Suffice it to say here, this book will offer a way of conceptualizing and exploring this important aspect of a text's organization. In doing so, it will slot into the ongoing revisionary trend of modern stylistics by taking on board issues of current relevance in linguistics.

Critical linguistics, like stylistics, seeks to interpret texts on the basis of linguistic analysis. This tradition of analytic enquiry can be traced directly to the work carried out during the 1970s by Roger Fowler and his associates at the University of East Anglia. Since the publication towards the end of that decade of two volumes outlining the critical linguistic 'manifesto' (Fowler *et al.* 1979; Kress and Hodge 1979), there has been a steady output of research within the tradition[5]. What characterizes this work, first of all, is the way in which it expands the horizons of stylistics by focussing on texts other than those regarded as literary. Media language has received particular scrutiny, although analyses have been conducted on discourse types as diverse as swimming-pool regulations (Fowler and Kress 1979a) and university guidelines on student enrolment (Fowler 1981: 24–45). Despite the heterogeneity of the texts examined, the motivating principle behind these analyses is to explore the value systems and sets of beliefs which reside in texts; to explore, in other words, *ideology* in language.

There is, unfortunately, a proliferation of definitions available for the term *ideology*, and many of these are contingent on the political framework favoured by the analyst. From a critical linguistic perspective, the term normally describes the ways in which what we say and think interacts with society. An ideology therefore derives from the taken-for-granted assumptions, beliefs and value-systems which are shared collectively by social groups. And when an ideology is the ideology of a particularly powerful social group, it is said to be *dominant*. Thus, dominant ideologies are mediated through powerful political and social institutions like the government, the law and the medical profession. Our perception of these institutions, moreover, will be shaped in part by the specific linguistic practices of the social groups who comprise them.

A central component of the critical linguistic creed is the conviction that language reproduces ideology. As an integrated form of social behaviour, language will be inevitably and inextricably tied up with the socio-political context in which it functions. Language is not used in a contextless vacuum; rather, it is used in a host of discourse contexts, contexts which are impregnated with the ideology of social systems and institutions. Because language operates within this social dimension it must, of necessity *reflect*, and some would argue, *construct* ideology.

The motivation for a critical linguistic analysis of language could be set out in the following way. First of all, dominant ideologies operate as a mechanism for maintaining asymmetrical power relations in society. As language can be used by powerful groups to re-inforce this dominant ideology, then language needs to be targeted as a specific site of struggle. Analysis for the sake of analysis is not sufficient; instead, the analyst makes a committed effort to engage with the discourse with a view to changing it. In other words, by highlighting insidious discursive practices in language, these practices themselves can be challenged. Nowhere has this 'consciousness-raising' element been more apparent than in the work on 'nukespeak' carried out in the 1980s (e.g. Chilton 1985). The avowed intent of this research was to expose the obfuscation and dissimulation which typified much of the political rhetoric on nuclear arms. Linguistic analysis became a means of clarifying the terms of the nuclear debate and foregrounding, particularly, the way in which dominant Western ideology masks the potential horror of nuclear confrontation.

The critical linguistic rationale outlined here raises a number of additional issues concerning the interrelationship of language and ideology. One of these is to do with the way in which dominant ideologies become ingrained in everyday discourse. They become rationalized as 'common-sense' assumptions about the way things are and the way things should be. A process of *naturalization* takes place, to the extent that people are often no longer aware of the hierarchies and systems which shape their social interaction. Fairclough offers the following useful illustration of one type of naturalization:

> the conventions for a traditional type of consultation between doctors and patients embody 'common sense' assumptions which treat authority and hierarchy as natural – the doctor knows about medicine and the patient doesn't; the doctor is in a position to determine how a health problem should be dealt with and the patient isn't; it is right (and 'natural') that the doctor should make decisions and control the course of the consultation and of the

treatment, and that the patient should comply and cooperate; and so on.

(1989: 2)

Ideology, Fairclough goes on to argue, is embedded in the language used to structure this type of social encounter. By foregrounding the linguistic code employed in such contexts, analysts can 'demystify' and 'denaturalize' what normally passes us by as real-time participants in everyday interaction.

Another issue arising from the critical linguistic rationale concerns the apparent 'pervasiveness' of ideology. As no use of language is considered truly neutral, objective and value-free, then theoretically critical linguistic analysis may be performed on any form of discourse. This explains the proliferation of analyses of diverse texts taken from a variety of contexts. However, the analyses which result from this pan-contextual search for ideology in language have been criticized for 'going too far', for seeing features of major ideological significance in inconsequential, prosaic discourse. Consider, for instance, Hodge and Kress's deconstruction of the word 'tinnie', an Australian English term for a tin of beer:

tins of beer, in spite of their phallic shape and association with male drinking and male solidarity, are classified with the 'ie' of implicitly feminine solidarity, as safe objects of male desire.

(1988: 102)

It is not clear if the *ie* of, say, *junkie* would be expected to carry the same degree of feminine solidarity. Extrapolating from the theory of the phallus-shaped beer tin, one might also conclude that all cylindrical containers were so-shaped because of this male sexist conspiracy and not because they just happen to be a useful way of storing products. There are times, perhaps, when a tin of beer is only a tin of beer.

This short survey of stylistics and critical linguistics, although important as a theoretical backcloth and point of entry to the book, has none the less been a highly condensed and eclectic summary of numerous strands of research. Readers new to the area may be alarmed at the introduction in so short a space of a flurry of abstract terms like *naturalization*, *ideology* – even *point of view* itself. Others may wonder what precisely constitute the 'techniques in linguistics' which underpin so much stylistic and critical linguistic enquiry. Well, fear not, because every concept introduced thus far will receive extensive explanation and illustration over the course of the book. As far as linguistic 'techniques' are concerned, the book will offer a series of detailed linguistic models which may be productively used in textual provided through sample analyses, and we will be in a better position to assess the merits and limitations of the stylistic and critical linguistic method in the light of these analyses. Before we move on to a fuller definition of the concept of point of view, a few comments on the book's layout should clarify further its structure, its aims and scope and the types of issues with which each chapter deals.

1.3 USING THIS BOOK

As the previous two sections indicated, this book sets out to deliver an integrated programme in stylistic and critical linguistic analysis. The 'package' offered is a general model for linguistic criticism. A common thread running through the entire book is, of course, the preoccupation with point of view in language, whether this be the ideological viewpoint adopted in a newspaper report or the more localized 'psychological' point of view exhibited by a work of narrative fiction. A guiding principle behind all of this is the premise that a particular style represents certain selections from a pool of available options in the linguistic system. By developing a particular style, a producer of a spoken or written text privileges certain readings, certain ways of seeing things, while suppressing or downplaying others. One of the tasks of an applied-linguistics programme of this sort is to provide a means of 'seeing through language', to adopt the subtly ambiguous title of Carter and Nash's recent study (Carter and Nash 1990). The purpose, in other words, is to probe under the surface of language, to decode the stylistic choices which shape a text's meaning. By examining the way things are 'made to look' in language we will be exploring the linguistic equivalent of the painting of Jodorowsky's third artist.

In terms of structure, the book is organized broadly into two main blocks, representing stylistic and critical linguistic interests respectively. A bridge between the two blocks is provided in chapter 4, half way through the book as a whole. This is not meant to suggest, however, that the two halves are to be viewed independently from one another. On the contrary, the theoretical compatibility of the two approaches is illustrated throughout. Furthermore, there is considerable cross-fertilization between the two blocks, with linguistic models assembled in the stylistics section being re-applied later in the book to newspaper and advertising language. Moreover, the later chapters contain many illustrations of how the linguistic models developed there can be equally productively applied to some of the passages of narrative fiction which were examined much earlier. It is the different aims and outcomes of the stylistic and critical linguistic approaches which makes some degree of separation sensible.

I have tried to keep this book as practical, accessible and 'user-friendly' as possible. To this effect, every chapter offers an equal balance of theory, analysis and interpretation. Chapters 2–5 also contain sections which provide detailed descriptions of specific linguistic models. These sections have been designed to be as self-contained as possible, so that readers may use them as mini-reference manuals on particular topics in linguistics. For instance, chapter 2 contains an introduction to the concept of *deixis* in language, as well as a section on techniques of *speech and thought presentation*. In chapter 3, the notion of *modality* is covered extensively, while chapter 4 includes a detailed account of the linguistic system of *transitivity*. Chapter 5 proposes a model of communication based on recent developments in *pragmatics* and *semantics*. The sixth chapter is different in that the models of language assembled over the previous four chapters are brought to bear on the specific question of gender and point of view. Although this chapter does not have a section devoted to a detailed analytic model, and is in consequence a little shorter than the other main chapters, the subject matter which it covers does provide an opportunity to undertake a critique of wider theoretical issues. One of these issues concerns the interrelationship between *language, thought* and *reality*. Furthermore, the chapter can be seen as a 'case-study' applying the language skills developed in previous sections to an important political issue. Throughout the book, finer academic points and remarks of a more 'scholarly' nature, unless absolutely necessary to the progression of the central argument, have been shunted into the 'Notes and further reading' sections which are appended to each chapter. There, of course, readers will also find suggestions on follow-up reading on all of the issues covered in the main body of the chapter.

The specific topics covered in each chapter are as follows. The next chapter begins the stylistic programme by examining point of view in narrative fiction. It surveys the history of the field, isolating three broad bands of research on narrative point of view. One of those bands is identified as especially promising stylistically, and, to this extent, it provides a point of entry to the 'modal grammar' of point of view which is proposed in chapter 3. The relatively neglected concept of *modality*, it will be argued, can account systematically for the different points of view exhibited by many works of narrative fiction. As is the case with stylistics generally, the term narrative fiction will cover not just established canonical texts, but novels from the popular science-fiction and thriller genres, as well as narratives produced by participants in stylistics workshops and tutorials. The first part of chapter 4 illustrates how this model of point of view can be enriched through reference to another layer of textual organization, *transitivity*. As the transitivity model has also proved popular in critical linguistic enquiry, chapter 4 is an appropriate place at which to begin the second part of our programme. The second half of the chapter, then, is devoted to the analysis of ideological point of view in print media. Both parts of the chapter allow for a more detailed critique of stylistic and critical linguistic methods than has been possible in this introductory chapter. Chapter 5 widens the scope of the exercise in two principal ways. Firstly, it introduces text-types beyond the news-reports and narrative fiction which have been the primary focus of attention up until then. More significantly, it devotes attention to the *process* of communication and proposes a pragmatic model which can account for the way in which meanings are produced and negotiated between writers and readers. The chapter contains numerous textual analyses which illustrate how a pragmatic study of point of view might be undertaken. The sixth chapter takes the discussion into the specific arena of feminist linguistics. It employs the analytic toolkit assembled over the book in a sustained investigation of the relationship between gender, ideology and point of view.

NOTES AND FURTHER READING

1 Five representative samples of work which combine stylistic and critical linguistic analysis are Fowler (1986), Birch and O'Toole (1988), Coupland (1988), Van Peer (1988), Carter and Nash (1990).
2 Useful surveys of the 'literary-language' debate can be found in Birch (1989: *passim*) and Carter and Nash (1990: 29–58).
3 This quotation, cited only as a representative sample, is from Hollander (1987: 129).
4 Two collections which reflect the recent 'pedagogical turn' in stylistics are: Brumfit and Carter (1986) and Short (1989).
5 An early statement of the critical linguistic 'code of practice' appears in Fowler and Kress (1979b). Subsequent modifications and extensions can be found in Fowler (1981: 24–45), Birch and O'Toole (1988: *passim*) and, most recently, Kress (1989).

2 Point of view in narrative fiction: preliminaries

I have tried to determine before anything else what the words in each visualization ask us to see and how they ask us to see it – that is to say, how the space is visualized in each literary object we are considering.

Alan Spiegel, *Fiction and the Camera Eye*

2.1 INTRODUCTION

This begins the first of two chapters devoted to the analysis of point of view in narrative fiction. The issue of point of view in literature has received much attention in recent years, with stylisticians, structuralists, linguists and even cognitive psychologists converging on the topic from their respective theoretical positions. One aim of this chapter is to cut through – or perhaps even wade through – the proliferation of models and theories which have developed as a result of this research. Another aim is to reach a consensus definition of the concept of point of view. Not only is this desirable in its own terms but it will also provide a suitable basis for the more detailed analyses which will be carried out in the next chapter.

Following the principle of scholars like Boris Uspensky and Roger Fowler, whose work will be discussed later, four important categories of point of view are identified here. The first two are *spatial* and *temporal* point of view, terms which, in addition to being fairly self-explanatory, will be developed in detail quite soon. The third category, by far the most important as far as this and the following chapters are concerned, is point of view on the *psychological* plane. Psychological point of view refers to the ways in which narrative events are mediated through the consciousness of the 'teller' of the story. It will encompass the means by which a fictional world is slanted in a particular way or the means by which narrators construct, in linguistic terms, their own view of the story they tell. Psychological point of view extends from authorial omniscience to a single character's perhaps restricted version of 'reality'. Uspensky sums up:

> In those cases where the authorial point of view relies on an individual consciousness (or perception) we will speak about the psychological point of view; we will conditionally designate the plane on which this point of view may be distinguished as the psychological plane.
>
> (1973: 81)

By the end of this chapter, a clearer picture of what is meant by psychological point of view and why it should be prioritized in the context of literary communication will, I hope, have emerged.

The fourth category of point of view, point of view on the *ideological* plane, has already received some attention in chapter 1. For the reasons explained there, discussion of this plane will be withheld until the analysis has been widened in scope to include discourse types other than narrative fiction.

Keeping in mind these general aims, this chapter will be structured as follows. The next section will introduce the concepts of *spatial* and *temporal* point of view and will suggest ways in which they may be studied from a linguistic perspective. Section 2.3 outlines the techniques which writers employ for the representation of speech and thought in narrative. This will be important generally to the issues covered in chapter 3, but it will also introduce terms which will feature in the more theoretical discussion undertaken in the section which immediately follows in this chapter. This discussion considers three broad bands of research which have influenced the study of point of view in narrative. For convenience, these three bands are labelled *structuralist*, *generative* and *interpersonal*, the last of these providing the point of entry to the more detailed, analytic focus of the next chapter.

2.2 SPATIAL AND TEMPORAL POINT OF VIEW

The expression 'spatial point of view' designates broadly the viewing position assumed by the narrator of a story. It concerns the 'camera angle' adopted in a text, whether this be a 'bird's-eye' view of events or the restricted viewpoint of a single observer. The suggested parallel with visual arts and particularly, filmic texts, is an important one; close-ups, long-shots and tracking shots all have linguistic counterparts in narrative fiction. Readers, like viewers, may be presented with objects, locations and characters in a host of different ways, ranging from the extreme close-up which characterizes much *film noir* to the panoramic tracking movement characteristic of the *mise-en-scène* technique. Interwoven with the spatial location of the viewing subject is the temporal dimension in which it is framed. The expression 'temporal point of view' refers to such a dimension, and relates generally to 'the impression which a reader gains of events moving rapidly or slowly, in a continuous chain or isolated segments' (Fowler 1986: 127). Again, filmic texts and narrative texts share many features of temporal point of view, with their flashbacks, gaps in the progression of time, and the interweaving of other stories and incidents which break up the linear development of the main body of the narrative.

Restricting ourselves for the moment to narrative fiction, we may give brief consideration here to some of the techniques which writers employ in constructing spatio-temporal points of view. Perhaps the most important linguistic component in this regard is the system of *deixis*. Deixis may be loosely characterized as those 'orientational' features of language which function to locate utterances in relation to speakers' viewpoints. *Spatial* deixis is realized through terms which denote the relationship of objects to a speaker, or which signal how a speaker is situated in physical space. *Temporal* deixis, by contrast, concerns the ways in which the time of the events referred to in an utterance interacts with the time of the utterance itself. With regard to spatial deixis first of all, the deictic adverbs *here* and *there*, and the demonstrative pronouns *this* and *that* are perhaps the purest indicators of directionality and location. The first items in each pair are *proximal* in that they express physical proximity to the speaker; the second are *distal* in that they normally suggest directionality away from the location of the speaker. There exists also a set of deictic verbs which often operate in combination with the deictic pronouns and adverbs. For instance, the verb *bring* suggests motion towards the deictic centre in

(1) Bring that here.

whereas *take* suggests orientation away from the speaking source:

(2) Take this there.

Generally related to the system of spatial deixis is the category of *locative* expressions. These are phrases which are governed by prepositions denoting place and direction and which function to identify the positioning of people and objects relative to the speaker and addressee. Locatives may be varied, as the following examples should show:

(3)   over there.
              behind you.
John is   by the hammock.
              beside the hut.
              under the tree.

Notice here how the interpretation of the exact location of objects in relation to John rests on a shared visual perspective between the speaker and addressee.

The proximal/distal distinction also extends in principle to time deixis. The pure deictic adverb *now* expresses proximal reference, which translates as something like 'at the time at which the speaker is speaking', whereas its distal counterpart, *then*, indicates that the events referred to took place at a time anterior to the time of speaking. Some examples should help clarify this:

(4) Give it to me *now*!
(5) I'm *now* working in Liverpool.
(6) He was a teenager *then*.
(7) She never laughed much *then*.

In the first two examples, *now* is generally co-terminous with the time of the utterance. In (6) and (7), the events referred to are displaced from the time of utterance to a point of relevance at some time in the past. These examples should also demonstrate that the system of tense may have a temporal-deictic function, although the interaction of tense with the non-deictic concept of time is complex and problematic. None the less, if illustrations are kept relatively simple, then some of the basic principles of tense and deictic reference may be set out. Consider the following utterance, spoken, say, in the course of a phone call:

(8) It's raining here now.

As the time of the event referred to is synchronous with the time of speaking, then the utterance as a whole expresses deictic *simultaneity*. The temporal orientation here is therefore proximal. If, however, the tense and temporal adverb are altered to their distal counterparts, retaining the spatial deictic *here*, then the following pattern emerges:

(9) It was raining here then.

The temporal relationship of the speaking time and the event referred to is now no longer synchronic, as the point of relevance has been shifted to a time which precedes that of the phone-call. In fact, the use of a past perfect creates further divisions in the suggested temporal arrangement of events:

(10) It had been raining here then.

The temporal point of view represented here is now three-tiered: there is the speaking time, the relevant point in the past to which the *then* refers, and a period anterior to this point, during which it rained. Clearly, the relationship of tense deixis to actual time is complex, not least because the grammatical category of tense and the non-linguistic co-ordinates of time are entirely different conceptual systems.

The next stage in the programme will be to examine the ways in which the notion of deixis might usefully be employed in an analysis of spatio-temporal point of view. To this effect, the remainder of this subsection will focus on some extracts from prose fiction. The analyses undertaken will be kept as informal as possible and, in order that we might proceed promptly to the remaining subsections, discussion of a more 'literary-critical' nature will be restricted to brief comments.

The establishment of spatio-temporal reference points provides just one point of entry into the universe of discourse developed in a text. Put another way, spatio-temporal point of view allows access to the 'fictional reality' which unfolds in the course of a story. The linguistic co-ordinates of space and time serve to anchor the fictional speaker in his or her fictional world, which, in turn, provides a window and vantage point for readers.

Illustrations of how spatio-temporal point of view operates are not difficult to find, but one which should provide a simple introduction to the principle is Ray Bradbury's short science-fiction story 'The Luggage Store' (1951). Set on a thinly populated Mars, it describes the experiences of a luggage-store proprietor who discovers that there is going to be a war on Earth. The isolation of the proprietor and the remoteness of Mars from Earth is established through clear spatial co-ordinates in the opening lines of the story:

> It was a very remote thing, when the luggage-store proprietor heard the news on the night radio, received all the way from Earth on a light-sound beam. The proprietor felt how remote it was.
> There was going to be a war on Earth.
> He went out to peer into the sky.
> Yes, there it was. Earth, in the evening heavens, following the sun into the hills. The words on the radio and that green star were one and the same.
>
> (collected in *The Martian Chronicles*, Triad edn, p. 165)

Oddly, and in spite of this narrative opening, almost all of the remainder of the short story is in the form of a dialogue between the proprietor and a priest who happens to be passing by. Yet peppered throughout this conversation are deictic signals which highlight and in some respects re-inforce the sheer physical distance between the speakers and the subject of their discussion, planet Earth. There is a proliferation of spatial and temporal terms, functioning to establish a clear viewing position in the story. Consider for instance, the following lengthier sequence which is rich in temporal and spatial deixis:

'Earth is . . . so far away it's unbelievable. It's not here. You can't touch it. You can't even see it. All you see is a green light. Two billion people living on that light? Unbelievable! War? We don't hear the explosions.'

5   'We will', said the proprietor. 'I keep thinking about all those people that were going to come to Mars this week. What was it? A hundred thousand or so coming up in the next month or so. What about them if the war starts?'

'I imagine they'll turn back. They'll be needed on Earth'.

10   'Well', said the proprietor, 'I'd get my luggage dusted off. I got a feeling there'll be a rush sale here any time.'

'Do you think everyone now on Mars will go back to Earth if this is the Big War we've all been expecting for years?'

'It's a funny thing, Father, but yes, I think we'll all go back. I 15 know, we came up here to get away from things – politics, the atom bomb, war, pressure groups, prejudice, laws – I know. But it's still home there. You wait and see. When the first bomb drops on America the people up here'll start thinking. They haven't been here long enough. A couple years is all. If they'd 20 been here forty years, it'd be different, but they got relatives down there.'

(p. 165)

In terms of spatial point of view, the alternation between proximal and distal terms identifies the vantage point clearly as that of the planet Mars. Deictic adverbs are especially foregrounded:

It's not *here*. (line 1)
we came up *here* (line 15)
But it's still home *there*. (lines 16–17)
they got relatives down *there*. (lines 20–21)

although there are also numerous demonstrative adjectives and pronouns in the passage:

Two billion people living on *that* light? (line 3)
I keep thinking about all *those* people (lines 5–6)
if *this* is the Big War (lines 12–13)

Two sets of directional verbs may also be identified: those which signal
movement away from the deictic centre and those which signal movement towards it. The proximal set is realized by the verb COME,
repeated many times in the passage, and the distal set by either GO
('we'll all *go* back' (line 14)) or TURN BACK ('they'll *turn back* (line 9)).
Vertical spatial relationships are also established with the 'up here' of
Mars contrasted with the 'down there' of Earth. This spatial framework is supplemented with temporal deictics which further contrast
the 'here and now' of Mars with the 'there and then' of Earth. For
instance, at lines 5–6, the proprietor refers to

those people that *were going* (distal)
come to Mars *this week* (proximal).

The second clause also highlights a textual pattern where proximal
deictics of time are positioned close to their spatial equivalents or to
direct references to Mars, the deictic centre of the story. Other
instances of this are:

everyone now on Mars (line 12)
coming up in the next month or so (line 7)
there'll be a rush sale here (line 11)

One significant point about this type of deictic patterning is that it is
mediated through the dialogue between two characters *within* the
story. The visual schema is not therefore one which is presented
directly by an external narrator; rather, it unfolds through the building
up of deictic devices in the speech of participants in the story. This is
what provides the spatio-temporal point of entry to the text and
establishes the 'universe of discourse' referred to earlier.

A good illustration of how spatio-temporal deixis is managed more
directly by a narratorial voice can be found near the beginning of
George Eliot's *The Mill on the Floss* (1859). In the second paragraph of
the novel, the speaking 'I' presents a view of Dorlcote Mill and its
surroundings in the following way:

And this is Dorlcote Mill. I must stand a minute or two here on the
bridge and look at it, though the clouds are threatening, and it is far
on in the afternoon. Even in this leafless time of departing February
it is pleasant to look at – perhaps the chill, damp season adds a
charm to the trimly-kept, comfortable dwelling-house, as old as the

elms and the chestnuts that shelter it from the northern blast. The stream is brimful now, and lies high in this little withy plantation, and half drowns the grassy fringe of the croft in front of the house.

(Dent & Dutton edn, p. 3)

Temporal and spatial deixis combine to make this highly 'proximal' stylistically. All of the key features of proximal spatial deixis are present: deictic adverbs ('I must stand . . . *here*'); demonstrative pronouns ('And *this* is Dorlcote Mill'); demonstrative adjectives ('*this* little withy plantation') and locative expressions which serve to anchor the viewing position as that of the narrating subject ('I must. . . look *at it*'; 'pleasant to look *at*'; 'the croft *in front of* the house'). Proximal temporal deictics are equally abundant, with deictic adverbs ('now'), demonstrative adjectives ('*this* leafless time') and noun phrases which align the temporal viewpoint with the time of narration ('it is *far on in the afternoon*'; 'I must stand *a minute or two*'). Significant also is the use of the so-called 'instantaneous' present tense throughout the passage, strengthening further the 'here and now' pattern.

Now, the general deictic system identified here is one which makes maximally close the events narrated and the time of narration. This type of pattern is not exclusive to prose fiction, however. On the contrary, it is a characteristic of a range of registers notably that of radio broadcasts where, in a comparable way to that of fiction, there are restrictions on the access that listeners have to the visual perspective of the speaking voice.[1] In order to generate a shared domain of discourse, broadcasters often need to develop texts with strong deictic profiles, and the results can be similar to the profile of the sequence from *The Mill on the Floss*. Evidence in support of this parallel is not difficult to provide. For instance, in stylistics seminars where this extract has been used but where its source has not been divulged immediately, students have been quick to identify it as a transcript of broadcast language. More remarkably, the source is often identified specifically as that of a radio travelogue. Even the archaic language of the passage ('brimful', 'withy') was not sufficient to sway the decision towards nineteenth-century prose fiction. Such responses are both extremely rich and highly coherent, because in support of their categorization, students were sensitive to those very deictic features that are the focus of attention in the present study. The 'here and now' words were picked out, and particular comment was made on the way the present tense conveyed the immediacy typical of many forms of broadcast language. Interestingly, those who recognized the source of the extract as that of *The Mill on the Floss* said very little about such stylistic features, preferring instead to discuss themes of wider literary significance. Perhaps the knowledge that this was the work of a major literary figure may have blocked some of the more basic perceptions of the style of the text.

Up to now, little attention has been given to the way in which locative expressions may act as perspective-framing devices in their own right. The fact that locatives are normally introduced by a preposition of direction or place enables the development of visual panorama, with key reference points intersecting in a mosaic-like fashion. A striking, and highly symmetrical, example of such a locative tapestry can be found in the second chapter of Gustave Flaubert's *Bouvard and Pecuchet* (1881). This sequence details the view from the window of the eponymous heroes' home, and for convenience, key locative expressions have been italicized in the passage:

> *Directly ahead* were the fields, *on the right* a barn, and the steeple of a church, and *on the left* a screen of poplars.
>
> Two main paths, *in the form of a cross*, divided the garden into four parts. The vegetables were arranged in beds, *from which* rose, *here and there*, dwarf cypresses and trained fruit-trees. *On one side* an arbor-way led *to a bower*; *on the other* a wall held up espaliers; and a lattice fence, *at the back* opened *onto the countryside*. There was *beyond the wall* an orchard; *behind the bower* a thicket; *beyond the lattice* fence a small track.
>
> (trans. Earp and Stonier; Jonathan Cape edn, p. 26)

A feature of this passage, which is true of the other two extracts examined so far, is that the viewing position is largely stationary. That is to say, the spatial perspective derives from a static source, whether this be a narrator or characters within the story. In contrast with this is the technique which Uspensky calls the 'sequential survey'. This is the situation where

> the narrator's viewpoint moves sequentially from one character to an other and from one detail to an other, and the reader is given the task of piecing together the separate descriptions into one coherent picture. The movement of the author's point of view here is similar to those camera movements in film that provide a sequential survey of a particular scene.
>
> (Uspensky 1973: 60)

A useful illustration of this kind of narrative 'tracking shot' is a brief episode from James Joyce's short story 'The Dead', which is discussed by Leech and Short (1981: 177) in their own chapter on point of view:

> Gabriel had not gone to the door with the others. He was in the dark part of the hall gazing up the staircase. A woman was standing near the top of the first flight, in the shadow also. He could not see her face but he could see the terracotta and salmon-pink panels of her skirt which the shadow made appear black and white. It was his wife.

The 'bird's-eye' vantage point of authorial omniscience is relinquished here, as the deictic centre in the passage is aligned with Gabriel Conroy. Indeed, the effect of this gradual discovery could easily have been nullified if the early reference to 'A woman' had simply read 'His wife'. Instead, this information is withheld temporarily – a technique which, incidentally, John Huston observes faithfully in his film of this short story. In the comparable scene in the film version, the camera tracks upwards from the viewing position of Gabriel, catching first the skirts of Gretta, and eventually incorporating the entire figure in the frame.

The principle of shifting focus also extends to the temporal plane. Earlier it was pointed out that temporal point of view encompasses flashbacks, previsions and disruptions on the 'normal' time sequence. One concept which may be added to this is that of 'duration' (Genette 1980: 86). Duration refers to the temporal span of a story, and, more specifically, to the ways in which the narration of some events may be accelerated or decelerated relative to the story as a whole. Where the temporal sweep of James Joyce's *Ulysses* covers only a single day, a short paragraph such as the following may compress a time span of nearly twenty years:

> I was born in 1927, the only child of middle-class parents, both English, and themselves born in the grotesquely elongated shadow, which they never rose sufficiently above history to leave, of that monstrous dwarf Queen Victoria. I was sent to a public school, I wasted two years doing my national service, I went to Oxford; and there I discovered I was not the person I wanted to be.
>
> (John Fowles, *The Magus*, Triad edn p. 15).

Re-orientations of time in the form of flashbacks or flashforwards may fragment the temporal development of a narrative. Consider, for instance, the startling opening of Flann O'Brien's novel *The Third Policeman* (1967):

> Not everybody knows how I killed old Philip Mathers, smashing his jaw in with my spade; but first it is better to speak of my friendship with John Divney.
>
> (Picador edn, p. 7).

First of all, there is a substantial gap between the time of narration and the events described. However, there is also a significant stretch of time between the formation of the protagonist's friendship with John Divney and the killing of old Mathers. The friendship with Divney, which is anterior to the killing, marks the beginning of the narrative proper, so the reference to the killing is thus a flashforward, or *prolepsis* if we adopt the term coined by Genette (1980: 40).[2]

So far in the discussion, terms like 'speaking voice' and 'external narrator' have been used informally, while the more technical emphasis has been placed on the linguistic realization of the co-ordinates of space and time. Little has been said on the nature of the medium through which the events of a story are mediated or 'focalized'. Yet the spatio-temporal orientation in a text is just one manifestation of the psychological disposition of the focalizer. The knowledge, attitudes and opinions of the medium through which the fiction is narrated are, after all, likely to govern the type of spatio-temporal viewpoint which develops. As Rimmon-Kenan points out, the determining factors of point of view rest on 'the cognitive and the emotive orientation of the focalizer towards the focalized' (1983: 79). It is this broader, psychological dimension of point of view which will occupy us shortly, but there remains one aspect of stylistic technique which needs some introduction. The technique in many ways straddles the gap between spatio-temporal point of view and psychological point of view and it concerns the ways in which speech and thought are presented in narrative fiction.

2.3 SPEECH AND THOUGHT PRESENTATION

The techniques of speech and thought presentation have been widely investigated in stylistics over the last two decades. Extensive treatments of the subject can be found in Page (1973), Pascal (1977), Banfield (1982), McHale (1983), Rimmon-Kenan (1983) and Ehrlich (1990). To my mind, the most accessible introduction to the topic remains that of Leech and Short (1981: 318–51). Amongst other things, Leech and Short base their categories on explicit linguistic criteria and offer numerous examples from prose fiction in support of their framework. This has enabled other stylisticians and linguists to apply this model not only to literary texts but to other forms of language use such as broadcast and print media.[3] Their categories are also sufficiently clear to be integrated with the discussion of psychological point of view which will be undertaken in this and the following chapter. The account which follows, then, will follow for the most part the typology proposed by Leech and Short.

Perhaps the two most widely used modes of speech presentation are Direct Speech (DS) and Indirect Speech (IS), of which the former may be regarded as a base-line reference point for the other modes. Direct Speech is characterized by the presence of an introductory report*ing* clause and a report*ed* clause enclosed in quotation marks. The orthographic separation of the reporting clause from that which is said is shown by the following two examples of DS:

> (11) a. 'I know these tricks of yours!', she said.
> (12) a. He said, 'I'll be here tomorrow.'

The quoted material in these examples could be reported indirectly, thus becoming Indirect Speech:

> (11) b. She said that she knew those tricks of his.
> (12) b. He said that he would be there the following day.

A number of important changes have been made in this conversion of DS to IS. First, the reported sequence, now introduced by *that*, has been embedded grammatically in the reporting clause. Second, the first- and second-person pronouns in the original quotations (*I, yours*) have been transposed to third-person equivalents. Third, the proximal deictics of space and time have been altered to their distal correlates: *these* becomes *those*, *here* becomes *there*, and *tomorrow* becomes *the following day*. Tense changes supplement these deictic shifts with the present tense of the reported clause becoming *backshifted* to the more remote past-tense version. In this instance, *know* is backshifted to *knew* whilst the modal *will* goes to its past-tense form *would*. One of the consequences of this cluster of changes is that the reported speech has been brought more tightly under narratorial control; tense and deixis, for instance, are now consonant with that of the dominant narrative framework.

Changes may be made to both DS and IS in order to render them more 'free'. For example, a DS form may be stripped of its reporting clause or its quotation marks – and if both changes take place, then the form which emerges is the maximally free form of Free Direct Speech (FDS). Here are some examples of FDS, arranged in increasing degrees of freedom.

> (11) c. I know these tricks of yours!, she said.
>   d. 'I know these tricks of yours!'
>   e. I know these tricks of yours!
> (12) c. He said, I'll be here tomorrow.

d. 'I'll be here tomorrow.'
e. I'll be here tomorrow.

A free form of IS may be constructed simply by removing the reporting clause and the *that* connective, should one be present. The result is referred to as Free Indirect Speech (FIS). Again, this form may display varying degrees of freedom and directness depending on how much of the flavour of the original speech a writer wishes to convey:

(11) f. She knew those tricks of his.
g. She knew those tricks of his!
(12) f. He would be there the following day.
g. He would be there tomorrow.

The second examples in each pair are slightly more direct than the first in that (11g) retains the exclamation mark of the DS form and (12g) the proximal temporal deictic. This mode of speech presentation (along with its counterpart in thought presentation) is arguably the richest and most intriguing of all the techniques available. It is often regarded as a fusion of narratorial and character voices, a 'dual' voice in the terms of Pascal (1977). Certainly, it would be difficult to identify precisely the source of the speaking voice in the FIS versions of examples (11) and (12) without at least some knowledge of the textual environment in which they occurred. Yet it is this very indeterminacy which gives FIS its special status.

There is a final category of speech presentation known as Narrative Report of Speech Act (NRSA). This form is more indirect again than IS and only provides a minimal statement about what was said. In this mode, no attempt is made to capture the original words used:

(11) h. She spoke of his trickery.
(12) h. He told her when he'd return.

In formal terms, the linguistic devices available for the presentation of *thought* are broadly analogous to those for speech presentation. Yet, despite their stylistic compatability, the two modes reflect vastly different degrees of novelistic licence. Leech and Short are comparably cautious at this point in their own discussion:

The modes of speech and thought presentation are very similar formally, but it should always be remembered that the representation of the thoughts of characters, even in an extremely indirect form . . . is ultimately an artifice. We cannot see inside the minds of other people, but if the motivation for the actions and attitudes of characters is to be made clear to the reader, the representation of their thoughts, like the use of soliloquy on stage, is a necessary licence.

(1981: 337)

Clearly, the representation of thought requires an omniscience that is not necessary for the presentation of speech. Indeed, a parallel may be drawn between this situation and that of naturally occurring conversation where participants may report verbatim the speech of their co-participants. Reporting their thoughts in a comparable manner is, however, another matter.

Following Leech and Short here, the five categories of thought presentation, along with appropriate examples of each, are as follows:

(13) a. Does she still love me? (Free Direct Thought: FDT)
   b. He wondered, 'Does she still love me?' (Direct Thought: DT)
   c. Did she still love him? (Free Indirect Thought: FIT)
   d. He wondered if she still loved him. (Indirect Thought: IT)
   e. He wondered about her love for him. (Narrative Report of a Thought Act: NRTA)

(Leech and Short 1981: 337)

Although this basic description should suffice for the purposes of the present study, a few caveats should be heeded. Firstly, the boundaries between the categories are not rigorously discrete, so it might be more appropriate to consider the presentation of both thought and speech as a continuum of varying degrees of freedom and directness. Secondly, there are one or two anomalies in the paradigm for thought presentation. Bizarrely, the unmarked DT-reporting verb *thought* is highly restricted in its distribution. If we take a fairly prosaic example of DT:

(14) a. 'John is a gentleman,' she thought.

and convert it into its corresponding IT form:

(14) b. She thought that John was a gentleman.

then an ambiguity arises. This is due to the way in which the verb *thought*, in addition to its reporting function, can be used 'non-factively' (see note 8 of chapter 5 for a brief explanation). Indeed, in (14b) there is a suggestion that the thinking subject does *not* believe that John is a gentleman. However, by far the most significant problem associated with the thought paradigm concerns the way in which extensive passages of narrative may be located within a participating character's consciousness but none of the 'official' modes of thought presentation are adopted. The example from 'The Dead' quoted in the previous section is a good illustration of such 'non-verbalized' thoughts where the focalizer is clearly a character in the story but none of the formal devices of thought presentation are used. One might consider extending the category of NRTA to account for such passages, although to do so would hardly provide much descriptive benefit. It might be more appropriate simply to regard thought presentation as a formalizing technique, a way of signalling what a character's thoughts would read like if they were actually verbalized. Not only would this be consistent with the account of point of view provided here, but it also allows for the way in narrative segments may be located within a character's active mind without the use of the formal devices of thought presentation.

To conclude this section, it is worth looking at some examples of speech and thought in operation, as it were. In particular, the more experimental free forms will require some illustration, so the discussion which follows will consider the Free Direct modes and the Free Indirect modes in turn.

The basic principle of Free Direct presentation is the removal, wholly or in part, of the authorial and orthographic clues which accompany a straightforward Direct presentation. A consequence of stripping away these clues is that the reported material, to varying degrees, is liberated from narratorial control. In terms of speech presentation, this often results in characters 'speaking for themselves' within dialogues that contain little, if any, authorial interference. Take, as a clear example of this technique, the opening of Malcolm Lowry's *Ultramarine* (1933) which consists entirely of FDS.

'What is your name?'
'Dana Hilliot, ordinary seaman.'
'Where were you born?'
'Oslo.'
'How old are you?'
'Nineteen.'
'Where do you live?'
'Sea Road, Port Sunlight.'
'Any advance?'
'Yes –'
'Next please! What is your name?'
'Anderson Marthon Bredahl, cook.'
'Where were you born?'
'Tvedestrand.'

'How old are you?'
'Thirty-nine.'

(Penguin edn p. 9)

In this rapid question–answer sequence, no identification of the inter-
locutors is offered. Yet despite the absence of reporting clauses, the
context of this speech event may still be constructed not only on the
basis of the content of the questions and answers, but also from the
highly ritualized manner in which the first speaker proceeds through a
standard set of questions. Dana Hilliot, the protagonist of the novel, is
indeed about to board a ship!

The use of Free Direct Thought generates a different, and arguably
more sophisticated, type of stylistic effect. As a useful comparison of
the differences between it and FDS, consider the deployment of both
modes in the following lengthier passage from 'The lotus eaters'
episode of Joyce's *Ulysses* (1922). In this scene, Leopold Bloom goes to
the chemist's to buy some skin lotion and soap for his wife, Molly:

> – Yes, sir, the chemist said. That was two and nine. Have you
> brought a bottle?
> – No, Mr. Bloom said. Make it up, please. I'll call later in the
> day and I'll take one of those soaps. How much are they?
> 5   – Fourpence, sir.
> Mr. Bloom raised a cake to his nostrils. Sweet lemony wax.
> – I'll take this one, he said. That makes three and a penny.
> – Yes, sir, the chemist said. You can pay all together, sir, when
> you come back.
> 10   – Good, Mr. Bloom said.
> He strolled out of the shop, the newspaper baton under his
> armpit, the coolwrappered soap in his left hand.
> At his armpit Bantam Lyons' voice and hand said:
> – Hello, Bloom, what's the best news? Is that today's? Show
> 15 us a minute.
> Shaved off his moustache again, by Jove! Long cold upper lip.
> To look younger. He does look balmy. Younger than I am.
> Bantam Lyons' yellow blacknailed fingers unrolled the baton.
> Wants a wash too. Take off the rough dirt. Good morning, have
> 20 you used Pears' soap? Dandruff on his shoulders. Scalp wants
> oiling.
> – I want to see about that French horse that's running today,
> Bantam Lyons said. Where the bugger is it?
> He rustled the pleated pages, jerking his chin on his high

25 collar. Barber's itch. Tight collar he'll lose his hair. Better leave
him the paper and get shut of him.

(Penguin edn, p. 86)

FDS and FDT can be seen operating in tandem here, along with a third
strand which Leech and Short refer to as *Narrative Report of Action*
(NRA) (1981: 324). This third strand maintains the ongoing 'action' of
the story as well as providing an external narrative framework around
which the strands of speech and thought are woven. Examples of NRA
from the passage are:

Mr. Bloom raised a cake to his nostrils. (line 6)
He strolled out of the shop, the newspaper baton under his armpit
(lines 11–12)
He rustled the pleated pages, jerking his chin on his high collar.
(lines 24–5).

The FDS sequences, by contrast, record the dialogue between Bloom
and the chemist and later, between Bloom and Bantam Lyons. Nowhere are inverted commas used, although Joyce's preferred
introductory dash and the presence of reporting clauses make some
sequences less free than others. Samples are:

– No, Mr. Bloom said. Make it up please. I'll call later in the day
and I'll take one of those soaps. How much are they?
– Fourpence, sir. (lines 3–5)

At his armpit Bantam Lyons' voice and hand said:
– Hello, Bloom, what's the best news? Is that today's? Show us a
minute. (lines 13–15)

Finally, there are the abrupt intrusions into the active mind of the
central character, Bloom, as in:

Shaved off his moustache again, by Jove! Long cold upper lip. To
look younger. He does look balmy. Younger than I am. (lines 16–
17)

Barber's itch. Tight collar he'll lose his hair. Better leave him the
paper and get shut of him. (lines 25–6)

These examples, like all the sequences of thought in the passage, are
maximally free and direct, receiving no explicit authorial intervention
whatsoever. They are, furthermore, highly elliptical in that many of the
more grammatically dispensable units are removed from the sentences
describing Bloom's thoughts. The resulting telegrammatic style evokes
the vividness, immediacy, speed and spontaneity of active human

cognition. Moreover, it often intersperses a character's impressions of their immediate physical environment with sudden recollections and flashbacks – notice, for example, the abrupt intrusion of the advertising jingle 'Good morning, have you used Pears' soap?' at lines 19–20.

One of the implications of this analysis is that we have moved quite close to a working definition of the so-called 'stream-of-consciousness' technique. Stream of consciousness, or 'interior monologue' as it is otherwise known, may be characterized as a form of Free Direct Thought which displays ellipsis. A little crude and simplistic, to be sure, but at least it is a definition which is related explicitly to stylistic criteria. A further implication of the use of FDT is that if it is sustained over a period the narrative gradually switches to first-person focalization. As Booth observes, 'any sustained inside view, of whatever depth, temporarily turns the character whose mind is shown into a narrator' (1961: 164). There is perhaps no clearer illustration of this cross-over than Molly Bloom's extended monologue in the last chapter of the novel on which the present discussion is based.

Turning now to the Free Indirect forms, the label Free Indirect Discourse (FID) is often used as a convenient blanket-term to cover both speech and thought which is presented in this mode. The stylistic significance of this technique is emphasized by the proliferation of other terms used to denote it, including 'style indirect libre', 'erlebte rede' and 'indirect interior monologue'. Perhaps its most important characteristic is the impression it gives of character and narrator speaking or thinking simultaneously. As was explained earlier, altered pronouns, distal deictics and backshifted verbs all serve to bring the reported material into line with the central narrative framework. These features of indirection contrast with their direct counterparts which, as we have seen, report speech and thought verbatim. FID, on the other hand, while 'free' in the sense that it has no reporting clause, is indirect in the way a character's voice is filtered through the narrator's viewpoint. For this reason, FID is often difficult to identify in a narrative, but this elusiveness is very much part of its stylistic effect.

As a sample of FID in an actual narrative, here is a short sequence from Malcolm Lowry's *Under the Volcano* (1947). In the extract, M. Laruelle is contemplating his future in Mexico when his thoughts turn suddenly to the more mundane problem of inclement weather:

> Yet in the Earthly Paradise, what had he done? He had made few friends. He had acquired a Mexican mistress with whom he quarrelled, and numerous beautiful Mayan idols he would be unable to take out of the country, and he had –

M. Laruelle wondered if it was going to rain.

(Penguin edn, p. 16)

The first paragraph is rich in the features of FID. Most significant, perhaps, are the backshifted verbs where the present tense of a direct report (e.g. 'with whom I quarrel') becomes past ('with whom he quarrelled'), whilst the present perfect of a direct version (e.g. 'I have made few friends') is now past perfect ('He had made few friends'). As is consistent with FID, no reporting clauses are used in this paragraph, although a reporting clause *is* used in the final sentence, marking a shift to Indirect Thought. This abrupt switch from FID to IT underscores the disparity in the content of M. Laruelle's thoughts, the deep soul-searching of the first paragraph compared to the banal reflection on the weather which follows. And the switch in reference, from pronouns to title and surname, strengthens this contrast further.

Less common, though still rich stylistically, is the use of FID in first-person narratives. While backshifted verbs and distal deictics signal FID in the same way as in third-person narratives, the pronoun system is a little more complex. Here, in sequences of speech which are addressed *to* the narrator, the pronouns move from the *you* of direct report to *I*, which, in this case, signals indirection. An example should help clarify this. In the following sequence from John Banville's *The Book of Evidence* (1989), the narrator, Freddie Montgomery, accuses his mother of selling his art collection in his absence:

I shouted, I waved my fists, I stamped about stiff-legged, beside myself. Where were they, the pictures, I cried, what had she done with them? I *demanded* to know. . . . Then, when I paused to take a breath, she started. Demand, did I? – I, who had gone off and abandoned my widowed mother.

(Minerva edn, p. 59).

Apart from one reporting clause, the mode used for reporting the speech of the narrator is generally Free Indirect. This should be clear from the use of the past tense ('I *demanded* to know') and the pronoun changes ('what had *she* done'). The speech of the protagonist's mother is also in the FIS mode, but noticeably the pronoun switch is from second person to first person ('Demand, did I? – I, who had gone off and abandoned my widowed mother'). A simple check for the presence of FID not only in this example but in narrative generally is simply to try to transpose the passage to a direct form. In the extracts from Banville and Lowry this should present no problem and should support the FID readings made of these examples.

A great deal more could be said on the uses and effects of FID. One issue not touched upon at all is the potential for creating irony through the use of this mode. Another is the relationship of FID to textual norms: how FIT signals an experimental leap away from the canonical IT employed in early prose fiction and how FIS, by contrast, represents a distancing from the more neutral DS form. Nevertheless, enough material will have been collected here for the purposes of the discussion which follows. Terms like FDT and FID will re-appear where appropriate, as the techniques of speech and thought presentation are crucially tied up with the concept of point of view.

2.4 APPROACHES TO POINT OF VIEW ON THE PSYCHOLOGICAL PLANE

The purpose of this section is to review three strands of research which are concerned, implicitly or explicitly, with the linguistic manifestation of the speaking voice(s) in narrative fiction. Inevitably, there will be some overlap between these three strands and perhaps, on the basis of finer theoretical distinctions, numerous other strands could be identified as relevant. The detail which would be required for such a comprehensive introduction, however, would warrant a full chapter in its own right and would delay the progress towards our own analyses of point of view. So what follows is a compromise: only three broad strands will be considered, and aspects of those strands which are most relevant to the concerns of the next chapter will be developed most fully. The third strand will receive particular attention, therefore, as it will be the one which informs the 'modal' approach to point of view outlined in chapter 3.

Because of its general adherence to the paradigm of structuralist poetics and narratology, I term the first approach to point of view *structuralist*. Such work is characterized generally by its preoccupation with uncovering the abstract principles of the system of literary communication, its oppositions and contrasts and its underlying positions and possibilities. Structuralist poetics, therefore, seeks to develop a 'grammar' of literature in much the same way as linguistics seeks to develop a grammar of a particular language. The parallel with linguistics is a central precept of structuralist theory and practice, the aim of which is a poetics which stands to literature as linguistics stands to language. The emphasis is not, therefore, on explaining what individual works mean but on explaining 'the system of figures and conventions that enable works to have the forms and meanings they do' (Culler 1980: 8). The way in which the theory and terminology of linguistics is used in structuralist poetics, however, is not straightforward. More often than not, linguistic units and categories are used in a metaphorical or 'analogical' way. That is to say, they are not employed directly in the analysis of texts but, rather, provide a kind of blueprint upon which the schemata of literary communication are modelled. This analogical use of linguistics is explicit in the following remark from Roland Barthes, a key figure in structuralist poetics:

> a narrative is a large sentence, just as any declarative sentence is, in a certain way, the outline of a little narrative.
>
> (1975: 241)

The theoretical justification for seeing narratives as 'big sentences' has never been easy to provide and, suffice it to say, some stylisticians are not convinced of the homology of the level of the sentence and the level of narrative.

Perhaps the best exemplum of where structuralist poetics and the analysis of point of view intersect, is Gerard Genette's *Narrative Discourse* (1980). Genette's study has proved influential not only as a theory of narrative composition but as an in-depth study of Marcel Proust's *A la recherche du temps perdu*. It has, furthermore, received modifications both from the author himself and from other narratologists and poeticians.[4] Genette, in keeping with the 'analogical' use of linguistics, attempts to define a series of narrative positions within the parameters of a quasi-grammatical theory. For example, the category of 'tense' is expanded to account for the 'stance of narrative discourse', whilst that of 'mood' is enlarged to 'the regulation of narrative information' (1980: 161–2). This widening of the scope of reference of grammatical terms is intended to handle larger narrative units at what Genette calls 'the macroscopic level' (88). The representation of time in fiction comes under particular scrutiny within this narrative framework – indeed, we have already touched upon some of Genette's classifications in the earlier discussion of temporal point of view (see section 2.2). However, those aspects of his model which touch upon more general aspects of point of view are of particular concern here.

In keeping with the structuralist method, Genette bases his model on sets of contrasts and oppositions. One key contrast, proposed at the outset, is that between *diegesis* and *narrative*.[5] Diegesis is the actual story which a narrative relates, the sequence of 'real' events organized in a linear chronological sequence. Diegesis thus incorporates the notion of 'plot'. Narrative, by contrast, is the means by which the story is told, the actual text with all its linguistic idiosyncrasies. Narrative may exhibit the strategies of flashback, flashforward or temporal fragmentation, or it may simply be isochronous with the story it relates. Some of Genette's own examples should help clarify the diegesis/narrative distinction. In a chapter on 'relations of frequency' between the narrative and diegetic levels (1980: 115–160), he discusses the ways in which utterances in a narrative are used to denote events at the story level, and, in doing so, identifies a number of asymmetries between the two levels. For example, an utterance like *He went fishing every time it rained* narrates once what may have happened any number of times in the actual story. In other words, a single narrative utterance takes upon itself several occurrences of a particular event. This 'iterative' narrative utterance is contrasted with the situation where a number of narrative utterances are used to relate an event which may have happened only once in the story. Genette's own illustrations of this are, he admits, rather contrived: he asks us to consider a series of statements like *Yesterday I went to bed early, Yesterday I went to bed before it was late, Yesterday I put myself to bed early*, as a means of relating just one event at the story level. However, although his examples are hypothetical, he does add the following proviso:

> Let us remember, however, that certain modern texts are based on narrative's capacity for repetition . . . the same event can be told several times not only with stylistic variations, as is generally the case in Robbe-Grillet, but also with variations in 'point of view', as in *Rasheman* or *The Sound and the Fury* . . . Let us also remember (and this is not as foreign to the function of literature as one might believe) that children love to be told the same story several times.
>
> (1980: 115)

This diegetic/narrative distinction provides a locus upon which further structural contrasts are based. One such contrast concerns the *position* of the narrator relative to the story. According to Genette, there are two basic positions: that where a narrator is *outside* the story and that where a narrator is a character *within* the story. The terms reserved for these positions are, respectively, *heterodiegetic* (meaning 'different to the story') and *homodiegetic* (meaning 'same as the story'). This distinction raises one or two issues which require comment. In the classic structuralist vein, and despite the fact that numerous examples are provided, terms *heterodiegetic* and *homodiegetic* are really abstractions referring to positions, not individuals, in a narrative. They may be thus more appropriately thought of as grammatical 'slots' which designate functions relative to other narrative functions. Furthermore, this contrast is not to be taken as a substitute for the more traditional distinction between first-person and third-person narration. Genette explains:

> The presence of first-person verbs in a narrative text can therefore refer to two very different situations which grammar renders identical but which narrative analysis must distinguish: the narrator's own designation of himself as such, as when Virgil writes 'I sing of arms and the man . . .', or else the identity of person between the narrator and one of the characters in the story, as when Crusoe writes 'I was born in the Year 1632, in the city of York . . .' The term 'first-person narrative' refers, quite obviously, only to the second of these situations.
>
> (1980: 244)

Heterodiegetic narratives, therefore, are defined on the basis of the absence of the narrator from the story and not through the non-occurrence of first-person pronouns. For instance, Fielding's *Tom Jones*, despite the narrator's frequent use of self-referential first-person pronouns, would be classified as nothing other than a heterodiegetic narrative.

Intersecting with the system of narrative positions is Genette's typology of narrative 'mood', which approximates most closely that dimension of narrative for which the term 'psychological point of view' has been reserved. Genette proposes a triadic system for this aspect of point of view, or *focalization*, as he prefers to call it. The three relevant categories of focalization are identified below, along with summaries of Genette's definitions (1980: 188–192):

1 *Zero focalization*: the narrative with omniscient narrator, where the narrator says more than any of the characters know.
2 *Internal focalization*: the narrative with restricted field or restricted omniscience, only fully realized in narratives of interior monologue (FID). Internal focalization may be *fixed*, as in the centre of consciousness in Henry James's *The Ambassadors*, or *variable*, as in the alternating focalization of Flaubert's *Madame Bovary*.
3 *External focalization*: the narrative where the narrator says less than a character knows. External focalization thus yields 'objectivist' or 'behaviourist' narratives, where access to the thoughts and feelings of characters is not provided. The work of Dashiell Hammet and Ernest Hemingway is representative of this mode.

The commitment to a particular mode of focalization need not be consistent over the whole length of a narrative. In Genette's words, 'any single formula of focalization does not, therefore, always bear on an entire work, but rather on a definite narrative section, which can be very short' (1980: 191). Significantly, the one mode which does not receive extensive explanation is the first of the three, zero focalization, which is referred to simply as 'the classical narrative'. Presumably this type differs from that of internal focalization in terms of the greater degree of omniscience which it manifests. But omniscience is the prerogative of all heterodiegetic narrators: it may be abrogated or relinquished as of necessity, even between one sentence and another in a narrative. Indeed, in the heterodiegetic narratives of internal and external focalization which Genette cites as examples, all of the narrators, including those of the Hemingway stories, possess at least the 'licence' of omniscience. Whether this licence is invoked or not is another issue. Noticeably, in her discussion and reformulation of this part of Genette's framework, Rimmon-Kenan (1983) drops completely the concept of zero focalization, preferring to develop the internal/external opposition instead. Another aspect of Genette's schema which requires greater clarification is the way in which the heterodiegetic/homodiegetic distinction intersects with the category of external focalization. For instance, the two types of narratives offered as exempla of external focalization are those by Dashiell Hammet (generally homodiegetic) and Ernest Hemingway (generally heterodiegetic). The narrator occupies substantially different positions within each type of story, and this clearly has important implications for the nature of the viewing position which emerges relative to each.

The categories proposed by Genette in his influential study are certainly useful and will be drawn upon where appropriate in the next chapter. However, in addition to the reservations expressed just now, there remains the issue of the 'analogical' method. The earlier cautionary remarks on this structuralist practice need not be re-introduced here, but one of the consequences of developing broad paradigms in this way is that the linguistic evidence offered is not explicit. Recognitions of categories such as internal and external focalization may vary from reader to reader, and while this is not undesirable, the view taken here is that it is possible to specify on clearer linguistic criteria the different types of point of view realized in narrative fiction. Point of view must, after all, be expressed in and through language and the techniques of modern linguistics, as was stressed in the chapter 1, are well-equipped to deal with such a phenomenon. It is to precisely such a narrower, linguistic theory of point of view that we now turn.

This second type of approach to the analysis of point of view in fiction is that which I term *generative*. The term generative is suggested because the linguistic perspective which informs this work is the transformational–generative (TG) model developed by Noam Chomsky and his followers. Such 'Chomskyan stylistics' is often characterized by the painstakingly detailed analysis of sets of sentences (attested or contrived) with a view to expounding a generative theory of narrative communication. Unlike the structuralist approach, which seeks to develop a grammar of narrative, the generative approach seeks to develop a grammar of the sentences which make up narratives. The former approach thus concentrates on the *macrostructures* of literary communication and the latter on its *microstructures*.

Ann Banfield's *Unspeakable Sentences* (1982) reads very much like a manifesto for generative stylistics. Rejecting the structuralist model completely, Banfield claims that the type of linguistic argumentation practised by transformational–generative linguists is necessary if an adequate definition of literary form is ever to be reached. The confidence with which this view is presented is almost belligerent:

> If the attentive reader, whether or not fluent in generative grammar, follows the arguments presented here, the nature of the specifically literary character of narrative will emerge from the backdrop formed by the different language of ordinary discourse and be revealed by its very essence – its very *linguistic* essence.
>
> (1982: 19; original emphasis)

Banfield goes on to identify two types of narrative sentence: 'sentences of narration' (roughly analogous to the Narrative Report of Action mode introduced in the previous section) and sentences of 'represented speech and thought' (yet another term for Free Indirect Discourse). Both types of sentence, she argues, are 'unspeakable'. Sentences of narration cannot be spoken not only because they are cut adrift from tangible co-ordinates of space and time but also because they contain no 'real' speaker and addressee. They are therefore 'objectified' in a manner which does not characterize the subjectified discourse of everyday interaction. Sentences of 'represented speech and thought' (referred to as FID from now on) are comparably 'unspeakable', but in this case it is because subjects cannot report their own speech and thought within this mode. For example, you might arrange a meeting with someone with:

I'll be in the pub this evening.

but never with:

He would be in the pub that evening.

This observation leads Banfield to reject vociferously the 'dual-voice' interpretation of sentences like the second which are represented in FID. She contends that it is impossible for two points of view to be represented simultaneously within a single sentence and that instances of FID reflect simply a single character's point of view. She rejects the idea that the second voice in FID is that of a narrator and points out that those who classify FID in this way do so by default: the presence of backshifted tenses and distal deictics are not sufficient indications that an external narratorial voice is genuinely present.

Scant though this summary of Banfield's theory is, it still highlights a number of the more controversial aspects of the generative approach. Significant at the outset is the way in which such work rests on *grammaticality judgements*. These are the predictions by the analyst about which sentences are well formed and which are not. Literary texts, perhaps not surprisingly, are something of a linguistic minefield in this regard, for here the conditions of grammaticality and acceptability are stretched to the limits. Yet Banfield appears to have no problem assigning grammaticality judgements to virtually all the sentences examined (whether contrived or taken directly from novels) and, in keeping with the introspective method of TG linguistics, it is assumed that these decisions about grammaticality will be shared by other native speakers. So, the following example of Direct Speech is considered grammatical:

(15) a. She replied, 'We may be parted for years, I and Peter.'

(p. 30)

whereas its Indirect Speech counterpart is not:

(15) b. She replied that they might be parted for years, she and Peter.

(p. 30)

It is difficult to assess how other speakers will judge example (15b), but to *my* mind (and this is perfectly sufficient for generative hypothesis building) it is not only perfectly acceptable but it also exhibits a subtle shift through the appended *she and Peter*, towards a more free form of IS. This principle leads us, in fact, to a second point of controversy. In Banfield's schema, there is little recognition of any continuum which might exist between her two types of narrative sentence. The sentences of narration and sentences of FID are regarded as distinct phenomena, with no possible shading of one type into another. Now, it was suggested in the previous section that the categories of speech and thought presentation, while useful as a system of generalized reference points, are not rigorously discrete and the boundaries of these categories are more fuzzy than clear. For instance, it is not easy to identify precisely which mode is being used for the reported speech in the following extract from Fielding's *Tom Jones* (1749):

> When Mrs. Western had finished, Sophia answered, 'That she was very incapable of arguing with a lady of her aunt's superior knowledge and experience, especially on a subject which she had so very little considered, as this of matrimony.'
>
> (Oxford edn, vol. I, p. 332)

Despite its inclusion within quotation marks of Direct Speech, Sophia's speech exhibits the pronoun and tense system characteristic of Indirect Speech. Precise classification is further complicated by the use of the *that* connective to introduce the reported material. As for the problem of 'slippage' between one mode and another within the confines of a *single* sentence, take the following short example from Neil Jordan's novel *Dream of a Beast* (1983):

> I told him slowly and carefully that yes, I did feel hungry.
>
> (Chatto & Windus edn, p. 66).

Here, the retention of 'yes' pushes this example away from IS towards FIS, but one would be hard put to place a single label on this sentence. A more general implication of this concerns Banfield's rejection of the 'dual-voice' theory outlined earlier. While it would be fair to say that there is only a single voice present in the example immediately above (it is, after all, a first-person narrative), the same could not be said as readily of the example from *Tom Jones*. Even in cases where none of the formal techniques of speech and thought presentation is used, it is still possible to identify the presence of more than one mediating voice. A simple, yet highly pertinent illustration of this is the opening sentence of Joyce's 'The Dead':

> Lily, the caretaker's daughter, was literally run off her feet.
>
> (Granada edn, p. 160)

Surely there are two voices present in this sentence: that of an external commentator who identifies Lily firstly by name and then, through apposition, by her position as the caretaker's daughter, and that of Lily herself whose (mis)use of 'literally' and 'run off her feet' suggests a pattern of language approximating her own idiolect.

A more general objection again to the 'unspeakable-sentence' approach relates to the way in which a theory of literariness is built on a distinction between just two types of narrative sentence. Sentences of

FID, Banfield argues, are 'unique to narrative' (p. 16) and the interaction between these and sentences of narration yields insights into the 'specifically literary character of narrative' (p. 19). Yet FID can occur outside narrative fiction and its deployment in print and broadcast media has been both well documented and well analysed (see note 3, above). Furthermore, FID is also endemic in fiction which is normally excluded from the literary canon: the romance fiction documented by Nash (1990) represents just one such excluded genre. So the assumptions that FID is particularly 'literary' or that 'literariness' resides solely in the interaction between this mode and sentences of narration need to be seriously questioned.

Challenging and thorough as *Unspeakable Sentences* is, it postulates a theory of point of view which is generally at odds with much subsequent research in stylistics. The present study is no exception, and while the views of Banfield deserve recognition – as do, indeed, those of Ehrlich (1990), who extends the framework beyond the limits of the single sentence – there are points of substantial theoretical disagreement between the generative approach and the approach adopted here. Only a few of those disagreements have been sketched in this short review.[6]

The third approach to point of view is one with which I concur generally and which is elaborated comprehensively in the following chapter. It is marked not only by its preoccupation with the compositional processes of both literary and everyday narratives but by its concern with the linguistic devices by which narrators slant and orientate their narratives towards readers. This emphasis on the compositional techniques of message construction prompts me to label this approach *interpersonal*. The term itself is borrowed from systemic–functional linguistics, where it is used to describe that function of language which is

> concerned with the establishment of social relations and with the participation of the individual in all kinds of personal interaction. Language, in this function, mediates in all the various role relationships contracted by the individual, and this plays an important part in the development of his personality.

> (Halliday 1970: 335)

Although the interpersonal approach shares both the structuralist concern with the macro-units of narrative and the generative interest in the sentence-level representation of point of view, what sets it apart is the way in which it attempts to isolate the linguistic features which create a text's 'personality'. For instance, an interpersonal analysis may examine the system of *modality*, which is the means by which a speaker's attitude towards what they are saying is conveyed. And different modalities, it may be argued, not only highlight the style of different narratives, but also help explain the generic differences between collections of narratives.

Two central analyses of narrative within the interpersonal framework are Uspensky (1973) and Fowler (1986). There exist other studies which are broadly interpersonal in orientation,[7] but the Uspensky–Fowler approach draws most explicitly on the features of language which realize this function. In the review which follows, I shall concentrate on the framework of point of view proposed by Fowler (1986: 127–47). This seems the best way forward, as Fowler blends his own ideas with those of Uspensky in developing a rather intriguing four-part model of psychological point of view.

In common with the scholars working within the structuralist model, Fowler proposes an initial distinction between *internal* and *external* narratorial viewpoints. Internal narrative is mediated through the subjective viewpoint of a particular character's consciousness, whilst in an external narrative events are described *outside* the consciousness of any participating character. Fowler then splits in two each of these types, thereby deriving a four-way classification. The first of these he names 'Internal type A' and identifies as a predominantly first-person mode of narration from the point of view of a participating character. It is characterized by a foregrounded *modality* (the grammar of explicit comment) and by the use of *verba sentiendi* (words denoting thoughts, feelings and perceptions). Type A is in this respect a highly 'subjective' mode of narration as it is located entirely within a participating character's consciousness, manifesting their judgements on other characters, and their opinions on both realized and unrealized events of a story. As an illustration of the type A mode, Fowler cites the opening sequence of F. Scott Fitzgerald's *The Great Gatsby* – the bulk of which is reproduced here:

Passage A

In my younger and more vulnerable years my father gave me some advice that I've been turning over in my mind ever since.

'Whenever you feel like criticizing anyone', he told me, 'just remember that all the people in this world haven't had the
5 advantages that you've had.'

He didn't say any more, but we've always been unusually communicative in a reserved way, and I understood that he meant a great deal more than that. In consequence, I'm inclined to reserve all judgements, a habit that has opened up many

10   curious natures to me and also made me the victim of not a few
     veteran bores. The abnormal mind is quick to detect and attach
     itself to this quality when it appears in a normal person, and so it
     came about that in college I was unjustly accused of being a
     politician, because I was privy to the secret griefs of wild,
15   unknown men.

(Fowler 1986: 135–6)

In a number of respects, this constitutes a paradigm case of type A
point of view. For one thing, it is a first-person narrative located within
the confines of a participating character's consciousness. It furthermore displays a foregrounded modality realized chiefly through
evaluative adjectives and adverbs ('more vulnerable' (line 1), 'unusually communicative' (lines 6–7), 'curious' (line 10), 'veteran' (line
11)) and generic sentences which proclaim timeless, universal truths
('The abnormal mind is quick to detect' (lines 11–12)). The passage
also includes many *verba sentiendi* highlighting, in this instance, the
preoccupation of the narrator with himself and his image ('turning over
in my mind' (line 2); 'I understood' (line 7); 'I'm inclined' (line 8)).

Fowler's second internal mode, type B, differs from A in that it is
consistently third-person narration. The perspective of type B is that of
an 'omniscient' narrator who claims knowledge of what is going on in
characters' minds. Despite the privileged access to the conciousnesses
of characters, authorial modality as such is not prominent, as the focus
is on characters and not the vantage point from which they are
described. However, as the author provides an account of the thoughts,
reactions and perceptions of characters, this mode will still be marked
by *verba sentiendi*. Fowler provides as an illustration of 'pure' type B a
passage from Mervyn Peake's *Titus Groan* which details an incident
where the kitchen-boy Steerpike plans his escape from captivity. I have
retained Fowler's italicization of significant *verba sentiendi* in the
passage:

Passage B
Again he *fastened his gaze* upon the first dozen feet of vertical stone,
choosing and *scrutinizing* the grips that he *would use*. His *survey* left
him uneasy. It *would be unpleasant*. The more he *searched* the wall
with his intense eyes the less he liked the *prospect*, but he could *see*
that it was feasible if he concentrated every *thought* and fibre upon
the attempt.

(Fowler 1986: 138)

The feature which links Fowler's remaining two categories is the
general avoidance, on the part of the narrator, of any description of

characters' thoughts and feelings. External type C is marked as the most impersonal form of third-person narration. Here the narrator declines to report any psychological processes, maintaining a position *outside* the consciousnesses of the characters in the story. Type C therefore exhibits neither modality nor *verba sentiendi* and the resulting style is one which is often perceived of intuitively as objective, neutral and impersonal – a style which typifies, Fowler argues, the ideal of 'objective realism' proposed by the French novelist Flaubert. The absence of evaluative modalities and narratorial judgements also makes this mode the formula for news-reporting, at least in theory if not in practice. Although it is virtually impossible to find texts that are completely devoid of modal devices, Fowler argues that much of the work of Hemingway comes close to a pure type C. He cites the following extract from *The Killers* as an illustration.

> *Passage C*
> Outside the arc-light shone through the bare branches of a tree. Nick walked up the street beside the car-tracks and turned at the next arc-light down a side-street. Three houses up the street was Hirsch's rooming-house. Nick walked up the two steps and
> 5 pushed the bell. A woman came to the door.
> 'Is Ole Anderson here?'
> 'Do you want to see him?'
> 'Yes, if he's in.'
> Nick followed the woman up a flight of stairs and back to the
> 10 end of a corridor. She knocked on the door.
> 'Who is it?'
> 'It's somebody to see you, Mr. Anderson', the woman said.
> 'It's Nick Adams.'
> 'Come in.'
> 15 Nick opened the door and went into the room.
>
> (1986: 141)

Although the third sentence could arguably be attributed to Nick's psychological inferencing (lines 3–4), there is virtually no interpretation of the cognitive processes of any of the characters. There is, furthermore, little authorial modality here. The general 'flatness' of the passage is also re-inforced by the techniques which Hemingway uses to present speech. The dominant mode is Free Direct Speech, where speech is reported directly without the mediation of a reporting clause. Where Direct Speech is used (line 12) the verb supplied in the reporting clause is simply 'said', which is the unmarked verb available for speech presentation.

The last of Fowler's categories, External type D, is in many ways the most intriguing and the most problematic. Despite its externality, the persona of the narrator is highlighted by explicit modality and in some cases by first-person pronouns. In this way an impression is created of a narrator who controls the telling of the story and who has definite views on the characters and events of the story, though, curiously, at the same time has no privileged access to the thoughts and feelings of those characters. It is worth quoting Fowler's development of type D at some length here:

> Externality in relation to the characters emerges when the narra-tor's modal activity includes what Uspensky calls 'words of estrangement': words such as 'apparently', 'evidently', 'perhaps', 'as if', 'it seemed', etc. as well as metaphors and comparisons. These expressions pretend that the author – or often, one character observing another – does not have access to the feelings or thoughts of the characters. They emphasize an act of interpretation, an attempt to reconstruct the psychology of the character by reference to the signs that can be gleaned by external observation. *Verba sentiendi* may be used, but only if introduced by words denoting appearance or speculation: 'He seemed tired', 'She was probably furious.' There is also, in texts which make extensive use of this technique, considerable reference to the physical characteristics and gestures of the characters.
>
> (1986: 142)

The example which Fowler provides of External type D narration is the following extract from Arnold Bennett's *Riceyman Steps*. I have retained Fowler's italicization of significant 'words of estrangement':

Passage D
On an autumn afternoon of 1919 a hatless man with a slight limp *might have been observed* ascending the gentle, broad acclivity of Riceyman Steps, which lead from King's Cross Road up to Ricey-man Square, in the great metropolitan industrial district of Clerkenwell. He was rather less than stout and rather more than slim. His thin hair had begun to turn from black to grey, but his complexion was still fairly good, and the rich, very red lips, under a small greyish moustache and over a short, pointed beard, were quite remarkable in their *suggestion* of vitality. The brown eyes *seemed* a little small; they peered at near objects. As to his age, an experi-enced and cautious observer of mankind, without previous knowledge of this man, *would have said* no more than he *must be* past forty. The man himself was *certainly* entitled to say that he was

in the prime of life. He wore a neat dark-grey suit, which *must have been* carefully folded at nights, a low, white, starched collar, and a 'made' black tie that completely hid the shirt-front; the shirt-cuffs could not be seen. He was shod in old, black leather slippers, well polished. He gave *an appearance* of quiet, intelligent, refined and kindly prosperity; and in his little eyes shone the varying lights of emotional sensitiveness.

(1986: 142–3)

This account of Fowler's four-category model should, for the moment, suffice. To progress further and suggest modifications and extensions will require some explanation of other relevant concepts, most notably that of modality in language. All of this will be done in the following chapter. However, one thing that this brief review of Fowler's model should reveal is that it is possible not only to identify structural categories in narrative but also to provide clear linguistic criteria for their recognition. Of course, while formalization of this sort is useful, it will always be a partial description and will never exhaust the range of linguistic markers of point of view in fiction.

2.5 SUMMARY

A substantial amount of material has been collected in this chapter, which, although diverse, is all relevant to the analysis of point of view in narrative fiction. The chapter began with a basic introduction to the concepts of spatial and temporal point of view, and the linguistic system of deixis was proposed as a useful means of exploring the way these co-ordinates of space and time are realized in fiction. Yet spatio-temporal point of view, it was argued, might be more appropriately regarded as a subsystem of point of view on the psychological plane. The case for subsuming spatio-temporal point of view into a broader-based category of psychological point of view is also argued by Uspensky:

the author may assume the point of view of one of his characters in all the possible aspects. . . . Thus the authorial position would fully concur with the position of the viewpoint character [*sic*] on the psychological plane. Also, the author would move through time and space together with this character, adopting his horizons – accordingly, the position of the author would concur with that of the character on the spatial-temporal plane.

(1973: 101)

This chapter also provides a short introduction to the techniques of speech and thought presentation. In addition to the intrinsic benefit this section should have had, it also provided some key terms and concepts, such as Free Indirect Discourse, which were to feature in the review of relevant work on point of view which followed. Of the three approaches discussed, the last, the interpersonal, was identified as the one with the most stylistic potential. It is, furthermore, still relatively underexplored. This is what provides the point of entry into the next chapter, where a grammar of point of view, based on interpersonal features of language use, will be proposed.

NOTES AND FURTHER READING

1 To give a clearer picture of what I mean by the interaction of deixis and register, consider the following short example from British television's 'Grandstand' programme. This is part of the regular preview of football matches for the day, and was recorded but two hours from writing the relevant section in the main body of the chapter. The proximal deictics of space and time and the use of the present tense should be easily identified:

> It's a beautiful day here at Hillsborough. The sun is shining now and the stage is set for an entertaining match. But the match is not just about Sheffield Wednesday and Aston Villa, it's about Ron Atkinson
>
> (John Motson)

2 The representation of time in fiction has become a central concern of narrative poetics in recent years. A short introduction of this sort cannot really do justice to what has become an extremely broad field, and to attempt to go further here would take us beyond the remit of this chapter. A comprehensive survey can be found in Toolan (1988: 47–89), where terms like prolepsis and duration are explored in much greater detail.

3 For applications of the speech and thought framework to texts outside the literary canon, see Mick Short's analysis of the experimental modes of speech presentation in a variety of British newspapers (Short 1988). Short proposes a supplement to his own model in the form of a category of 'speech summary', a category designed to account for the discoursal conditions of text-types other than the novel. Also relevant here is McKenzie (1987), who offers a perceptive study of a booklet produced by South African students reporting their discussions with the African National Congress. McKenzie demonstrates how Free Indirect Speech provides a perfectly legal means of coping with the ban on direct quotation of the ANC which was then in operation. Roeh and Nir (1990) argue that different modes of speech presentation reflect different underlying ideological stances. They illustrate their argument with examples of Indirect Speech and Free Indirect Speech taken from Israeli radio broadcasts.

4 Genette reviews his own model in a number of places, but most comprehensively in Genette (1988). Bal (1977) offers a critique of some of Genette's earlier versions of the theory of focalization, and her later work (1985) is a generally relevant contribution to structuralist theories of narrative. More

recent modifications and extensions of Genette's work are Edmiston (1989) and Nelles (1990).

5 Just about every theory of formalist and structuralist poetics establishes some such contrast. Some parallel distinctions, in the order diegesis–narrative, are; *fabula/sjuzhet; histoire/discours;* story/discourse. The proliferation of terms in this area is an unfortunate one, as are some of the attempts to establish triadic, as opposed to binary, contrasts. Rimmon-Kenan (1983) and Toolan (1988) provide accessible reviews of these developments.

6 Ehrlich's (1990) account, unlike that of Banfield, attempts to isolate the formal devices which enable a fictional character's viewpoint to be maintained *across* sentence boundaries. She thus proposes an intersentential model of FID and, in addition to the generative base, draws on relevant work on cohesion and coherence in order to develop this model. A compact and useful book, but the dense metalanguage which characterizes work in this tradition may be off-putting to the uninitiated ('the RTs of the SCPs' parentheticals serve as the RTs for the SCPs' root-Ss', p. 66)!

7 Three such studies, which may be considered interpersonal in the broadest sense, are Dolezel (1976) and Weber (1984, 1989).

3 Point of view in narrative fiction: a modal grammar

> Ineluctable modality of the visible: at least that if no more, thought through my eyes.
>
> (from the 'Proteus' episode, *Ulysses*, by James Joyce)

3.1 INTRODUCTION

British television's Channel 4 runs a regular light-entertainment programme called *Whose Line is it Anyway?* Part of the show involves a sketch where four guest celebrities improvise on a topic in a style of their choosing. The topics, suggested *ad hoc* by the studio audience, can cover anything from motor-cycle maintenance to a visit to the dentist, and the styles adopted by the celebrities normally mimic well-known writers. It is not surprising, therefore, to hear a discourse on tropical-fish keeping in the style of D.H. Lawrence, or a monologue on air-traffic control conducted, rather alarmingly, in the manner of Samuel Beckett. What is intriguing is the degree of success of these improvisations. The studio audience often recognizes instantly the style being adopted, suggesting that there are some fairly widespread assumptions about what sounds typically Lawrentian, Joycean or Kafkaesque. Explaining this measure of agreement is in a sense what this chapter sets out to do. It will be argued that much of the 'feel' of a text is attributable to the type of point of view it exhibits, and, furthermore, that sufficient generalizations can be made about the ways in which writers consistently draw on particular points of view. The linguistic feature which will underpin this discussion is the concept of *modality* which was introduced informally towards the end of the previous chapter. What follows is a more comprehensive description of the term, and this will prepare the way for the modal grammar of point of view which is the central concern of this chapter.

3.2 MODALITY IN LANGUAGE

So far in the discussion, the term *modality* has been used rather loosely to refer to 'attitudinal' features of language. In his own account Fowler quite properly identifies a variety of grammatical means for conveying modal commitment, amongst which are included modal auxiliaries, modal adverbs (or sentence adverbs), evaluative adjectives and adverbs, generic sentences and verbs of knowledge, prediction and evaluation. What might constitute a useful supplement to this kind of framework, however, is some identification of the different *types* of modality found in English. Such an identification will in fact prove central to the point-of-view model that will be outlined in the following section. What follows here, then, is an account of the more important modal systems, and, in keeping with the basic procedure adopted in this book, this account draws on a number of primary sources.[1] Three points should be borne in mind in relation to this. First, though sufficiently comprehensive, this modal framework is relatively self-contained and, as such, should provide readers with a workable model with which they may conduct their own analyses of modality. Second, for the benefit of those readers who do not wish to consult the at times intimidating primary sources, a number of theoretical and terminological difficulties have been ironed out. And finally, those features of modality which are especially relevant to the analysis of point of view will be assigned particular importance in the modal 'package' which follows.

As was pointed out earlier, *modality* refers broadly to a speaker's attitude towards, or opinion about, the truth of a proposition expressed by a sentence. It also extends to their attitude towards the situation or event described by a sentence. Modality is therefore a major exponent of the *interpersonal* function of language which was outlined in section 2.4 of the previous chapter. For convenience, I shall identify and describe four modal systems of English. These are the *deontic* system, along with the closely related *boulomaic* system; the *epistemic* system with its subsystem of *perception* modality. Deontic modality, first of all, is the modal system of 'duty', as it is concerned with a speaker's attitude to the degree of obligation attaching to the performance of certain actions. For instance, in the following examples, the deontic modal auxiliaries realize a continuum of commitment from *permission* (1) through *obligation* (2) to *requirement* (3):

(1) You may leave.
(2) You should leave.
(3) You must leave.

As we shall see later, modal auxiliaries have a variety of functions, and some of these forms may 'double up' as epistemic forms.

Deontic expressions may also combine adjectives and participles in 'BE . . . THAT' and 'BE . . . TO' constructions representing a comparable continuum of commitment. The following examples exhibit different degrees of obligation and possibility, and the grammatical formulae used in each are explained alongside:

(4) You are permitted to leave.   (BE + *participle* + TO)
(5) It is possible for you to leave.   (BE + *adjective* + TO)
(6) You are obliged to leave.   (BE + *participle* + TO)
(7) It is necessary that you leave.   (BE+ *adjective* + THAT)
(8) You are forbidden to leave.   (BE + *participle* + TO)

Clearly, the deontic system is of crucial relevance to the strategies of social interaction, especially to tactics of persuasion and politeness. Indeed, when we come to consider some of the linguistic features of persuasive discourse such as advertising language, deontic modality will provide a valuable analytic tool (see chapter 5).

Closely related to deontic modality is *boulomaic* modality, which is extensively grammaticized in English in expressions of 'desire'. Modal lexical verbs, indicating the wishes and desires of the speaker, are central in the boulomaic system, as the following examples should make clear:

(9) I hope that you will leave.
(10) I wish you'd leave.
(11) I regret that you're leaving.

Again, adjectival and participial constructions in a 'BE . . . TO' or 'BE . . . THAT' framework can carry boulomaic commitment, although related modal adverbs may also be used:

(12) It is hoped that you will leave.   (BE + *participle* + THAT)
(13) It's good that you're leaving.   (BE + *adjective* + THAT)
(14) It is regrettable that you're leaving. (BE + *adjective* + THAT)
(15) Hopefully, you'll leave.   (*modal adverb*)
(16) Regrettably, you're leaving.   (*modal adverb*)

The epistemic system is possibly the most important regarding the analysis of point of view in fiction. And as the epistemic modal adverb in the previous sentence (spot it!) should suggest, epistemic modality is concerned with the speaker's confidence or lack of confidence in the truth of a proposition expressed. In the following examples, the modal auxiliaries are now used in their epistemic sense. They convey varying degrees of epistemic commitment to the basic proposition *You are right*:

(17) You could be right.
(18) You may be right.
(19) You must be right.
(20) You might have been right.
(21) You should have been right (i.e. in the context of 'If you followed the instructions carefully').

Despite the obvious centrality of the modal auxiliaries in the system, epistemic modality may be grammaticized through a range of other devices. Modal lexical verbs are one means:

(22) I think you are right.
(23) I suppose you're right.
(24) I believe you are right.

as are adjectives in the familiar 'BE . . . TO' and 'BE . . . THAT' constructions:

(25) You are sure to be right.
(26) It's certain that you're right.
(27) It's doubtful that you're right.

There is also a group of epistemic modal adverbs which includes, but is not restricted to, the following: *arguably, maybe, perhaps, possibly, probably, certainly, supposedly, allegedly*.

Note, however, that speakers also have the option of expressing the basic proposition in its 'raw' form; or in other words, as a *categorical assertion*:

(23) You are right.

As Lyons (1977: 763) points out, categorical assertions express the strongest possible degree of speaker commitment. In this respect, they are 'epistemically non-modal'. Epistemic expressions thus function to distinguish non-categorical assertions from categorical ones by signalling that the speaker's commitment to the truth of the proposition encoded in the utterance is qualified. This distinction is crucial, yet it may strike some as counter-intuitive to argue that *You are right* is actually epistemically stronger than the modalized *You must be right*. Perhaps the best solution to this is to quote at some length Lyons's formulation of the categorical/modalized distinction. He argues thus:

> Although it might appear that a statement is strengthened by putting the proposition that it expresses within the scope of the

operator of epistemic necessity, this is not so, as far as the everyday use of language is concerned. It would be generally agreed that the speaker is more strongly committed to the factuality of 'It be raining' by saying *It is raining* than he is by saying *It must be raining*. It is a general principle, to which we are expected to conform, that we should always make the strongest commitment for which we have epistemic warrant. If there is no explicit mention of the source of our information and no explicit qualification of our commitment to its factuality, it will be assumed that we have full epistemic warrant for what we say.

(Lyons 1977: 808–9).

Therefore, the use of epistemic modal operators such as *must, certainly*, and *necessarily* renders the speaker's commitment to the factuality of propositions explicitly dependent on their own knowledge. The following schema may help clarify the ways in which epistemic statements differ from categorical assertions:

Basic proposition —

   Unmodalized, categorical assertions (*John is right*; *Mary has gone*)

   Modalized assertions

- Strong commitment (*John must be right*; *Mary must surely* have gone)
- Medium commitment (*John may be right*; *Mary may probably* have gone)
- Weak commitment (*John could be right*; *Mary might possibly* have gone)

Perception modality, as Perkins (1983: 81) points out, is best regarded as a subcategory of epistemic modality. It is distinguished by the fact that the degree of commitment to the truth of a proposition is predicated on some reference to human perception, normally visual perception. Adjectives in 'BE . . . THAT' constructions are especially important, as are related modal adverbs:

(29) a. It's clear that you are right.
    b. You're clearly right.
(30) a. It's obvious that you're right.
    b. You're obviously right.
(31) a. It's apparent that you're right.
    b. Apparently, you're right.
(32) a. It's evident that you're right.
    b. You're evidently right.

It is worth adding that verbs which represent straightforward mental processes do not *de facto* constitute part of the perception modal system. Statements of the sort *I saw the game* or *I heard the noise* are simply categorical assertions presenting observations on the part of the speaker. By contrast, examples (29)–(32) incorporate some linguistic justification for the speaker's commitment to the truth of a proposition based on reference to external signs.

The following schema might help summarize the function of the modal systems introduced in this section. The boxed enclosures are attempts to capture the interrelatedness of some categories, and the non-linguistic concepts which each category represents are explained to the right.

Modal system   Non-linguistic concepts represented

DEONTIC ──────────────→	obligation, duty and commitment
BOULOMAIC ──────────→	desire

EPISTEMIC ──────────────→	knowledge, belief and cognition
PERCEPTION ──────────→	perception

The four modal systems outlined here will provide support for the framework of point of view that follows. It will be argued that the modal systems are distributed unevenly across the point of view categories and that certain modalities are specific to, or at least dominant in, particular categories.

Before moving on to this, I want to look more closely at some aspects of the Fowler model. One reason for doing so is to explain why such an apparently elegant model, based on principled linguistic criteria, should need any reworking at all. As a step towards this, consider the following passage from Samuel Beckett's novel *Molloy* (1950). In this episode, Molloy has been arrested and taken to a police station for having been found 'resting' astride his bicycle. The passage is somewhat lengthy, but it will prove important in the discussions here and in the following section:

Passage 1
   And suddenly I remembered my name, Molloy. My name is Molloy, I cried, all of a sudden, now I remember. Nothing compelled me to give this information, but I gave it, hoping to please, I suppose. They let me keep my hat on, I don't know

5 why. Is it your mother's name? said the sergeant, it must have
been a sergeant. Molloy, I cried, my name is Molloy. Is that your
mother's name? said the sergeant. Yes, I said, now I remember.
And your mother? said the sergeant. I didn't follow. Is your
mother's name Molloy too? said the sergeant. I thought it over.
10 Your mother, said the sergeant, is your mother's – Let me think!
I cried. At least I imagine that's how it was. Take your time, said
the sergeant. Was mother's name Molloy? Very likely. Her
name must be Molloy too, I said. They took me away, to the
guardroom I suppose, and there I was told to sit down. I must
15 have tried to explain. I won't go into it. I obtained permission, if
not to lie down on a bench, at least to remain standing, propped
against the wall. The room was dark and full of people hastening
to and fro, malefactors, policemen, lawyers, priests and journalists I suppose. All that made a dark, dark forms crowding in a
20 dark place. They paid no attention to me and I repaid the
compliment. Then how could I know they were paying no
attention to me, and how could I repay the compliment, since
they were paying no attention to me? I don't know. I knew it and
I did it, that's all I know. But suddenly a woman rose up before
25 me, a big fat woman dressed in black, or rather in mauve. I still
wonder today if it wasn't the social worker. She was holding out
to me, on an odd saucer, a mug full of a greyish concoction which
must have been green tea with saccharine and powdered milk.

(Picador edn, p. 23)

A stylistician working within the Fowler framework might encounter
some problems with this passage. In many respects, it reads as a
straightforward case of Internal type A: it is first-person narration
from a participating character, it is peppered with *verba sentiendi* and it
has a foregrounded modality. However, difficulties arise when one
looks more closely at the *type* of modality that is used. For the most
part, epistemic modal expressions are prominent, realized chiefly
through modal auxiliaries ('it *must* have been' (lines 5–6); 'I *must* have
tried' (lines 14–15); '*must* have been' (line 28)) and modal lexical verbs
('I suppose' (repeated often); 'I imagine' (line 11); 'I . . . wonder'
(lines 25–6)). With regard to the second category, the modal lexical
verb KNOW is used frequently with both positive and negative polarity –
a technique which obfuscates thoroughly parts of the narrative:

I don't know why. (lines 4–5)
I know . . . (line 21)
I don't know. (line 23)

I knew it (line 23)
I know . . . (line 24)

Such epistemic modal expressions typify Fowler's 'words of estrangement'. Molloy's modality, as it were, is one of uncertainty,
bewilderment and alienation. There is a general reluctance to interpret
events and actions, and when such interpretations are made, they are
based on references to stimuli in the immediate physical environment.
In short, these are all the characteristics of External type D. Furthermore, this clash in potential readings is often borne out in workshops
and seminars that I have conducted on point of view: students often
remark that this passage 'feels' like D, but it 'can't be D' because its
first-person narrative viewpoint pushes it towards type A. The strictures of the analytic framework thus produce a counter-intuitive
reading in this instance.

The following passage is the opening paragraph of John le Carré's
The Little Drummer Girl (1983):

Passage 2
It was the Bad Godesberg incident that gave the proof, though the
German authorities had no earthly means of knowing this. Before
Bad Godesberg, there had been growing suspicion; a lot of it. But
the high quality of the planning, as against the poor quality of the
bomb, turned the suspicion into certainty. Sooner or later, they say
in the trade, a man will sign his name. The vexation lies in the
waiting.

(Pan Books edn, p. 11)

Classification of this paragraph within Fowler's framework is not
straightforward. On the face of it, it is Internal type B – this is certainly
the dominant mode of the novel as a whole. Evidence for such a
classification is the third-person narrative framework and the exercis-
ing of omniscience through reference to the thoughts of characters
(e.g. 'the German authorities had no earthly means of knowing this').
But part of the type B profile is the absence of authorial modality, and
in this short example authorial modality is far from absent. Take, for
instance, the final two sentences of the paragraph:

Sooner or later, they say in the trade, a man will sign his name. The
vexation lies in the waiting.

These are generic sentences, in fact, and of the sort identified in the
highly modalized language of the passage from *The Great Gatsby*
which was discussed in section 2.4.

A further point concerns the interrelationship of Internal type A and External type C. In a recent workshop on stylistics, I asked groups of participants to produce short narratives of personal experience. Normally the narratives elicited under such conditions fall into the type A category and this was generally true of those produced in this workshop. However, one of the groups provided the following story:

Passage 3
Last night a Colombian presidential candidate was on a flight from Bogota to Cali. A twenty-two year old passenger walked up to him, drew a gun and fired. The candidate fell onto the floor. One of his bodyguards shot the attacker.

This is clearly a type C narrative. It is written in the third person, has no authorial modality and remains outside the thoughts and feelings of the characters in the story. In this respect, it is very much like passage C discussed in section 2.4 of chapter 2 or, for that matter, like any standard news-report of such an incident. Having noted the characteristics of their narrative, the group who produced this story pointed out that it originally 'began life' as a type A narrative with the following structure:

Passage 3a
This morning, I read in a paper that a Colombian presidential candidate was on a flight from Bogota to Cali last night. A twenty-two year old passenger walked up to him, drew a gun and fired. The candidate fell onto the floor.

What had happened was that the original first-person framework had been removed, leaving the remainder of the narrative intact. This consequently necessitated a re-classification to type C. Nevertheless, both versions are substantially similar in feel and hardly merit the difference in classification that results from a strict application of the Fowler model. This furthermore raises the question of the possibility of having a type A narrative with *no* modality; in other words, of having a story which presents events through categorical assertions without any mediating commentary by the narrator. As we shall see in the section that follows, such narratives do exist.

As the points above should suggest, some classifications within the Fowler framework tend to be counter-intuitive; a text which exhibits an 'alienated' narrative viewpoint, for instance, may none the less have to be categorized as type A, simply on the grounds that the alienation is experienced by a participating character and not an invisible, external narrator. Comparable analytic overlaps were noted above and still others will be touched upon, where necessary, in the following section. Indeed, it seems that some expansion of Fowler's model is warranted – if only to avoid a situation where texts which share superficially similar linguistic features will be assigned to drastically different point of view categories.

3.3 A MODAL GRAMMAR OF POINT OF VIEW IN NARRATIVE FICTION

In the framework which follows, an initial distinction will be made between *category A* narratives and *category B* narratives. Category A narratives are defined as those which are narrated in the first person by a *participating character* within the story. In this respect, this category corresponds to Genette's *homodiegetic* narration in that the narrator, in some manifestation of her or his self, takes part in the story she or he narrates. Category A narratives, as will be explained shortly, can be subdivided further on the basis of three broad patterns of modality. These patterns, for reasons which will become clear soon, will be referred to as *positive*, *negative* and *neutral*. Category B narratives are somewhat more complex. They all possess a third-person narrative framework and are told by an invisible, 'disembodied', non-participating narrator. This category corresponds most closely, therefore, to Genette's *heterodiegetic* narration. Category B narratives, however, may be divided into two modes, depending on whether events are related outside or inside the consciousness of a particular character or characters. Where a third-person narrative is told from a 'floating' viewing position, outside that of any character, then it is said to be category B, in *Narratorial mode*. In this situation the only 'voice' is that of the narrator. If such a third-person narrator invokes the 'licence of omniscience' and moves, whether momentarily or for a prolonged period, into the active mind of a particular character, then that character becomes, to use the common label, the *Reflector* of fiction. Thus, when a third-person narrative takes place within the confines of a single character's consciousness it is said to be category B in *Reflector mode*. Furthermore, like their category A counterparts, category B narratives, in either mode, may be subdivided on the basis of positive, negative or neutral modalities. The result of this is a model which comprises nine point-of-view polarities. Figure 3.1 summarizes the model, and the remainder of this section will be devoted to explanations and illustrations of each of its categories.

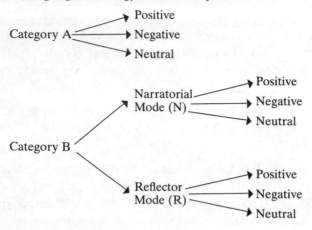

Figure 3.1 A model of point of view

3.3.1 Category A narratives

The first of the category A narratives, *A positive* (*A +ve*), is virtually identical to Fowler's Internal type A. The criteria for the recognition of such narratives include *verba sentiendi* and evaluative adjectives and adverbs. The decision to refer to this type as *positive* derives from the 'positive shading' which attaches to the modality displayed by such narratives. In general, the deontic and boulomaic systems are prominent, foregrounding a narrator's desires, duties, obligations and opinions *vis-à-vis* events and other characters. The epistemic and perception systems, by contrast, are suppressed, so propositions are not predicated on the perhaps limited knowledge of the narrator. There is, furthermore, little inferencing based on references to external signs. It is thus unusual to find epistemic modal adverbs such as *possibly, probably, maybe* and *perhaps,* and modal auxiliaries in verb phrases like *might have been, could have been* and *must have been* tend to be rare. Perception modal adverbs such as *evidently* and *apparently* are also uncommon. In short, there is an absence of 'words of estrangement' in the Uspensky–Fowler sense, and the resulting narrative is more co-operatively orientated towards the reader. Although assertions are often embedded under predicators referring to the thoughts and feelings of the narrator, they are not normally supplemented with the epistemic markers which render the events of the narrative less palpable. The opening of *The Great Gatsby*, discussed in some detail in section 2.4, has already provided a good illustration of what is virtually a pure A+ve narrative, and to be sure, A+ve narratives are not difficult to find. Perhaps the clearest example of a text which is almost dominated by this mode is Charlotte Brontë's *Jane Eyre* (1847). In the following passage, what amounts to an early feminist critique of occupational roles is assigned to the homodiegetic narrator. It is particularly rich in the deontic and boulomaic modalities of obligation and desire, and the modal operators through which these systems are realized have, for convenience, been italicized.

Passage 4
It is vain to say human beings *ought to be* satisfied with tranquillity: they *must have* action, and they will make it if they cannot find it. Millions are condemned to a stiller doom than mine, and millions are in silent revolt against their lot. Nobody knows how many rebellions beside political rebellions ferment in the masses of life which people earth. Women *are supposed to be* very calm generally: but women feel just as men feel; they *need* exercise for their faculties, and a field for their efforts as much as their brothers do; they suffer from too rigid a restraint . . . and it is narrow-minded in their more privileged fellow-creatures to say that they *ought to* confine themselves to making puddings and knitting stockings, to playing on the piano and embroidering bags. It is thoughtless to condemn them, or laugh at them, if they *seek* to do more or learn more than custom *has pronounced necessary* for their sex.

(Penguin edn, p. 141)

Other *A +ve* markers abound in the extract. Note, for instance, the use of evaluative adjectives ('It is *vain*'; 'It is *thoughtless*'), *verba sentiendi* ('women *feel*'; 'they *suffer*') and generic sentences which possess universal or timeless reference ('Millions are condemned to a stiller doom'; 'women feel just as men feel'). In summary, this is a condensed sequence of A+ve narration, co-operatively orientated towards an implied reader through its clear rationalization of obligations, duties and desires.

To close, for the moment, discussion of the A+ve category, here is another short sample of homodiegetic narration. This is taken from the first chapter of Jerome K. Jerome's novel *Three Men in a Boat* (1889).

Passage 5
George has a cousin, who is usually described in the charge-sheet as a medical student, so that he naturally has a somewhat family-physicianary way of putting things.

I agreed with George, and suggested that we should seek out some retired and old-world spot, far from the madding crowd, and dream away a sunny week among its drowsy lanes – some half-forgotten nook, hidden away by the fairies, out of reach of the noisy world – some quaint-perched eyrie on the cliffs of Time, from whence the surging waves of the nineteenth century would sound far-off and faint.

Harris said he thought it would be humpty. He said he knew the sort of place I meant; where everybody went to bed at eight o'clock, and you couldn't get a Referee for love or money, and had to walk ten miles to get your baccy.

(Dent edn, p. 7)

All the main characteristics of A+ve are here: *verba sentiendi*, evaluative adjectives and adverbs, a foregrounded deontic and boulomaic modality and an absence of the more 'alienating' forms of epistemic and perception modality.

Category A narratives with negative shading (*A–ve*) exhibit precisely the sort of epistemic and perception modalities which are absent from A+ve. Epistemic modal auxiliaries, modal adverbs and modal lexical verbs (such as *I suppose, I imagine* and *I assume*) are much in evidence, as are the perception adverbs *evidently* and *apparently*. There is, furthermore, a development of comparative structures which have some basis in human perception (*it looked as if . . .*; *it seemed . . .*; *it appeared to be . . .*). This intuitively 'negative' shading is what makes A–ve feel very like Fowler's External type D – although in this instance, of course, the bewilderment and estrangement derives from within a participating character's consciousness. A clear example of A–ve is provided by the extract from Beckett's *Molloy*. (See passage 1 above.) Here Molloy's language is rich in epistemic and perception modalities which highlight, if anything, his *uncertainty* about characters and events.

Whereas the Beckett novel is one where A–ve forms the dominant paradigm throughout, other narratives make use of abrupt transitions into this mode from another dominant mode. Sudden transitions of this sort often result in a disorientating lack of purchase on events narrated, with things no longer as tangible and palpable as they were before the transition into the A–ve mode. In John Banville's *The Book of Evidence* (1989), just such a transition occurs. Although broadly an A+ve type narrative, at one point in the novel, after the narrator protagonist has committed a brutal and seemingly unmotivated murder, there is an extended sequence of A–ve narration. One of the functions of this (in this specific instance) may be to render the sensation and experience of shock:

Passage 6
Not a soul to be seen, not a grown-up anywhere, except, away down

the beach, a few felled sunbathers on their towels. I wonder why it was so deserted there? Perhaps it wasn't, perhaps there were seaside crowds all about, and I didn't notice, with my inveterate yearning towards backgrounds. . . . Yet I could not worry, could not make myself be concerned. I seemed to float bemused, in a dreamy detachment, as if I had been given a great dose of local anaesthetic. Perhaps this is what it means to be in shock? No: I think it was just the certainty that at any moment a hand would grasp me by the shoulder.

(Minerva edn, pp. 126–8)

In a manner comparable to the Beckett passage discussed earlier, this excerpt foregrounds the epistemic and perception modal systems. The modal adverb *perhaps* is repeated many times, although other epistemic operators such as modal lexical verbs ('I wonder'; 'I think') are prominent. Modal lexical verbs of perception are also used, as in 'I didn't notice' and 'I seemed to float', as well as the familiar *as if* comparator which frequently supplements the perception system.

One of the functions of such transitions into A–ve sequences is to relay the kind of self-questioning which often occurs at key stages in homodiegetic narratives. In the following extract from Ronald Sukenick's experimental novel *The Endless Short Story* (1986), the dialogic function of A–ve is heightened to the extreme:

Passage 7
Then suddenly it wasn't funny. Absurd, perhaps. Inexplicable. Maybe somebody up there with a literary bent heard about the book by word-of-mouth and just wanted a freebie, pure literary curiosity. Gordon Liddy, maybe? While it was true that the President had just authorized the C.I.A. to engage in domestic intelligence again, I couldn't believe that included literary intelligence. Maybe they'd concluded my novel is a secret code. I mean, my work is not for everyone. Still who knows what might be considered political these days? Possibly the very fact my work is not for everyone was considered political. Maybe I was considered an 'elitist'. Maybe, for all I knew, they liked the fact that I was an elitist. Maybe they were going to try to recruit me. Didn't the very fact that they neglected to include payment with their book order imply a certain complicity, as if they could expect everybody's cooperation?

(Fiction Collective edn, p. 25).

A brief, yet important, final remark is necessary on the A–ve category. In A–ve narrative, the position where epistemic and perception markers are placed within a sentence has crucial implications for the type of cognitive processing involved in understanding that sentence. In the Banville example (passage 6), modal operators tended to be *pre-posed*. That is to say, the modal commitment towards the particular proposition expressed is signalled early on and, consequently, any events subsequently described are brought within the scope of the modal operator. For instance, the adverb *perhaps* is used sentence-initially in every instance:

Passage 6a
Perhaps it wasn't, perhaps there were seaside crowds all about. . . .
Perhaps this is what it means to be in shock?

At the other extreme, is the strategy adopted in the passage from *Molloy* (passage 1) which, in perceptual terms, is much more disorientating. Here modal operators are often *post-posed*, with epistemic modification *following* the proposition which it governs. For example:

Passage 1a
I gave it, hoping to please, I suppose. . . . Is it your mother's name? said the sergeant, it must have been a sergeant. . . . They took me away, to the guardroom I suppose . . . a big fat woman dressed in black, or rather in mauve.

This tactic has important conceptual consequences. Given the 'on-line' nature of the reading process, there is the natural tendency to interpret what precedes these epistemic markers as categorical assertions; in other words, as statements to which no doubt or uncertainty is attached. No sooner has this information been accessed, however, than it is immediately jeopardized by the post-posing of epistemic weakeners, which leave the exact nature of the events described uncertain. Without trying to sound glib, it seems that in the case of *Molloy*, the more you read the less you know!

The remaining category A narrative is *A neutral*, so named because of the complete absence of narratorial modality which characterizes this mode. Rather than presenting qualified opinions and judgements on events and other characters, the narrator withholds subjective evaluation and tells the story through categorical assertions alone. Texts exhibiting a dominant A neutral point of view normally comprise extended sequences of straightforward physical description with little attempt at psychological development and, not surprisingly, such texts are rare. Passage 3a, the 'workshop' example discussed above, is a rather contrived instance of A neutral. It is, however, still possible to find A neutral narrative in many novels. One which draws extensively on this 'flat' technique is Albert Camus' *The Outsider* (1942). The following sequence is almost 'pure' A neutral, written in a thoroughly unmodalized, non-reflective, categorical style:

Passage 8
While I was helping her [Marie] to climb on to a raft, I let my hand stray over her breasts. Then she lay flat on the raft, while I trod water. After a moment she turned and looked at me. Her hair was over her eyes and she was laughing. I clambered up on to the raft, beside her.

(Penguin edn, p. 28)

The opening sentence of the same novel highlights the often startling effect created when this mode is used to narrate events to which emotional involvement is normally attached, although notice how the remainder of this opening paragraph undergoes an abrupt transition to A–ve very much in the manner discussed above:

Passage 9
Mother died today. Or, maybe, yesterday; I can't be sure. The telegram from the Home says: 'Your mother passed away. Funeral tomorrow. Deep sympathy.' Which leaves the matter doubtful; it could have been yesterday.

(Penguin edn, p. 13)

In fact, much of the novel exhibits this type of oscillation between the A neutral and A–ve modes.

The A neutral point of view also characterizes much of the style of the 'hard-boiled' detective novel, although, as before, this will tend to be interlaced with the other A categories. Here is a brief illustration from Raymond Chandler's *Farewell, My Lovely* (1940) comprised entirely of categorical assertions. Note also the general lack of connectivity and causality between the sentences:

Passage 10
We went on up the stairs. He let me walk. My shoulder ached. The back of my neck was wet.

(Penguin edn, p. 10)

The flat, almost 'journalistic' feel which this mode generates has not escaped the attention of other stylisticians. Nash (1990), in a study of the language of popular fiction, examines the following fight scene from the same novel:

Passage 11
The bouncer tried to knee him in the groin. The big man turned him in the air and slid his gaudy shoes apart on the scaly linoleum that

covered the floor. He bent the bouncer backwards and shifted his right hand to the bouncer's belt. The belt broke like a piece of butcher's string. The big man put his enormous hand flat against the bouncer's spine and heaved. He threw him clear across the room, spinning and staggering and flailing with his arms. Three men jumped out of the way. The bouncer went over the table and smacked into the baseboard with a crash that must have been heard in Denver. His legs twitched. Then he lay still.

(Penguin edn, p. 12)

In his discussion of this passage, Nash highlights a number of interesting stylistic contrasts. Despite the astonishing violence depicted, the style throughout is 'cool, distanced, whimsical' (1990: 133). Furthermore, although the narrator, Philip Marlowe, uses few self-referential first-person pronouns and says virtually nothing about his own private feelings, the 'feeling of reportage', as Nash points out, still serves to convey Marlowe's character to us – a character which is 'cynically humorous, detached, street-wise, missing nothing' (134). I would suggest that this stylistic effect is in some part also due to the extensive use made of the A neutral category.

3.3.2 Category B narratives

The B category, as was suggested earlier, is slightly more complicated than category A. This is because it is split in two on the basis of whether the narrative is related from a position outside the consciousness of any of the characters, or whether it is mediated through the consciousness of a particular character. The terms reserved for these two modes are: *B in Narratorial mode* (B(N)), and *B in Reflector mode* (B(R)). In the case of the second mode, the term Reflector was adopted to identify the character (or even animal or inanimate object) whose psychological perspective is represented in a text. The B(N) and B(R) modes each realize three subcategories yielding a total of six types of category B narrative.

The first of these, *B(N)+ve*, has much in common with its category A counterpart: it has a foregrounded deontic and boulomaic modality, evaluative adjectives and adverbs and generic sentences. It differs, of course, in that the narrative is in the third person, and is related via an invisible, non-participating narrator. The opening paragraph of le Carré's *The Little Drummer Girl* (passage 2, discussed in section 3.2) typifies B(N)+ve, and, in fact, much of the novel is framed within this often ironic speaking voice. A similar voice presides over much of the narrative of Joseph Conrad's *The Secret Agent* (1907). Consider the following extract, for instance, which details the death of Mr Verloc at the hands of his wife and note particularly the use of the generic sentence in the second line:

Passage 12
The knife was already planted in his breast. It met no resistance on its way. Hazard has such accuracies. Into that plunging blow, delivered over the side of the couch, Mrs. Verloc had put all the inheritance of her immemorial and obscure descent, the simple ferocity of the age of caverns, and the unbalanced nervous fury of the age of bar-rooms. Mr. Verloc, the secret agent, turning slightly on his side with the force of the blow, expired without stirring a limb.

(Penguin edn, p. 234)

B(N)+ve is also one of the techniques Joyce uses in the 'Nausicaa' episode of *Ulysses*. Narratorial modality is especially prominent in the ironic introduction to Gerty MacDowell:

Passage 13
Gerty MacDowell, who was seated near her companions, lost in thought, gazing far away into the distance, was in very truth as fair a specimen of winsome Irish girlhood as one could wish to see. She was pronounced beautiful by all who knew her though, as folks often said, she was more a Giltrap than a MacDowell.

(Penguin edn, p. 346)

One of the criteria for the recognition of the B(N)+ve mode is that the story, or part of it, should be narrated from a position outside the consciousness of any of the characters. This 'externality' interacts in interesting ways with spatial deixis, often developing the 'bird's-eye view' or 'floating viewpoint' described in chapter 2 (section 2.2). Precisely this kind of 'camera angle' is adopted in the following extract from Fielding's *Tom Jones*, where a panoramic view of Squire Allworthy's estate is provided:

Passage 14
The left hand scene presented the view of a very fine park composed of very unequal ground, and agreeably varied with all the diversity that hills, lawns, wood, and water, laid out with admirable taste, but owing less to art than to nature, could give. Beyond this the country gradually rose into a ridge of wild mountains, the tops of which were above the clouds.

It was now the middle of May, and the morning was remarkably serene, when Mr. Allworthy walked forth on the terrace, where the dawn opened every minute that lovely prospect we have before described to his eye. . . .

Reader, take care, I have unadvisedly led thee to the top of as high a hill as Mr. Allworthy's, and how to get thee down without breaking thy neck, I do not well know. However, let us e'en venture to slide down together, for Miss Bridget rings her bell, and Mr. Allworthy is summoned to breakfast, where I must attend, and, if you please, shall be glad of your company.

(Oxford edn, vol. I, pp. 43–44)

Here, the panoramic sweep is framed entirely by the heterodiegetic narrator, who, despite the self-referential pronouns, is still situated outside the story. Indeed, the suggested altitude of this bird's-eye view is a source for parody by the narrator: 'how to get thee down without breaking thy neck, I do not well know'.

So far in the discussion, a distinction has been carefully drawn between the concepts of author and narrator. What is of interest here is a typology of narrators and narrative styles, not a bibliographical account of authors and their works. Clearly, any attempt to align some of the more ironic B(N)+ve styles examined above with the sentiments of 'real' authors is not feasible. In fact, as far as Scholes and Kellogg are concerned, the perceived gulf between author and narrator is itself sufficient for a definition of irony. They remark that narrative irony is 'a function of disparity' between the narrator and the author (1966: 240). In the case of the B(N)+ve mode, however, there are situations where the distance between author and narrator seems to diminish, or where there appears no feasible justification for maintaining a distinction between the two. Many instances of such 'coalescence' can be found in the work of D.H. Lawrence, where the action of the story is suspended in favour of a highly modalized discourse located within the B(N)+ve mode. Take as an example the following paragraph from *The Plumed Serpent* (1926):

Passage 15
Men and women should know that they cannot, absolutely, meet on earth. In the closest kiss, the dearest touch, there is the small gulf which is none the less complete because it is so narrow, so *nearly* non-existent. They must bow and submit in reverence, to the gulf. Even though I eat the body and drink the blood of Christ, Christ is Christ and I am I, and the gulf is impassable. Though a woman be dearer to a man than his own life, yet he is he and she is she, and the

gulf can never close up. Any attempt to close it is a violation, and the crime against the Holy Ghost.

(Penguin edn, p. 265)

This is B(N)+ve in its most extreme form; a paragraph stuffed full of generic sentences and deontic modal operators of obligation and duty. Yet it is difficult to attribute such sententious moralizing to any character within the story, nor is there any real suggestion of an ironic gap between author and narratorial speaking voice. Scholes and Kellogg refer, in fact, to the 'lifelong trouble' Lawrence had with point of view, and their elaboration of this is perhaps the most charitable way of closing this discussion of Lawrence's use of the B(N)+ve mode:

> His art and his ethos converge and conflict in the handling of point of view. It is his weakest point, opening structural flaws in most of his long works which only his great skill with the texture of language could make tolerable.

(1966: 279)

The second category B narrative, B(N) negative, comes very close to Fowler's External type D with its 'words of estrangement' and lack of detail concerning the thoughts of characters. In the present model, it is similar in feel to A–ve in that the epistemic and perception modal systems are highlighted, thus generating a comparable quality of 'alienation' and 'bewilderment'. The passage from *Riceyman Steps* discussed in section 2.4 of the previous chapter provides a good illustration of a B(N)–ve narrative. The opening of Franz Kafka's *The Trial* (1925) also possesses many of the features of this category:

Passage 16

> Someone must have been telling lies about Joseph K., for without having done anything wrong he was arrested one fine morning. His landlady's cook, who always brought him his breakfast at eight o'clock, failed to appear on this occasion. That
> 5 had never happened before. K. waited for a little while longer, watching from his pillow the old lady opposite, who seemed to be peering at him with a curiosity unusual even for her, but then, feeling both put out and hungry, he rang the bell. At once there was a knock at the door and a man entered whom he had never
> 10 seen before in the house. He was slim and yet well knit, he wore a closely fitting black suit, which was furnished with all sorts of pleats, pockets, buckles, and buttons, as well as a belt, like a tourist's outfit, and in consequence looked eminently practical, though one could not quite tell what actual purpose it served.

15 'Who are you?' asked K., half raising himself in bed. But the man ignored the question, as though his appearance needed no explanation.

(Penguin edn, p. 7)

Note the prominent narratorial modality here, realized chiefly through epistemic expressions ('Someone must have been . . .' (line 1); 'one could not quite tell . . .' (line 14)) and comparators based on reference to physical appearance ('like a tourist's outfit' (line 13); 'looked eminently practical' (line 13); 'as though his appearance . . .' (line 16)). This pattern of modality may account for the alienating or disquieting effects which critics have identified as a hallmark of Kafka's style. Intuitive responses to this linguistic pattern may also have prompted remarks like that of Heller (1974: 88), who states that 'Kafka's art of conclusively stating inconclusiveness is unsurpassed and probably unsurpassable.'

One further point might be made regarding the modal verb of perception in line 6 of the Kafka passage ('the old lady opposite, who *seemed* to be peering at him'). The modal operator here arguably relates to Joseph K.'s view of events and not that of the external narrator. This may therefore represent a subtle stylistic shift into K.'s consciousness, but one in which the same negative modal shading is retained. In other words, it is the Reflector of fiction who has now become the site of epistemic and perception modalities and not the external narrator. Further development of this particular point is best left, therefore, to the discussion of the B(R)–ve category which follows shortly.

Fowler (1986) also cites the authors Mervyn Peake and Charles Dickens as primary exponents of the B(N)–ve mode, although he is careful to point out that neither writer operates exclusively within this category. As Fowler provides a useful analysis of the work of the first of these, here is a short sample from the second with relevant epistemic and perception markers italicized.

Passage 17

He [Mr Bounderby] was a rich man: banker, merchant, manufacturer, and what not. A big, loud man, with a stare and a metallic laugh. A man made out of a coarse material, which *seemed* to have been stretched to make so much of him. A man with a great puffed head and forehead, swelled veins in his temples, and such a strained skin to his face that it *seemed* to hold his eyes open and left his eyebrows up. A man with a pervading *appearance* on him of being inflated like a balloon . . .

A year or two younger than his eminently practical friend, Mr. Bounderby *looked* older: his seven or eight and forty *might have had* the seven or eight added to it again, without surprising anybody. He had not much hair. One *might have* fancied he had talked it off.

(*Hard Times* (1854), Penguin edn, p. 58)

It is worth adding that this narrative technique especially when accompanied by alienating metaphors, is often reserved for a portrayal of villains and grotesques. Fowler explains why:

It is not only that the emphasis on their physical peculiarities presents them as bizarre and threatening; the exaggerated refusal to go *below* the surface, the ostentatious guesses at what unimaginable motives might lurk beneath, present the characters as inhuman, beyond the comprehension of an ordinary human belief system.

(1986: 143)

The last of the B(N) subcategories, *B(N) neutral*, has been well documented, under different terminology, in the literature on point of view. It corresponds to Fowler's External type C, Genette's 'external focalization' (see section 2.3) and Rimmon-Kenan's 'objective' focalization (1983: 80). As this cluster of labels should suggest, this narrative style tends to be the most impersonal, with a narrator providing little or no modalized language. It is also marked by the absence of direct description and analysis of the thoughts and feelings of characters. In the present model, B(N) neutral is similar to A neutral, but differs in the significant feature of its third-person – as opposed to first-person – narrator. The text which is often cited as a canonical example of this mode is Hemingway's *The Killers*, a section of which was discussed in section 2.4 of the previous chapter. As a further illustration, consider the following short vignette from Hemingway's *In Our Time* collection, which, if anything is even more depersonalized:

Passage 18
They shot the six cabinet ministers at half past six in the morning against the wall of a hospital. There were pools of water in the courtyard. There were wet dead leaves on the paving of the courtyard. It rained hard. All the shutters of the hospital were nailed shut. One of the ministers was sick with typhoid. Two soldiers carried him downstairs and out into the rain.

(from *The Essential Hemingway*, Jonathan Cape edn, p. 285)

Apart from the occasional suggestion of how one event precipitates another and the use of a few evaluative adjectives and adverbs ('It rained *hard*'), this story is told entirely without authorial modality or psychological portraits of characters. The dominance of categorical assertions over any type of modalized expressions may possibly account for the characteristically 'flat' feel of much of Hemingway's writing. Another related feature of this style is the preference for *additive*, rather than *adversative* or *causal* conjunctions, so that connectivity is straightforwardly linear and not dependent on cause and effect relationships. Take, for instance, the following sentences from 'The Revolutionist', another of Hemingway's short stories:

Passage 19
He was very shy and quite young and the train men passed him on from one crew to another. He had no money, and they fed him behind the counter in railway eating houses.
(Jonathan Cape edn, p. 302)

Even in the second sentence, the two clauses which form the conjunct are linked by 'and', and not, as one might expect in such a discourse context, by 'so' or 'but'. The suppression of complex connectivity in this way seems to have baffled some critics, with comments on the famous Hemingway 'and' ranging from the vague to the faintly nonsensical:

As a matter of fact, Hemingway takes pains to avoid the *mot juste*, probably because it sounds too literary to him, preferring the general unspecific word like 'and'.
(Peterson 1974: 23–4)

Two final comments are necessary on the B(N) neutral category. First, of all the styles surveyed here it is the one most frequently compared to that of journalism in terms of its factuality and ostensibly objective approach to characters and events. Yet some caution needs to be exercised in this comparison. While journalistic style may be generally devoid of subjective positively shaded modalities, there are other grammatical means by which point of view can be conveyed. The representation of point of view in journalism will in fact be part of the concern of subsequent chapters. Second, one major literary exponent of this style, Gustav Flaubert, has not been mentioned so far. Much attention has been devoted to so-called 'Flaubertian realism' in fiction, which is defined by Ezra Pound as 'an attempt to set things down as they are, to find the word that corresponds to the thing, the statement that portrays, and presents, instead of making a comment, however brilliant, or an epigram' (1960: 74). This is an issue to which we will return when we consider later the final category in this point-of-view framework.

Each of the three B(R) subcategories bear similarities to their B(N) counterparts and for that matter to their category A counterparts. *B(R) positive*, for instance, exhibits the same type of modality as B(N)+ve and A+ve: the main difference, of course, is that in the case of B(R)+ve the narrative is mediated in the third person through the consciousness of a Reflector. A canonical example of this mode is Henry James's novel *The Ambassadors* (1903). Despite its third-person narrative framework, virtually all of it is narrated from the perspective of its protagonist, Strether, who forms the 'centre of consciousness' or 'central intelligence' of the story. This Jamesian technique of selective or restricted omniscience has been well catalogued in studies of point of view: Genette refers to it as 'fixed' internal focalization (1980: 189), whilst Scholes and Kellogg detail it thus:

> James favours a single perspective over multiple perspectives, and he further insists that his single perspective be that of a character who is inside the frame of the action rather than that of a disembodied presence who addresses the reader from outside the action.
>
> (1966: 273)

Examples from James are not difficult to find, but here is one from the penultimate chapter of *The Ambassadors* which is especially rich in the deontic modal operators which typify the B(R)+ve mode:

Passage 20
He [Strether] was to delay no longer to re-establish communication with Chad, and we have just seen that he had spoken to Miss Gostrey of this intention on hearing from her of the young man's absence. It was not, moreover, only the assurance so given that prompted him; it was the need of causing his conduct to square with another profession still – the motive he had described to her as his sharpest for now getting away. If he was to get away because of some of the relations involved in staying, the cold attitude towards them might look pedantic in the light of lingering on. He must do both things; he must see Chad, but he must go. The more he thought of the former of these duties the more he felt himself make a subject of insistence of the latter.

(Penguin edn, p. 379)

The interaction of spatial deixis (see section 2.2) with not only this mode, but all of the B(R) modes, often creates subtle visual perspectives in narrative. Normally, the Reflector of fiction becomes, momentarily or for more prolonged periods, the deictic centre for the spatial viewpoint. For example, in James Joyce's short story 'Two

Gallants' (1914), one of the eponymous 'heroes', Lenehan, forms the deictic centre for much of the story. In this short sequence, he watches, from a distance, while his friend attempts to extort money from a woman.

Passage 21
His eyes searched the street: there was no sign of them. Yet it was surely half-an-hour since he had seen the clock of the College of Surgeons. Would Corley do a thing like that? He lit his last cigarette and began to smoke it nervously. . . . Suddenly he saw them coming towards him. He started with delight and, keeping close to his lamp-post, tried to read the result in their walk. They were walking quickly, the young woman taking quick short steps, while Corley kept beside her with his long stride.

(Granada edn, p. 54)

The combination of psychological description ('He started *with delight*') and proximal spatial deictics ('he saw them *coming towards* him') functions to identify the viewing position as that of Lenehan.

The techniques of speech and thought presentation (introduced in section 2.3 of the previous chapter) also interact in subtle ways with this type of point of view. In keeping with its 'special' status, Free Indirect Discourse is perhaps the most intriguing of the techniques available. One may recall that this is the situation where the speech and thought of a character is presented with freedom and immediacy, though in a form which retains the third-person pronouns and backshifted tense systems characteristic of the general format of a third-person narrative. The following passage, taken from Malcolm Lowry's *Under the Volcano* (1947), is a good illustration of the use of FID in the B(R)+ve mode. Here the Reflector of the fiction is Yvonne, the estranged wife of the consul, Geoffrey Firmin. Note particularly the preponderance of *verba sentiendi*, evaluative adjectives and adverbs and deontic and boulomaic modal expressions:

Passage 22
The Consul, sitting down again, was shaking so violently he had to hold the bottle of whisky he was pouring himself a drink from with both hands. 'Have a drink?'
'—'
Or should she? She should: even though she hated drinking in the morning she undoubtedly should: it was what she had made up her mind to do if necessary, not to have one drink alone but a great many drinks with the Consul. But instead she could *feel* the smile leaving her face that was struggling to keep back the tears she had

forbidden herself on any account, thinking and knowing Geoffrey knew she was thinking: 'I was prepared for this, I was prepared for it.' 'You have one and I'll cheer', she found herself saying. (As a matter of fact she had been prepared for almost anything. After all, what could one expect? She had told herself all the way down on the ship, a ship because she would have time on board to persuade herself her journey was neither thoughtless nor precipitate, and on the plane when she knew it was both, that she should have warned him, that it was abominably unfair to take him by surprise.)

(Penguin edn, pp. 52–3)

Another feature of the intersection between speech and thought presentation and point of view concerns the use of Free Direct Thought, especially when it is conveyed through that elliptical variant which we identified as 'stream of consciousness' (see section 2.3). If sustained, this technique turns the Reflector into Narrator; in other words, the distinction between the B(N) and B(R) modes collapses and the narrative takes on the appearance of homodiegetic category A. In the relevant part of the discussion of FDT in the previous chapter, an example from Joyce's *Ulysses* was used to highlight the striking effects created by abrupt transitions in and out of this mode. Here is another short illustration from the 'Calypso' episode of the same novel where Bloom, ever cognizant of life's more mundane exigencies, is feeding his cat:

Passage 23
 – Milk for the pussens, he said.
 – Mrkgnao! the cat cried.
 They call them stupid. They understand what we say better than we understand them. She understands all she wants to. Vindictive too. Wonder what I look like to her. Height of a tower. No, she can jump me.

(Penguin edn, p. 57)

After the sequence of Direct Speech, the sustained focalization through the Reflector pushes this narrative towards first-person category A.

The second B(R) subcategory, *B(R) negative*, shares many of the features of A–ve and B(N)–ve. It is rich in 'words of estrangement', with a high proportion of epistemic and perception modal expressions. However, in B(R)–ve the modality is a product of the consciousness of a particular character and not an external narrator. To illustrate this, it is worth re-introducing part of the Kafka passage quoted earlier:

Passage 16a

K. waited for a little while longer, watching from his pillow the old lady opposite, who seemed to be peering at him with a curiosity unusual even for her. . .

What appears to be happening here is that the point of view has switched from a more external perspective into the active mind of the central character, but, significantly, the same modal features are present in Joseph K.'s depiction of events ('*seemed* to be peering'). Thus, we have a transition from B(N)–ve into B(R)–ve which, interestingly, signals that the 'bewilderment' or 'alienation' works on *two* levels in this passage. In many ways, this two-level point of view is comparable to Genette's concept of 'double focalization' which he develops to account for passages where antitheses are created which share 'the logic of narrative representation' (1980: 209–11).

Spatial deixis also interlocks with the B(R)–ve mode in ways parallel to that of B(R)+ve, but in this case distal rather than proximal spatial deictics are often used to supplement the disorientating effect created by the epistemic and perception modalities. The following extract, taken from John le Carré's *The Little Drummer Girl*, is a good illustration of negative modal shading interacting with a spatial dimension whereby viewing subject and object viewed are far apart. This particular episode is narrated from the perspective of Charlie, a (female) member of a group of artists staying on a Greek island. Charlie is obsessed by the arrival of a mysterious stranger to their beach:

Passage 24

Even when he lay as dead, a mysterious alertness seemed to wink from his lithe brown body, carried to her by the sun. Sometimes the tension seemed to snap in him, and he would leap suddenly to his feet, remove his hat, stroll gravely down his dune to the water like a tribesman without his spear, and dive in soundlessly, hardly troubling the water's skin. She would wait; then still wait. He had drowned, without a doubt. Till at last, when she had given him up for good, he would surface far across the bay, swimming in a leisurely overarm freestyle as if he had miles to go, his cropped black head glistening like a seal's.

(Pan books edn, p. 71)

This is the sort of passage that might present problems for an analysis within the Fowler–Uspensky framework. On the one hand, it is mediated by an omniscient narrator who clearly has access to the thoughts and feelings of characters, thereby realizing an Internal point of view. On the other hand, it exhibits the modality of an External narrative. In the terms of the present framework, it is hoped that this overlap is to some extent avoided.

The last of the B(R) subcategories, *B(R) neutral*, is rather more elusive than the other two. This is largely due to the type of criteria which the model predicts for the identification of this category: that is to say, the events of the narrative must be mediated through the consciousness of a Reflector but in a style where categorical assertions take precedence over modalized expressions. It is this 'objectivity' which makes it difficult to distinguish between the Narratorial mode and the Reflector mode – in either case, events and characters are viewed dispassionately and without recourse to the four available modalities. This principle should become clearer if we recall one of the examples of the B(N) neutral mode provided earlier. This is passage 18, the Hemingway vignette. The point-of-view perspective can be adjusted towards that of a potential Reflector simply by inserting some signals that events are being mediated through the consciousness of a particular individual. So, in this way passage 18 can be converted to:

Passage 18a
X recalled how they shot the six cabinet ministers at half past six in the morning against the wall of a hospital. There were pools of water in the courtyard, and X remembered that there were wet dead leaves on the paving of the courtyard.

Apart from the addition of a Reflector, nothing really alters the 'feel' of the passage. Evaluative modalities are still absent and categorical assertions still the dominant mode of expression.

Quite often, the only indication that the B(R) neutral, as opposed to B(N) neutral, mode is in operation is some signal that events are being viewed from the spatial location of a character and not from the 'floating' or 'bird's-eye' position that characterizes the Narratorial mode. For instance, in this short sequence from Joyce's 'The dead', Gabriel Conroy is clearly the focalizer, and, for this brief period at least, is a passive and unreflective focalizer at that:

Passage 25
His eyes moved to the chair over which she had thrown some of her clothes. A petticoat string dangled to the floor. One boot stood upright, its limp upper fallen down: the fellow of it lay upon its side.
(Granada edn. pp. 199–200)

In her study of point of view, Rimmon-Kenan discusses an illuminating passage from Flaubert's *Madame Bovary* (1856). This is the scene where Emma Bovary looks at her garden at Tostes before the period of her great *ennui* and, according to Rimmon-Kenan, it is 'neutral in character':

Passage 26

The garden, longer than wide, ran between two mud walls covered with espaliered apricot trees, to a thorn hedge that separated it from the field. In the middle was a slate sundial on a brick pedestal; four flower-beds with eglantines surrounded symmetrically the more useful vegetable garden. Right at the bottom, under the spruce bushes, a plaster priest was reading his breviary.

(Rimmon-Kenan 1983: 80)

Here the spatial perspective which unfolds derives from the viewing position of the passive Emma, providing a clear example of the B(R) neutral mode. It may also be of interest to compare this passage with the extract from *Bouvard and Pecuchet* discussed under the broad remit of spatial point of view in the previous chapter (see section 2.2).

As a final illustration of the B(R) neutral category, consider the following extract from James Joyce's short story 'A Painful Case'. Here various witnesses offer their accounts of the death of Mrs Sinico:

Passage 27

James Lennon, driver of the engine, stated that he had been in the employment of the railway company for fifteen years. On hearing the guard's whistle he set the train in motion and a second or two afterwards brought it to rest in response to loud cries. The train was going slowly.

P. Dunne, railway porter, stated that as the train was about to start he observed a woman attempting to cross the lines. He ran towards her and shouted but, before he could reach her, she was caught by the buffer of the engine and fell to the ground.

A juror – You saw the lady fall?

Witness – Yes

Police Sergeant Croly deposed that when he arrived he found the deceased lying on the platform apparently dead. He had the body taken to the waiting-room pending the arrival of the ambulance.

(Granada edn, p. 104)

It is no coincidence, given the definition of the neutral mode, that these accounts occur in the context of a newspaper report. Indeed, it will be recalled that news reporting often takes this form of categorical, unmodalized discourse.

Positive shading
deontic, boulomaic systems foregrounded; generics and *verba sentiendi* present

Negative shading
epistemic and perception systems foregrounded; supplemented with generalized 'words of estrangement'

Neutral shading
unmodalized categorical assertions dominant; few *verba sentiendi* and evaluative adjectives and adverbs

A positive
'Co-operative' first-person narrative; canonical example: *Jane Eyre*

A negative
less 'co-operative' first-person narrative through distancing effect of negative shading; canonical example: *Molloy*

A neutral
'flat' or unreflective first-person narration; characteristic of much of 'hard-boiled' detective fiction genre

B(N) positive
disembodied narrator offering opinions and judgements (often ironic) on the story; mode used extensively by Fielding and Joyce

B(N) negative
disembodied narrator trying to 'make sense' of characters and events; distancing and 'bewilderment' common; canonical example: *The Trial*

B(N) neutral
external narrator refusing privileged access to thoughts and feelings of characters; technique used extensively by Hemingway

B(R) positive
action located within viewing position of character, offering their opinions and judgements; canonical example: *The Ambassadors*

B(R) negative
'estrangement' situated in mind of character: hence 'double focalization' in Kafka; often used to suggest spatial distance between viewer and object

B(R) neutral
action situated in viewing position of passive character, though evaluative modalities still withheld; much used by Flaubert

Category A (homodiegetic)

Narratorial mode

Reflector mode

Category B (heterodiegetic)

Figure 3.2 Relations between modal categories

As quite a lot of theory, data and analysis has been presented in this section, it might be a good idea to collect the various strands of the discussion together in the form of a simple schema. Figure 3.2, which should complement figure 3.1 above, is intended to illustrate how the nine modal categories interrelate. Each box in the diagram represents the convergence of hetero- and homodiegetic narration with modal shading, and, where possible, 'typical' examples of each type have been suggested.

3.4 TRANSPOSITIONS AND TRANSITIONS

Throughout the description of the point of view framework, attention was drawn repeatedly to the stylistic similarity of cross-category modes. That is to say, the positive modal shading which characterizes, for instance, an A+ve narrative will also be a prominent feature of its equivalent B(N) and B(R) modes. This makes all three categories similar in 'feel', at least on the level of modal patterning. Similarly, the A–ve mode will share many of the 'estranging' characteristics of B(N)– ve and B(R)–ve, while A neutral will display the same 'flatness' as its B(N) and B(R) counterparts. Further support for this aspect of the framework can be obtained if we develop *transposition* tests on a few of the many passages introduced in the previous two sections. The practice of transposition in linguistic analysis is a crucial one and, as was pointed out in chapter 1, it will underpin many parts of this book. It is invaluable not only as a means of lending support to an argument but also as a foregrounding device whereby unrealized possibilities can be considered in relation to realized ones. This is aside from its function as a language 'game'; a form of experimentation often undertaken in creative writing programmes.[2]

For our first transposition exercise, the first passage to be introduced in the chapter will be recalled. This is the extract from Beckett's *Molloy* from which the final sentence only is reproduced below:

Passage 1a
She was holding out to me, on an odd saucer, a mug full of a greyish concoction which must have been green tea with saccharine and powdered milk.

This, it was argued, occurred in the context of an A–ve narrative. Yet transposition to the equivalent modes within the B category is remarkably easy. First, consider how the simple alteration of 'me' to 'Molloy' (or even 'him') converts the point of view to B(N)–ve:

Passage 16

She was holding out to Molloy, on an odd saucer, a mug full of a greyish concoction which must have been green tea. . .

Interestingly, this transposition has shifted the epistemic commitment for the utterance away from Molloy towards an external narrator. In the following conversion to B(R)–ve, however, this commitment returns to Molloy, who has now become the Reflector of fiction:

Passage 1c

She was holding out to him, on a odd saucer, a mug full of a greyish concoction which Molloy thought must have been green tea. . .

One consequence of juggling modes around in this way is that it allows for useful comparisons with other texts by the same author. For instance, it would be interesting to know what a *real* Beckett B(R)–ve narrative would look like if such a thing existed. Well, as it happens, his novel *Watt* (1953) is a largely third-person narrative where this mode dominates and, in places, its resemblance to the transposition from *Molloy* in passage 1c is uncanny. Although rather lengthy, the following passage from *Watt* will provide a good illustration of the B(R)–ve mode. Here, the description of the two Galls is filtered through the consciousness of the central character, Watt:

Passage 28

We are the Galls, father and son, and we are come, what is more, all the way from town, to choon the piano.

They were two, and they stood, arm in arm, in this way, because the father was blind, like so many members of his
5   profession. For if the father had not been blind, then he would not have needed his son to hold his arm, and guide him on his rounds, no, but he would have set his son free, to go about his own business. So Watt supposed, though there was nothing in the father's face to show that he was blind, not in his attitude
10   either, except that he leaned on his son in a way expressive of a great need of support. But he might have done this, if he had been Watt, or merely tired, on account of his great age. There was no family likeness between the two, as far as Watt could make out, and nevertheless he knew that he was in the presence
15   of a father and son, for had he not just been told so. Or were they not perhaps merely stepfather and stepson. We are the Galls, stepfather and stepson – those were perhaps the words that should have been spoken. But it was natural to prefer the others.

Not that they could not very well be a true father and son,
20 without resembling each other in the very least, for they could.
(Picador edn, p. 67)

The features of negative modal shading are abundant in this passage.
Perception modal operators are especially common, and are often
couched in the form of negative references to the Galls' physical
appearance viewed from the perspective of Watt ('there was nothing
. . . to show . . .' (lines 8–9); 'no family likeness' (line 13); 'without
resembling each other' (line 20). The familiar epistemic operators are
here also: modal auxiliaries ('he *might* have done this' (line 11); 'they
could not very well be' (line 19); modal adverbs ('Or were they not
perhaps . . .' (lines 15–16); 'those were *perhaps* the words . . .' (line
17) and the particularly telling modal lexical verb 'suppose' ('So Watt
supposed . . .' (line 8) It is worth adding that the technique of post-
posing modals, discussed in section 3.3.1, operates here almost to the
point of perversion. The first delayed signal that much of this description is speculation comes in the form of 'So Watt supposed', where
what precedes suddenly ceases to be the harder currency we first
imagined. From then on, the passage is peppered with the epistemic
weakeners that function to make the picture of the Galls progressively
more obscure.

A good illustration of the cross-category similarity of the A+ve and
B+ve modes can be developed from the opening paragraph of le
Carré's *The Little Drummer Girl* (passage 2, first introduced in section
3.2). Although the modality exhibits positive shading, it is not clear, on
the basis of this paragraph alone, whether this is going to be a category
A or category B narrative. The reader, in fact, has to wait for some
explicit signal in subsequent text. As it happens, the narrative category
unfolds as B(N)+ve, but a sequence like the following, written in
A+ve, would have been entirely compatible with the first paragraph:

Passage 2a
Sooner or later, they say in the trade, a man will sign his name. The
vexation lies in the waiting.
   I knew that the bomb exploded much later than intended,
probably a good twelve hours later, at twenty-six minutes past eight
on Monday morning. I'd been told that several defunct wrist-
watches, the property of victims, confirmed the time.[3]

Comparable transpositions can be performed on the neutral modes.
The B(N) neutral story from Hemingway (passage 18, above) can
easily be adjusted to its parallel form in category A, and, as is

consistent with category A, the Narrator is now a participating character within the story:

Passage 18b
We shot the six cabinet ministers at half past six in the morning against the wall of a hospital. There were pools of water in the courtyard. There were wet dead leaves on the paving of the courtyard.

What is remarkable about this rewrite is that it reads very much like the following *real* example of a Hemingway A neutral narrative. This is part of another vignette from the *In Our Time* collection:

Passage 29
We were in a garden in Mons. Young Buckley came in with his patrol from across the river. The first German I saw climbed over up the garden wall. We waited till he got one leg over and then potted him. . . . Then three more came over further down the wall. We shot them. They all came just like that.

(Jonathan Cape edn, p. 272)

Here again the predictive potential of the transposition exercise is highlighted, with the modal pattern of a rewritten narrative matching that developed from a genuine text by the same author.

Intracategory transpositions are not as straightforward as cross-category transpositions. Generally, intracategory transpositions are unidirectional, moving from neutral through negative to positive, but not the other way round. The reason for this is not complicated: large sequences of positive and negative narratives are psychological interpretations of characters and events, and such interpretations are barred from the strongly categorical format of the neutral mode. Indeed, entire sections of narratives in the positive and negative modes will evaporate if an attempt is made to transpose them into their relative intracategorical neutral modes. (Just try performing such an operation on, for instance, passages 28 and 6a above.) Acknowledging, then, the unidirectionality of such transpositions, conversions of neutral to positive and negative modes are still possible if extra material is added to the basic format. Taking as an example the B(N) neutral extract from *The Killers* (passage C, in section 2.4), the first paragraph can be transposed to the more 'alienated' B(N)–ve point of view. This and subsequent rewrites are highly unlikely to oust Hemingway from his position among the greats, but it is hoped that the reader will accept if not the quality at least the spirit of the enterprise!

Passage Ca

Outside an arc-light could be seen shining through the bare branches of a tree. Nick walked up the street beside what looked like car-tracks and turned at the next arc-light into a side-street. Three houses up the street was Hirsch's rooming-house, apparently. Nick walked up some steps and pushed what must have been a bell. Someone came to the door.

The transposition to B(N)+ve works particularly well on the sequences of reported speech in passage C. As was pointed out earlier, the B(N) neutral mode generally employs either FDS, or DS with unmarked reporting clauses. These can readily be supplemented with markers of authorial modality:

Passage Cb

'Is Ole Anderson here?', asked Nick with some firmness.

'Do you want to see him?', came the rather timid reply.

'Yes, if he's in', answered Nick.

With growing confidence, Nick followed the woman up a flight of stairs and back to the end of the corridor. She knocked gingerly on the door.

Not an earthshattering literary embellishment, to be sure, but the fact that this now no longer sounds remotely like Hemingway is very much the point of the transposition exercise.

While transposition exercises have been developed primarily as a means for demonstrating how components of the point-of-view model interlock, the study of *transition* takes us in a different direction. As a preliminary to this, it is worth stressing that nowhere in this chapter have I claimed that a single text always realizes a single mode. Rather, it has been suggested that a particular mode may dominate a text, contributing perhaps to the special 'feel' of that text. Moreover, as we have already seen, abrupt transitions between modes may occur, often resulting in startling re-orientations of point of view. These transitions may even take place within the confines of a single sentence. Going back, for instance, to the opening of Joyce's 'The Dead', discussed in 2.3, it was argued there that narrator and character voices were both represented in this short sentence: 'Lily, the caretaker's daughter, was literally run off her feet.' The example from Camus' *The Outsider* (passage 9) also displayed a striking oscillation in point of view, with a transition from the unmodalized proposition of its opening sentence 'Mother died today' into a series of highly disquieting modalized assertions

Or, maybe, yesterday; I can't be sure. The telegram from the Home says: 'Your mother passed away. Funeral tomorrow. Deep sympathy'. Which leaves the matter doubtful; it could have been yesterday.

It is difficult to say, given the normally emotional nature of what is described, which of the two textual strategies used is the more alarming: the cold, factuality of the opening sentence or the untroubled vacillation of the remainder of the paragraph.

More systematic transitions, developed over larger narrative units, can also be identified. Here is (yet!) another example from Hemingway, this time from his short novel *The Old Man and the Sea* (1952). In this episode, the old man battles with the huge marlin he has hooked and for sustenance is forced to eat raw tuna fish. Notice how each paragraph signals a particular viewing position:

Passage 30

1 He knelt down and found the tuna under the stern with the gaff and drew it toward him keeping it clear of the coiled lines. Holding the line with his left shoulder again, and bracing on his left hand and arm, he took the tuna off the gaff hook and put the gaff back in place. . . .

2 'I don't think I can eat an entire one', he said and drew his knife across one of the strips. . . .

3 'What kind of a hand is that', he said. 'Cramp then if you want. Make yourself into a claw. It will do you no good.'

4 Come on, he thought and looked down into the dark water at the slant of the line. Eat it now and it will strengthen the hand. It is not the hand's fault and you have been many hours with the fish. But you can stay with him for ever. Eat the bonito now.

5 He picked up a piece and put it in his mouth and chewed it slowly. It was not unpleasant.

6 Chew it well, he thought, and get all the juices. It would not be bad to eat with a little lime or with lemon or with salt.

7 'How do you feel, hand?', he asked the cramped hand that was almost as still as rigor mortis. 'I'll eat some more for you.'

8 He ate the other part of the piece that he had cut in two. He chewed it carefully and then spat out the skin.

(Granada edn, pp. 48–9)

Here two strands of point of view are interwoven: the B(N) neutral mode for passages of speech and action and the B(R)+ve mode for the transitions into the active mind of the old man. Paragraphs 1, 5 and 8 present Narrative Report of Action (see section 2.3), with events related from outside the consciousness of the old man. Paragraphs 2, 3 and 7 report the speech of the old man, framing it within the Direct Speech mode with the unmarked reporting verbs 'said' and 'asked'. Both strands of the narrative are thus located in a B(N) neutral point of view. The third strand, realized by paragraphs 4 and 6, exhibits a departure from this point of view: the use of Free Direct Thought, by representing the workings of the active mind of a character, signals that the old man has now become the Reflector of fiction. The point of view category which this technique engenders is now B(R)+ve. What is remarkable about this, however, is that this pattern of alternation between modes is not only highly regular but is virtually unbroken over the entire central section of the novel. The rhythmical effect which this consistent pattern generates has been touched upon implicitly by a number of critics, with more than one going as far as to suggest that this rhythm parallels the movement of the sea on which the events of the novel take place.[4]

Further examples of transitions between modes and their stylistic effects could be collected here, but what is at issue really is the principle of transition itself. The feasibility of transition from one mode to another and the stylistic complexity of texts which exhibit multiple transitions is what the present model seeks to accommodate. It also attempts to explain how a particular mode may dominate a text despite momentary infractions into other subordinate modes. Genette reserves the term 'alteration' for such situations, elaborating thus:

> a change in focalization, especially if it is isolated within a coherent context, can also be analyzed as a momentary infraction of the code which governs the context without thereby calling into question the existence of the code – the same way that in a classical musical composition a momentary change in tonality, or even a recurrent dissonance, may be defined as a modulation or alteration without contesting the tonality of the whole. Playing on the double meaning of the word *mode* , which refers us to both grammar and music, I will thus give the general name *alterations* to these isolated infractions.
>
> (1980: 195)

Finally, the model presented here is in no way intended to provide an exhaustive account of all types of prose fiction. At best, it can be considered a relatively systematic method of accounting for dominant patterns in different text types. In this respect, and as was pointed out in chapter 1, it can help account for why one style of writing may simply 'feel' different from another. Perhaps the best way of picturing the nine components of the model, then, are as directions on a compass or nodes on a grid, providing handy points of reference by which styles can be measured. There will, of course, be exceptions which are not easily accommodated within the framework.[5] Like other stylistic frameworks, the modal grammar of point of view presented here is intended to account for the linguistic experimentation, complexity and subtlety which characterizes many works of prose fiction, although, as subsequent chapters will show, modality is only one layer of a multi-layered communicative process. None the less, if, as a result of this discussion, we are nearer an understanding of why, say, Hemingway sounds as 'deadpan' as he does, or why Beckett's fiction is often so perversely 'uninformative', then the modal grammar presented here will have had some measure of success.

3.5 SUMMARY

This chapter began with an introduction to the concept of modality in language. The purpose of this was threefold. First, as is the case elsewhere in the book, a schematic description of an important aspect of linguistics was presented in such a way as to be relatively self-sufficient and of some heuristic benefit in itself. Second, it was designed to form a bridge with the work which was reviewed towards the end of the previous chapter, particularly that of Uspensky and Fowler. And third, it was developed to facilitate the systematic analysis of point of view in fiction. To this effect, the main body of the chapter was concerned with the formalization of a grammar of point of view within a modal framework. Modality thus became the criterion against which different styles of writing could be measured, and different genres identified. There will, no doubt, be exceptions, flaws and overlaps in the model – but this is the very stuff which fuels linguistic debate and leads to revisions and modifications of models of language structure. Of course, there is the problem that modality is only one dimension of the complex, multidimensional process of linguistic communication. The purpose of the next chapter, then, will be to introduce another dimension and, in doing so, to widen the scope of the analysis to incorporate forms of language use other than that of prose fiction.

NOTES AND FURTHER READING

1 The account of modality offered in this section is really an amalgam of the following sources: Lyons (1977), Coates (1983), Perkins (1983), Palmer (1986), Simpson (1990). Other useful surveys are Stubbs (1986) and Coates (1987).

2 Anyone interested in the creative-writing potential of the model may care to consider the following protocol. This is an activity which was developed for use in a recent series of workshops involving speakers of English as a second language. Depending on second-language competence, participants could choose to work individually or in groups of three to four:

1 Write down a short narrative of personal experience. Your story may detail any event that may have happened to you – no matter how banal. (These narratives need not be attempts at major literary enterprises!)

2 In terms of the framework of *point of view*, identify the category within which you have written your narrative. (e.g. B(N)–ve, A neutral, B(R)+ve and so on).

3 Now attempt to rewrite your narrative (a) in a different category, but within the same mode (e.g. A–ve to B(N)–ve) and (b) in a different mode within the same category (e.g. A–ve to A neutral or A+ve). What linguistic changes are necessary for your rewrites? Are some rewrites easier than others? If so, why?

Such an activity helps to provide greater linguistic awareness of aspects of prose fiction which may have been only intuitively or subliminally perceived. It also tends to assist the development of language skills in areas like narrative construction and the use of modalized expressions. Even when transpositions are not particularly successful (as in many attempted conversions of A+ve to A neutral) there is still some benefit. For one thing, such 'failed' transpositions foreground the amount of psychological description that occurs in a A+ve style narratives, and illustrate how impoverished those narratives become if this psychological detail is stripped away. As it happened, groups still managed to develop useful transpositions on some of the more complex conversions. For instance, our earlier 'newspaper-style' narrative (passage 3, section 3.2), which was originally produced in such a workshop, was rewritten, to my mind entirely commendably, as the following, highly modalized, A+ve style variant:

> The young man, spurred on by hatred and jealousy, stepped up to the candidate and in slow motion, pulled the trigger and watched his leaden body slump to the floor. He had only a second to feel immense jubilation and relief before an arrow of fire was dealt between his own shoulderblades.

3 Readers may be interested to know that in the original B(N)+ve version of this narrative, the second paragraph begins as follows:

> It exploded much later than intended, probably a good twelve hours later, at twenty-six minutes past eight on Monday morning. Several defunct wristwatches, the property of victims, confirmed the time. As with its predecessors over the last few months, there had been no warning.

4 Simpson (1987) presents a detailed (if over-long!) analysis of a passage from the *The Old Man and the Sea*, concentrating primarily on the way modes of speech and thought presentations are deployed. It is argued that regular oscillations between the modes creates an almost subliminal rhythmical effect, which is sustained over the prolonged period during which the old man is at sea. Certainly, the notion of 'rhythm' in this text is one which has been mooted by a number of critics, some of whom are quoted in my article.

5 One exception which springs immediately to mind is the use of a second-person narrative framework. Here is a brief illustration from Ray Bradbury's short story 'The Night' (1948):

> You are a child in a small town. You are, to be exact, eight years old, and it is growing late at night. Late, for you, accustomed to bedding in at nine or nine-thirty; once in a while perhaps begging Mom or Dad to let you stay up later to hear Sam and Henry on that strange radio that is popular in this year of 1927. But most of the time you are in bed and snug at this time of night.
>
> (Granada edn, p. 154)

In terms of a point of view framework, it is largely a question of whether this technique warrants the development of an extra category, say a 'category C'. Or is such category C writing too peripheral to justify such an extension? These are problems which I must leave the reader to resolve.

4 Encoding experience in language: the system of transitivity

Something must have happened to me sometime.

(Joseph Heller, *Something Happened*)

4.1 INTRODUCTION

Picture, if you will, the following scenario. You are sitting in your boss's office anxiously awaiting news about your recent application for promotion. But just before announcing the outcome of your application, your boss is called away to take a phone call in another office. You sit nervously, rubbing together the palms of your hands. On the desk in front of you is an expensive-looking miniature replica Ming vase. You pick up this little cobalt-blue *objet d'art* and turn it deftly in your hands. Then, of course, catastrophe strikes: as you're turning it, it slips through your fingers and smashes into a dozen or so fragments on the varnished oak floor. You stare at it vacuously. After what seems like a lifetime, your boss returns. She stares at the pieces on the floor and then frowns at you in clear anticipation of an explanation. What do you say to her?

Let us suppose you decide to make a clean breast of it and offer the following remark by way of explanation:

(1) I broke the vase.

In this grammatically *active* sentence, the 'doer' has been placed first whereas the object affected has been positioned last. This certainly foregrounds your involvement in the incident, leaving no doubt about your responsibility for the breakage. Perhaps this 'up-front' approach is the sort of thing your boss respects. Or perhaps not. You decide therefore that (1) is a little too direct, and that the following is more appropriate:

(2) The vase was broken by me.

By converting (1) to its *passive* equivalent in this way, you have re-arranged the original sequence of information. The object affected is now placed first, whilst the agent responsible for the breakage is now shifted towards the end of the sentence. Perhaps this more subtle explanation is what your boss would prefer. Then again, maybe not. You feel the passive form is basically a good idea, but it sounds a little clumsy. You also feel that the removal of the 'doer' of the process is desirable. On balance, then, (3) seems the best policy:

(3) The vase was broken.

This strategy exploits a feature of the passive in that it has been possible to remove the optional 'by –' phrase from the end of the sentence. However, although the 'by –' phrase has disappeared, your boss can still react to (3) by asking *Who by?* Maybe the safest tactic is to construct a sentence which will not support a *who by?* question. You opt therefore for the following:

(4) The vase broke.

Like all of the options you have considered, (4) is a true statement about what happened. The 'pay-off' here, as far as you are concerned, is that in (4) the 'doer' has been excised completely from the process, fending off the awkward *who by?* question. On the other hand, there is the risk that the boss may think you're being disingenuous or that you are rather spineless. Perhaps a more direct approach, like that of (1) say, is needed.

The four possibilities considered here represent different ways of encoding in language our experience of a particular event. Something has happened and circumstances dictate that we must select words to describe it. In this case the particular selections which we make are from the system of *transitivity* and it is this system which forms the remit of the present chapter.

The fact that transitivity has proved a useful analytic model in both stylistics and critical linguistics makes it a useful bridge between the analysis of narrative fiction and other discourse types. This chapter will reflect this multifunctionality by examining both narrative and media language, demonstrating, I hope, that the potential range of this model is extensive. The concept of transitivity will be introduced in the next section. In keeping with the precedent set earlier, this will take the form of a montage of various theories,[1] all pared down to form as neat and economical a model as possible. Section 4.3 will apply this model to some samples of prose fiction. This should supplement the analyses undertaken in the previous two chapters and should add another dimension to our expanding stylistic framework. The following section (4.4) will apply the same model of analysis to examples of media language, and the concept of ideological point of view will become progressively more prominent as we investigate this type of discourse. After that, in section 4.5, the implications of using transitivity as a general method of analysis will be considered, and some of the problems associated with its application will be noted.

4.2 THE TRANSITIVITY MODEL

In this study, the term *transitivity* is used in a much wider sense than that employed in traditional grammars. Here it refers generally to how meaning is represented in the clause. It shows how speakers encode in language their mental picture of reality and how they account for their experience of the world around them. Modality, as we saw earlier, is an important part of the interpersonal function of language. By contrast, transitivity, because it is concerned with the transmission of ideas, is part of the *ideational* function of language. The way in which transitivity carries out this ideational function is by expressing *processes*. Halliday explains what this means:

> What does it mean to say that a clause represents a process? Our most powerful conception of reality is that it consists of 'goings-on': of doing, happening, feeling, being. These goings-on are sorted out in the semantic system of the language and expressed through the grammar of the clause.
>
> (1985: 101)

The semantic processes expressed by clauses have potentially three components. These are:

(1) *process* itself, which will be expressed by the verb phrase in a clause.
(2) The *participants* involved in the process. These roles are typically realized by noun phrases in the clause.
(3) The *circumstances* associated with the process, normally expressed by adverbial and prepositional phrases.

Processes can be classified according to whether they represent actions, speech, states of mind or simply states of being. What I propose to do is to account for the major processes realized in the system and the participant roles that are associated with them.

4.2.1 Material processes

These are simply processes of *doing*. Material processes have two inherent participant roles associated with them. The first of these is the ACTOR, an obligatory element which represents the 'doer' of the process expressed by the clause. The second is an optional GOAL which represents the person or entity affected by the process. Here are two examples illustrating these configurations:

	ACTOR	PROCESS	GOAL
(5)	John	kicked	the ball.

	ACTOR	PROCESS
(6)	The lion	sprang.

Because a GOAL element is present in (5), we can re-arrange this sentence into a passive form:

	GOAL	PROCESS	ACTOR
(7)	The ball	was kicked	by John.

Although both the original participants are still present in this clause, the GOAL element is placed first and the ACTOR shifted to the end of the sentence.

Material processes can be subdivided on the basis of finer distinctions in meaning. If the process is performed by an animate actor, it is referred to as an *action* process. The term *event* process is reserved for those processes which, by contrast, are performed by an inanimate actor. Action processes may themselves be further subdivided into *intention* processes (where the actor performs the act voluntarily) and *supervention* processes (where the process just happens).

We can develop a network for this system of material processes. The schema below illustrates how the subcategories interrelate with one another and provides sample sentences for each type. Distinctions become more 'delicate' as the system progresses rightwards.

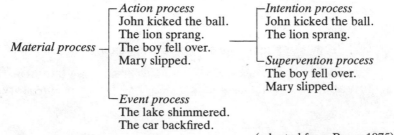

(adapted from Berry 1975)

Two brief comments are necessary on material processes before we move on to the next category. First, it is not always easy to separate out the three subdivisions of material processes on the basis of the criteria provided above. It is often not clear, for instance, whether a particular participant role exhibits animacy or inanimacy, or whether a process has been done intentionally or not. So these subdivisions should be regarded more as handy approximations than as strictly delineated categories. Second, for the purposes of simplicity, *circumstantial* elements have been omitted from the examples so far. These are the elements which provide extra information on the 'how, when, where and why' of the process, although they are normally grammatically subordinate in status to the process. To this extent, circumstantial elements are often 'deletable', whereas the process itself never is. By way of illustration, examples (5), (6) and (7) can easily be embellished to include circumstantial elements:

/CIRCUMSTANCES

(5) a. John kicked the ball hard.

/CIRCUMSTANCES

(6) a. The lion sprang from the bushes.

CIRCUMSTANCES /

(7) a. From the edge of the penalty area, the ball was kicked by John

4.2.2 Verbalization processes

These are processes of *saying*. The participant roles associated with verbalization processes are that of SAYER (the individual who is speaking) and TARGET (the addressee to whom the process is directed). To this we may add the role of VERBIAGE which, used in its original non-derogatory sense, means 'that which is said'. Some examples are:

	SAYER	PROCESS	VERBIAGE	
(8)	He	said	that.	

	SAYER	PROCESS	VERBIAGE	TARGET
(9)	They	announced	the decision	to me.

	SAYER	PROCESS	TARGET	VERBIAGE
(10)	John	told	Mary	his life story.

4.2.3 Mental processes

This third category accounts for processes of *sensing*. These processes are 'internalized' and as such are quite different in quality to the 'externalized' processes of doing and speaking. Mental processes may be more delicately defined as *perception* processes ('seeing', 'hearing'), *reaction* processes ('liking', 'hating') and processes of *cognition* ('thinking', 'understanding'). There are two inherent participant roles associated with mental processes, which are SENSER (the conscious being that is perceiving, reacting or thinking) and PHENOMENON (that which is perceived, reacted to or thought about). Below is a system network for mental processes which is followed by a set of examples broken down into their constituent parts.

Mental process

— *Perception*
John saw Mary.
She heard the concert.

— *Reaction*
She likes Bach.
He hates wine.

— *Cognition*
She considered the question.
I thought hard.

	SENSER	PROCESS	PHENOMENON
(11)	John	saw	Mary.

	SENSER	PROCESS	PHENOMENON
(12)	She	likes	Bach.

	SENSER	PROCESS	PHENOMENON
(13)	She	considered	the question.

	SENSER	PROCESS	CIRCUMSTANCES
(14)	I	thought	hard.

4.2.4 Relational processes

This final category expresses processes of *being*. Quite often, they signal that a relationship exists between two participants but without suggesting that one participant affects the other in any way. Relational processes may be (a) *intensive*, expressing an '*X is a*' relationship; (b) *possessive*, expressing an '*X has a*' relationship; or (c) *circumstantial*, expressing an '*X is at/on a*' relationship. Here is a network illustrating these distinctions:

Relational process —————————
- *Intensive*
  Mary is wise.
  Tom seems foolish.
- *Possessive*
  Gill has a guitar.
  John owns a piano.
- *Circumstantial*
  Bill is at home.
  The queen was in the parlour.

Now, the participant roles associated with relational processes can be quite complex. For the present purposes, the terms CARRIER (roughly the 'topic' of the clause) and ATTRIBUTE (a description or comment about the topic) should suffice. In the examples on the system network, the CARRIER element is first in all cases, with the ATTRIBUTE following the verb in all cases.

4.2.5 The standard analysis and the ergative analysis

I wish to add one final component to the analytic model outlined in this section. This component concerns the ways in which *agency* and *causation* relate to the processes expressed by the clause, especially those clauses which express material processes. This should form a useful extra dimension in our framework of analysis.

Let us re-introduce two of the examples used in the 'office sketch' which opened this chapter, placing them together for ease of comparison:

(1) I broke the vase.
(4) The vase broke.

In relation to both examples, the question might be asked: which participant is affected by the process expressed by the clause? Clearly, it is the vase – in either case, it breaks. Now, in our transitivity framework a standard breakdown of these examples would look like the following:

	ACTOR	PROCESS	GOAL
(1)	I	broke	the vase.

	ACTOR	PROCESS
(4)	The vase	broke.

The problem here is that the vase appears as the GOAL in (1) but as the ACTOR in (4), despite the fact that it is the affected participant in both cases. This is because there is a special set of verbs in English (like *to break*) which can express both patterns, and each pattern is said to bear an *ergative* relationship to the other. To account for this kind of situation it is sometimes useful to isolate one participant that is the key figure in the process and without which the process could not have come into existence. In examples (1) and (4), the vase represents this key participant role and may thus be labelled the MEDIUM, on the basis that it is the medium through which the process comes into existence. In material processes of this sort, the MEDIUM will always be equivalent to the ACTOR in an intransitive (non-goal-directed) clause and the GOAL in a transitive clause. Consider the following examples, which all realize processes which behave in a similar way to that expressed by (1) and (4):

The police exploded the bomb.	The bomb exploded.
The wind shattered the windows.	The windows shattered.
John cooked the rice.	The rice cooked.

According to the criteria noted above, the MEDIUM will be represented by *the bomb*, *the windows* and *the rice* in each pair of examples. However, in each of the examples on the left, there is another participant functioning as an external cause of the process. This participant, which is responsible for engendering the process from outside, may be referred to as the AGENT. The AGENT will thus be equivalent to the ACTOR in goal-directed material processes – as can be seen by the participant function of *the police*, *the wind* and *John* in the left-hand examples. Consequently, these examples display an AGENT + PROCESS + MEDIUM sequence, whilst those on the right simply display a MEDIUM + PROCESS sequence. The ergative interpretation suggested here need only be invoked for the special types of process identified in this section. It forms a useful supplement, an extra layer, to the standard analysis of transitivity which suffices for most purposes. To show how both types of analysis interrelate with one another, here is a 'double' analysis of examples (1) and (4):

Ergative analysis:	AGENT	PROCESS	MEDIUM
Standard analysis:	ACTOR	PROCESS	GOAL
(1)	I	broke	the vase.

Ergative analysis:	MEDIUM	PROCESS
Standard analysis:	ACTOR	PROCESS
(4)	The vase	broke.

The ergative interpretation bears an important relation to the system of *voice*. A clause that displays no feature of agency is neither active nor passive but middle (*The bomb exploded*). On the other hand, clauses which display agency can be either active or passive and are therefore non-middle in voice (*The police exploded the bomb*). In non-middle clauses the feature of agency may be *explicit*, as in *The police exploded the bomb* and its passive equivalent *The bomb was exploded by the police*. On the other hand, it may be left *implicit*, through the removal of the optional 'by–' phrase (*The bomb was exploded*). In reaction to clauses which bear implicit agency, one can still ask *Who by?*, whereas in the case of a middle clause (*The bomb exploded*) one cannot.

The system of options available for ergativity and voice have important pragmatic and contextual implications. It should be clear by now that the choice whether to include or omit agency from a process constitutes an important part of message construction. Going back to our office sketch, in the construction of a strategically more 'neutral' explanation, a speaker may select a middle clause displaying no agency. This is precisely the type of strategy realized by example (4):

(4) The vase broke.

More informative (although more 'incriminating') are those clauses which signal greater degrees of involvement by the speaker in the action referred to. The first of these, example (1), is both non-middle and features explicit agency:

(1) I broke the vase.

as does its passive equivalent, example (2)

(2) The vase was broken by me.

Example (3) signals greater mitigation, as the agency here is now left implicit:

(3) The vase was broken.

The communicative function of transitivity and ergativity will be explored further in the following three sections. But for the moment, a short summary of the main types of process introduced in this section might be helpful. The list of categories below should provide a checklist of the important features of transitivity:

Process name	Process type	Participant role(s)
Material	'doing'	ACTOR (obligatory); GOAL (optional);
Verbalization	'saying'	SAYER (obligatory); TARGET (optional); VERBIAGE (optional)
Mental	'sensing'	SENSER (obligatory); PHENOMENON (optional)
Relational	'being'	CARRIER (obligatory); ATTRIBUTE (obligatory)

The next stage will be to examine the ways in which transitivity can be used in the analysis of a range of text types.

4.3 STYLISTICS AND TRANSITIVITY

The transitivity model has proved a popular analytic framework ever since Halliday's influential analysis of William Golding's *The Inheritors*, published as long ago as 1971. More recently, there has been Kennedy's analysis (1982) of a central scene from Conrad's *The Secret Agent* and Burton's (1982) feminist-stylistic analysis of a sequence from Sylvia Plath's *The Bell Jar*. Rather than review these studies just yet, I prefer for a number of reasons to develop some illustrations of my own. For one thing, these earlier stylistic analyses have employed versions of the transitivity model in various stages of its development, so to avoid adding to the confusion it is better to provide a demonstration using a single, up-to-date version such as that outlined in the previous section. Furthermore, there will be an opportunity here to re-introduce some of the material discussed in the previous chapter, thereby creating extra insights into the same texts through the use of a different linguistic technique. This should underscore the multifunctional nature of language and highlight the possibility of multidimensional textual analysis.

At first, it is best to keep the analysis as straightforward as possible. To this effect, I propose to return to a short section from Hemingway's *The Old Man and the Sea* examined in section 3.4 of the previous chapter (passage 30). It was introduced there as part of the discussion of point of view transitions, where the B(N) neutral mode which characterized passages of physical description alternated with sequences of B(R)+ve in the form of transitions into the old man's consciousness. The passages of B(N) neutral – the externalized, unmodalized narrative 'facts' – are quite interesting in terms of transitivity. The following extract is the first paragraph of passage 30, this time quoted in its entirety and sentence numbers added for ease of reference. As you read the passage, ask yourself a question which has become the first principle of a transitivity analysis: who or what does what to whom or what?

(1) He knelt down and found the tuna under the stern with the gaff and drew it toward him keeping it clear of the coiled lines. (2) Holding the line with his left shoulder again, and bracing on his left hand and arm, he took the tuna off the gaff hook and put the gaff back in place. (3) He put one knee on the fish and cut strips of dark red meat longitudinally from the back of the head to the tail. (4) They were wedge-shaped strips and he cut them from next to the backbone down to the edge of the belly. (5) When he had cut six strips he spread them out on the wood of the bow, wiped his knife on his trousers, and lifted the carcass of the bonito by the tail and dropped it overboard.

Following up the 'who does what' axiom reveals a number of dominant stylistic traits in the passage. Almost invariably, the old man is the 'doer', doing some action to some entity. The clauses in which he features are all in the simple past and are normally arranged in a sequence which reflects the temporal sequence of the events described. They contain virtually no interpretative intrusions by the narrator. In short, they reflect pure B(N) neutral narrative and with a single exception, all express material processes of doing. In all of these material processes, the old man is the ACTOR so the processes are of the *action* type. As nothing 'just happens' to him in any of these clauses, and he is firmly in control of everything he does, then a full description will specify that these clauses express material action processes of *intention*. Here are breakdowns of some typical patterns:

	ACTOR	PROCESS
1	He	knelt down . . .

	ACTOR	PROCESS	GOAL	CIRCUMSTANCES
2	he	took	the tuna	off the gaff

	ACTOR	PROCESS	GOAL	CIRCUMSTANCES
4	he	cut	them	from next to the backbone

Often, the ACTOR role is ellipted when clauses are strung together, although it is still easily inferred through reference to preceding clauses. The symbol ∅ can be used to denote this sort of implicit agency:

	ACTOR	PROCESS	[connector]		
1	He	knelt down	and		

	ACTOR	PROCESS	GOAL	CIRCUMSTANCES	[connector]
	∅	found	the tuna	under the stern...	and...

	ACTOR	PROCESS	GOAL	CIRCUMSTANCES
	∅	drew	it	toward him

Another feature of this highly stable pattern of transitivity is the invariable use of the active voice. Passive variants, where the GOAL element is fronted and the ACTOR either shifted rightwards or removed completely, are never used. Indeed, in the context of the passage as a whole, conversions to the passive would seem a little odd:

> 5(a) When six strips had been cut, and they were spread out by him on the wood of the bow . . .

Of a total of seventeen processes expressed in this paragraph, only one is non-material. This is a relational process which occurs in the first clause of sentence 4. By way of contrast with the dominant material – action – intention pattern, here is a breakdown of this clause:

	CARRIER	PROCESS	ATTRIBUTE
4	They	were	wedge-shaped strips

Although there is not the space to develop a detailed interpretation of the analysis of this paragraph, a few comments are necessary before we move on to our next example. One of the stylistic consequences of the dominant material paradigm, where mental and other processes signifying reflection and deliberation are suppressed, is that it creates a highly 'actional' descriptive framework. Now, in the context of the longer passage in which this paragraph appeared (see section 3.4), it was shown that this type of description alternated systematically with paragraphs of speech and thought presentation. This offers an excellent illustration of the convergence of transitivity and point of view.

There is a controlled oscillation between sequences of material processes depicting an externalized view of events, sequences of verbalization processes in the form of the represented speech of the old man and sequences of mental processes representing intrusions into the old man's consciousness signalled by the use of Direct Thought and Free Direct Thought. This regular pattern, it was argued, is not restricted to a few paragraphs but to the entire central section of the novel.

A further consequence of the brief analysis undertaken here is that it provides a rationale for more coherent judgements about Hemingway's style. All of the material processes identified display an inflexible pattern of transitivity, where the use of the active voice ensures that the ACTOR element always precedes the process. This invariability may simply be another aspect of the stylistic 'flatness' which typifies the B(N) neutral category of point of view. It certainly appears to have eluded many critics writing about Hemingway's style. For instance, in a much-publicized article, Levin remarks of Hemingway that 'in the technical sense, his syntax is weak' and 'his verbs not particularly energetic' (1972: 331). There is no technical sense in which syntax can be weak or verbs energetic, yet despite the 'pre-linguistic' nature of these remarks it is still possible to see what the critic is getting at. I hope the twin features of modality and transitivity, operating in tandem, will have provided some clearer understanding of the mechanics of Hemingway's prose style.

The second illustration of the stylistic potential of the transitivity model is somewhat more complex. The example chosen for analysis is one which displays positively shaded modality with events being mediated, often ironically, through an opinionated speaking voice. Part of the object of the analysis which follows will be to demonstrate how patterns of transitivity enrich this ironic technique.

In section 3.2 and later during the discussion of category B narrative viewpoints, use was made of the opening of John le Carré's spy-novel *The Little Drummer Girl* (passage 2). This passage, it may be recalled, was concerned broadly with 'the Bad Godesberg incident' – an explosion resulting from a bomb planted in the centre of a diplomatic community by an international terrorist group. This incident forms the nucleus of the first four pages of the novel, although, bizarrely, the actual explosion and its immediate consequences are never engaged with directly for any sustained period. Instead, much of the narrative is concerned with events that took place prior to or subsequent to the explosion. This is supplemented with discursive summaries of the Rhineland weather and tourist-brochure style descriptions of the residences of the diplomatic community. All of this is narrated in the third person with the highly modalized language of the B(N)+ve mode.

There is, however, one point in the sixth paragraph of the novel where the narrative does move closer to its ostensible topic as the effects of the explosion on a school bus are described. As will be seen, description of the direct consequences of the explosion is almost submerged in the generic sentences which signal a dominant B(N)+ve modality:

> Somewhere in every bomb explosion there is a miracle, and in this case it was supplied by the American School bus, which had just come and gone again with most of the community's younger children who congregated every schoolday in the turning-circle
> 5 not fifty metres from the epicentre. By a mercy none of the children had forgotten his homework, none had overslept or shown resistance to education on this Monday morning. So the bus got away on time. The rear windows shattered, the driver went side-winding into the verge, a French girl lost an eye, but
> 10 essentially the children escaped scot-free, which was afterwards held to be a deliverance. For that also is a feature of such explosions, or at least of their immediate aftermath: a communal, wild urge to celebrate the living, rather than to waste time mourning the dead. The real grief comes later when the shock
> 15 wears off, usually after several hours, though occasionally less.
>
> (Pan edn, p. 13)

Most of the first paragraph either proclaims universal truths in the form of generics ('Somewhere in every bomb explosion there is a miracle') or offers *post hoc* interpretations of the consequences of the explosion ('. . .but essentially the children escaped scot-free'). There is, however, a sequence of three clauses which intrudes into this framework and offers a direct, if highly condensed, account of the actual effects of the explosion. This sequence begins at line 8:

> The rear windows shattered, the driver went side-winding into the verge, a French girl lost an eye . . .

Like the narrative clauses identified in the paragraph from Hemingway, these clauses are temporally ordered and express material processes. But there the similarity stops. The second and third clauses constitute our first encounter with material action processes of *supervention*. In these clauses, human ACTORS perform the actions involuntarily; the processes seem to 'just happen'. The first clause requires some elaboration. It expresses an *event* process on the basis that it is performed by an inanimate ACTOR. However, the verb 'shatter' expresses one of those special types of process which permits an *ergative* interpretation (see above). Both layers of analysis are captured below:

Ergative analysis:	MEDIUM	PROCESS
Standard analysis:	ACTOR	PROCESS
	The rear windows	shattered

This is a particularly salient choice of process here. It was pointed out earlier that non-goal-directed clauses of this sort, which are neither active nor passive, are middle in voice. Consequently, the processes associated with middle clauses normally appear endogenous; that is to say, they are brought about by the single participant associated with them (the MEDIUM) and not by any external AGENT. Alternative representations of this clause would have to specify some sort of agency, either explicitly in the form of active or passive non-middle clauses:

X shattered the rear windows.

The rear windows were shattered by X

or implicitly, in the form of a passive with the AGENT deleted:

The rear windows were shattered.

If we consider the three narrative clauses of the original text together, there is the impression that the processes expressed by them are simply self-engendered, uninduced by any external cause. This is odd, given that they depict the violent effects brought about precisely *by* an external cause. The impact of the bomb explosion is further diminished and, for that matter, trivialized, through the syntactic frame which incorporates these three clauses. For instance, each clause is presented in an asyndetic 'listing' fashion without the use of formal connectors. Furthermore, the consequences of the explosion – especially the French girl's loss of an eye – are clearly undermined by the following adversative clause ('but essentially the children escaped scot-free'), the content of which is manifestly at odds with what has gone before.

It might be added as a footnote to this analysis that other descriptions of violence in *The Little Drummer Girl* exhibit similar transitivity patterns. Consider the following extract from the penultimate chapter of the novel, where a sickening description of a savage attack is mediated through the viewing position of a Reflector of fiction:

She saw Khalil's face burst, she saw him spin round and spread his arms to the wall, appealing for its help. So the bullets went into his back, ruining his white shirt. His hands flattened against the wall – one leather, one real – and his wrecked body slipped to a rugger player's crouch.

(Pan edn, p. 510)

A detailed analysis of this scene is not necessary, as by now the basic pattern of transitivity has been established. Suffice it to say, there is no suggestion of external agency in those event and supervention processes which involve directly the victim of the attack ('Khalil's face burst'; 'His hands flattened'). Significant also is the way in which the entire scene is represented through a mental process of perception which is attributed to the female protagonist of the novel ('She saw'; 'she saw').

What this brief analysis has sought to demonstrate is how a certain type of transitivity pattern, especially when developed in conjunction with a positively-shaded modality, can function as an ironizing technique. In the le Carré example, this convergence of modality and transitivity served to highlight the persona of the speaking voice whilst distancing the purported central event of the narrative. So, where the physical horror of certain events is suppressed, the opinionated subjectivity of the narrator is foregrounded. The use of the ironic narrative technique has been commented upon by critics of le Carré, one of whom remarks specifically of *The Little Drummer Girl* that

Where explanations seem unnecessary they are given, where a particularly horrifying incident seems to demand the narrator's acknowledgement of that horror, none is forthcoming. Often there is a throwaway matter-of-factness to descriptions or, again, a disturbing faux-naiveté. Such techniques give a cool pathos to parts of the narrative.

(Barley 1986: 162)[2]

While endorsing these observations in general terms, I would want to add that a stylistic analysis will go some way towards explaining just why and how such 'throwaway matter-of-factness' and 'cool pathos' is created. Indeed, the rationale behind much modern stylistics is that not only does the use of linguistic models offer greater 'purchase' on texts but that it also provides the basis for comparative analyses of other texts using those same linguistic models. This comparative principle will further underpin the discussion of the final extract in the stylistic part of our transitivity programme.

In order to provide a complete picture of the point of view spectrum, a text which exhibits negative modal shading will be used to round off this section. This will be a short sample of 'Gothic' horror fiction which represents a genre of writing not covered so far and which should be worth exploring in terms of transitivity. In the extract below, which exhibits a dominant A–ve point of view, a first-person narrator discovers that he is in the company of a less than personable companion:

> Was It – the dark form with the chain – a creature of this world, or a spectre? And again – more dreadful still – could it be that the corpses of wicked men were forced to rise, and haunt in the body the places where they had wrought their evil deeds? And was
> 5 such as these my grisly neighbour? The chain faintly rattled. My hair bristled; my eyeballs seemed starting from their sockets; the damps of a great anguish were on my brow. My heart laboured as if I were crushed beneath some vast weight. Sometimes it appeared to stop its frenzied beatings, sometimes its pulsations
> 10 were fierce and hurried; my breath came short and with extreme difficulty, and I shivered as if with cold; yet I feared to stir. It moved, it moaned, its fetters clanked dismally, the couch creaked and shook.
>
> 'Horror: a true tale', *Blackwoods* 89 (1861)

The markers of negative modal shading take the form of epistemic modal verbs ('*could* it be'), modal lexical verbs of perception ('my eyeballs *seemed* starting'; 'it *appeared* to stop') and comparators based on reference to physical stimuli ('My heart laboured *as if* I were crushed'; 'I shivered *as if* with cold'). The ways in which transitivity patterns intersect with this modal shading are interesting. Despite the control that the narrator appears to have over his mental faculties, all suggestions of physical self-control disappear. Material processes of *supervention* signal the lack of command that the narrator has over, so to speak, his body parts. Here are a few illustrations:

ACTOR	PROCESS	
My hair	bristled (lines 5–6)	

ACTOR	PROCESS	CIRCUMSTANCES
My eyeballs	seemed starting	from their sockets (line 6)

ACTOR	PROCESS	
My heart	laboured (line 7)	

The abject fear which this linguistic strategy is presumably designed to convey is one feature of the extract, but the attempt to convey suspense, I would suggest, relies on another textual feature. This second pattern relates to the transitivity patterns associated with the protagonist's 'grisly neighbour'. If we look closely at the type of process in which the apparition is *directly* involved (lines 11–12), all it really does is 'move' (material action) and 'moan' (verbalization?). Of course, there is the suggestion that it is responsible for more 'happenings' than are attributed to it directly. Consider, for instance, the ominous sequence

The chain faintly rattled. (line 5)

The process of 'rattling' is one which allows an ergative interpretation. Although it may therefore permit agency, it can still be represented, as it is here, in the form of an agentless, middle clause. In other words, the chain just rattles, and any responsibility for the rattling is left unspecified and must be inferred from the context. Similarly, cause and effect relations are also suppressed in the final three material processes of the extract, where agentless, middle clauses help develop a picture where inanimate objects appear to have a will of their own:

its fetters clanked dismally, the couch creaked and shook.
(lines 12–15)

This pattern of transitivity squares neatly with the viewing position of the narrator. The apparition's involvement in the movement of inanimate objects, although not perceived directly, is none the less imputed. The spatial point of view established here is therefore very much akin to a cinematographic technique which is employed almost to the point of cliché in horror films. This is the technique where the action is shot from within a darkly lit room. The camera pans towards the door and then brings in the door-handle in extreme close-up. The door-handle turns. Then the door creaks as it begins to open . . . Although certainly not consciously contrived to do so, the sequence of clauses just used to describe the movement of the door in my example exhibits the same type of transitivity pattern as that used in the passage of horror fiction examined above!

The three short analyses undertaken in this section were designed to illustrate the potential of the transitivity model in stylistics. Although this type of analysis will not provide an exhaustive account of a text's meaning, it should at least offer some insights into one important feature of message construction. Furthermore, some of the ways in which transitivity and modality interact have been assessed, and this has, I hope, enriched further our understanding of point of view in narrative fiction. What has not been dealt with here is the way in which transitivity can be used as an analytic tool in the study of non-literary discourse. This will be the objective of the following section.

4.4 TRANSITIVITY AND CRITICAL LINGUISTICS

This section takes the analysis in a number of new and important directions. It will re-introduce the work of the critical linguists which was reviewed briefly in chapter 1. While compatible in many respects with stylistics of the sort practised in 4.3, a critical linguistic approach will normally expand the analytic focus to include not only media language but all sorts of institutional discourses. Moreover, what was defined earlier as point of view on the *ideological* plane will become progressively more central in the analysis and discussion which follow.

Transitivity has been a popular part of the analytic toolkit of work within the critical linguistics tradition. It has been employed to uncover how certain meanings are foregrounded while others are suppressed or obfuscated. In this way, the transitivity model provides one means of investigating how a reader's or listener's perception of the meaning of a text is pushed in a particular direction and how the linguistic structure of a text effectively encodes a particular 'world-view'. This world-view will, of course, be that of the producer(s) of the text. Fowler provides a useful summary of this feature of textual meaning:

> Linguistic codes do not reflect reality neutrally; they interpret, organize, and classify the subjects of discourse. They embody theories of how the world is arranged: world-views or ideologies.
>
> (1986: 27)

The final part of this quote offers a useful perspective on the notion of ideology which was discussed in the introduction to the book.

As a preliminary to the critical linguistic analysis which follows, a brief recap of the transitivity model, illustrated with examples of media language, might be of some benefit. What follows is a breakdown of all the main processes along with attested examples taken from a variety of British newspapers.

Material processes.
(1) Action/intention:
  Two thugs attack policeman during Middlesbrough game.
  Police attacked isolated groups of miners.
(2) Action/supervention:
  He careered off the road.
  She broke down in the public gallery.

(3) Event:
Bomb explodes in city centre.
The rear door opened at the traffic lights.
Verbalization processes:
(1) Special Branch says students are members of Iraqi Armed Forces.
(2) Ministers call for curbs on repossessions.

Mental Processes:
(1) Perception:
Residents nearby heard the explosion.
(2) Reaction:
She despised her psychopath boyfriend.
(3) Cognition:
Detectives believed her story.

Relational processes:
(1) Intensive:
Hurd becomes Foreign Secretary.
(2) Possessive:
United have four point advantage over Liverpool.
(3) Circumstantial:
Capacity crowd at Nat West final.

Now, it was pointed out earlier that a critical linguistic analysis will seek to *interpret*, rather than simply *describe* the linguistic structure of texts. With specific reference to transitivity, one study which has become in many respects a flagship for the critical linguistics approach is Tony Trew's widely referenced article on media language (1979). Trew analyses the news coverage of an event of civil disorder in pre-independence Zimbabwe. He examines, amongst other things, the headlines and opening texts of two British newspapers of 2 June 1975 which cover this event. Part of these are reproduced here:

POLICE SHOOT 11 DEAD IN SALISBURY RIOT
Riot police shot and killed 11 African demonstrators.
(the *Guardian*, p. 1)

RIOTING BLACKS SHOT DEAD BY POLICE
Eleven Africans were shot dead and 15 wounded when Rhodesian police opened fire on a rioting crowd.
(*The Times*, p. 1)

Lexical choices in these two texts are clearly significant: the 'African demonstrators' of the *Guardian* are transformed into 'Rioting Blacks' in *The Times*. These lexical differences are also accompanied by important differences of the transitivity structure of the two reports. the *Guardian* employs active constructions thereby making the ACTOR the first element in the clause and shifting the GOAL towards the end of the clause. This places considerable emphasis on the agents involved in the process ('POLICE . . . Riot police . . .'). *The Times*, by contrast, adopts passive constructions which put the GOAL (the affected participants) in a position of focal prominence ('RIOTING BLACKS . . . Eleven Africans . . .') whilst placing the ACTOR element (the agents of the killings) in a less prominent position. Furthermore, in *The Times*'s opening text, agency is actually deleted from the processes expressed by the first clause and can only be identified by inference from the second. Here is a breakdown of this sentence following the format established for this chapter:

GOAL	PROCESS		GOAL	PROCESS
Eleven Africans	were shot dead	[and]	15	wounded
ACTOR	PROCESS		GOAL	
[when] police	opened fire on		a rioting crowd	

Trew contends that in *The Times* the effects of passivization and agency deletion serve to shift attention away from those who did the shooting and onto the victims. In other words, while retained within some notional parameter of 'truth', the two messages are slanted in crucially different directions. This slanting can be aligned with the political orientation of the two newspapers; the *Guardian* reflecting the political left and *The Times* the political right. This type of interpretation, extrapolating from textual analysis to questions of political bias, encapsulates the critical linguistic method. From this perspective, texts are never regarded as neutral, value-free chunks of language; rather, they are viewed as embodiments of a host of institutional and political discursive practices.

Going back to Trew's examples for a moment, it is significant that the processes expressed in both extracts still support the 'who by?' question. That is to say, agency is explicit or at least implicit in these processes, so the relevant aspect of message construction resides more in the configuration of participants in the clause. Thus, a response will still be possible to the axiomatic transitivity question: 'who or what does what to whom or what?' However, there are situations where the question breaks down somewhat and responses are difficult to sustain. It is to one such situation that we shall now turn.

On 4 July 1986 a verdict was reached in the trial of a police constable who, in August of the previous year, broke into a home in Birmingham and shot a five-year-old boy as he slept in bed. The officer was acquitted of unlawfully killing the boy. British television's BBC evening news chose to describe the event which led to the trial in the following way:

The boy died when the policeman's gun went off.

At best, this is a needless obfuscation of what was publicly available information; at worst, an astonishing act of linguistic dissimulation.[3] In language terms, the resources of the system of transitivity are exploited to the full. Two middle clauses expressing material processes are conjoined by the connector *when*. The first process is of the supervention type, and the second of the event type:

Ergative analysis:	MEDIUM	PROCESS	
Standard analysis:	ACTOR	PROCESS	
	The boy	died	[when]
Ergative analysis:	MEDIUM	PROCESS	
Standard analysis:	ACTOR	PROCESS	
	the policeman's gun	went off	

The processes of both of these clauses, unlike the examples *break* or *shatter* examined in section 4.3.5, can *never* take agency. They defy analysis, therefore, in terms of the standard 'who or what does what . . .' formula, nor will either clause support a 'who by?' question. Consider, for instance, the anomaly of the following exchange:

A: The boy died
B: Who by?

So, unlike *shatter*, *break* or any of the special 'double-function' processes examined earlier, the processes of *die* and *go off* cannot be expanded into equivalent active and passive forms:

*X died the boy.
*The boy was died by X.
*Y went off the gun.
*The gun was went off by Y.

The use of the 'when' connector is also interesting. This signals a relationship of temporal contiguity rather than one of causation. Strictly speaking, it denotes 'X happened *at the same time as* Y' rather than 'X happened *because of* Y', although, of course, causation may be implied through the use of the first strategy. In any case, the 'when' contributes further to what seems to be a general refusal to simply tell it the way it was.

One might wonder what motivates the BBC to employ this particular configuration of transitivity. A possible explanation is that this discourse pattern has an underlying political motive; that it is biased, in this instance, in favour of a powerful political institution. In this respect, it functions as a conscious suppression not so much of the 'truth', because this example is arguably still a true representation of the circumstances, but of a reasonable version of 'reality'. Exploring the distinction between truth and reality in this way is another part of the critical linguistic creed. As particular linguistic codes embody particular realities, then nothing in language can be regarded as truly objective or neutral. Certainly, while it is difficult to challenge this piece of language on the criterion of truth, the issue of which version of reality it functions to present is entirely another matter.

In chapter 6, the transitivity model will be re-introduced, where, in parallel with other linguistic frameworks, it will feature in the discussion of gender and ideology. As far as this section is concerned, one final illustration of its potential in the critical linguistic analysis of news-reporting should prove useful. In 1988, an industrial dispute developed between British nurses and government health ministers. The following two extracts are the headlines and opening texts of the reports of the dispute carried by the *Guardian* and *The Times* on 15 November. Bearing in mind what was said about the political orientation of these papers during the discussion of Trew's analysis, readers may care to identify for themselves which report belongs to which paper:

NURSES THREATEN TO RESIGN IN PAY ROW
Fifty-five midwives yesterday threatened to resign in the pay dispute over regrading.

MINISTERS ATTACK NURSES' PROTESTS
Health ministers yesterday launched a propaganda offensive over the nurses' grading dispute.

Both transitivity structure and lexical selections vary markedly between one report and the other, and it is difficult to attribute this disparity to anything other than different attitudes towards the nurses' cause. In the first extract, which in case you hadn't guessed comes from *The Times*, the nurses are represented as the only active participants throughout. More technically, the phrase 'NURSES' realizes the ACTOR role in the headline, with 'Fifty-five midwives' performing a similar function in the opening text. The associated processes can be identified by asking the question 'What do the nurses *do*?' and, in the case of both clauses, the answer will be: THREATEN TO RESIGN. By contrast, in the two clauses which comprise the *Guardian*'s account, the ACTOR role is occupied by 'MINISTERS' and 'Health ministers' and the two associated processes are respectively, 'ATTACK' and 'launched a propaganda offensive'. The *Guardian*'s account also features a GOAL element in its headline which is realized by the phrase 'NURSES' PROTESTS'. As it is the protests of the nurses which come under attack, this transitivity configuration only just stops short of accusing the ministers of attacking the nurses directly.

If anything, lexical choices are just as strong an indicator of the respective political stances adopted in both extracts. A number of words are used which have affective connotations and most of these carry conventionally negative evaluations of the activity to which they refer. In the example from *The Times*, for instance, the nurses issue 'threats', an activity normally interpreted unfavourably in most contexts. In the *Guardian* by contrast, it is the health ministers whose behaviour is evaluated negatively: they 'attack' and 'launch offensives', and to support their campaign of aggression they promulgate 'propaganda'.

The question of the conventional associations that attach to particular words is one which will be dealt with much more systematically in the next chapter. There, the notion of *presupposition* will be developed to account for such aspects of utterance meaning. But for the moment, some of the theoretical consequences of the use of the transitivity model need to be addressed. In particular, the issue of *interpretation* requires some discussion and this and other related issues will be the concern of the next section.

4.5 PROBLEMS OF ANALYSIS AND INTERPRETATION

At the beginning of section 4.3, I referred to M. A. K. Halliday's influential article on *The Inheritors* which was first published over two decades ago. In a number of respects, this article has become the blueprint of a modern stylistics which seeks to uncover patterns of meaning through the systematic analysis of linguistic structure. Halliday's article was, moreover, one of the first to adopt a specifically systemic–functional model and by doing so it not only illustrated the validity of the model itself but also offered a viable alternative to the transformational–generative model which was favoured in much contemporaneous stylistic work.

One of Halliday's chief concerns was to illustrate how the analysis of transitivity might contribute to an understanding of the particular 'mind-style' projected in a text. In the specific case of *The Inheritors* the bulk of the story is narrated from the point of view of Lok, one of a group of Neanderthal people. Towards the end of the book, Lok and his tribe are supplanted by a more advanced tribe and the narrative point of view shifts concomitantly towards that of these 'new' people. Halliday demonstrates convincingly that there is a marked difference in the linguistic styles which are used to signal these two narrative viewpoints. Where the world depicted from the perspective of 'new' people is very much like our own, the world seen by Lok and his tribe is distinctly unfamiliar. Within the limits of Lok's understanding, people appear to move aimlessly, seldom acting directly on objects in their physical environment. This sense of discontinuity, Halliday argues, is created through particular selections from the system of transitivity. For instance, where material processes are used, they tend to be non-GOAL directed. So, when human ACTORS feature in such processes they tend not to act on anything and if they do it is often only on themselves. Furthermore, many of these human ACTOR elements are more accurately classified as parts of the body and not complete beings. One consequence of this corporal fragmentation is that much of the action is attributable to what Nash has recently described as *meronymic* (body part) agency. This he contrasts with *holonymic* (complete body) agency (Nash 1990: 139). Thus, instead of a transitivity pattern like 'Lok smelled this stuff' we obtain the actual form 'His nose examined this stuff.' Similarly, a sequence like 'Lok twitched his ears' is dispreferred in favour of 'His ears twitched.' Furthermore, while much of the movement within Lok's visual perspective is often caused by his antagonists, Lok fails to understand the ways in which these antagonists act upon and control their environment. So, when a hostile tribesman twitches the bushes in front of Lok, an event-type material process is used to describe this:

> The bushes twitched.

The linguistic pattern which signals the central character's limited cognitive capacity is even more striking in the following sequence, which describes an enemy drawing a bow and shooting an arrow at Lok:

> A stick rose upright and . . . began to grow shorter at both ends. Then it shot out to full length again.

Again, event processes highlight Lok's inability to comprehend cause-and-effect relationships; there is no conception here at all of how a human agent is responsible for the action described.

This pattern of transitivity is one which constructs a fictive world in which there is constant activity, but where there is no distinction between human and inanimate movement and where there is little apprehension of how any of this movement is caused. After illustrating

how stylistic choices express 'this combination of activity and helplessness', Halliday offers the following very telling conclusion to his
analysis: 'No doubt this is a fair summary of the life of Neanderthal
man' (1971: 350). Equating the grammatical structure of a text with the
world-view it portrays is an interpretative manoeuvre which is common
to much stylistic analysis. Yet it is one which has been attacked
vociferously by critics, and Stanley Fish, in particular, has pilloried
Halliday for this particular piece of interpretation (Fish 1981: 59–64).
The criticism rests primarily on what might be termed the *interpretative
positivism* shown by stylisticians who simply invoke linguistic descriptions as a way of confirming the decisions they have already taken
about a text's meaning. Not only does this practice assume a one-to-
one correspondence between the stylistic profile of a text and the
world-view it portrays, but it also serves as a way of conferring value on
the formal methods of analysis themselves. After all, these formal
methods are, as Fish has argued, really only constructs developed by
linguists and stylisticians: they are not, therefore, ratifiable as ontologically stable categories.

I am aware that the problem of interpretative positivism, as presented here, is both abstract and complex. However, it constitutes part
of a polemic which is too serious to ignore and which needs to be
resolved at this stage of our analysis. So, in order to provide a clearer
idea of the problem and its potential consequences, I propose the
following illustration, which supplements Halliday's analysis with a
short analysis of my own.

At the start of one of William Golding's other novels, *Pincher
Martin* (1956), the eponymous first-person narrator is thrown into the
sea as a result of a U-boat attack on his ship. The first three chapters of
the novel describe Martin's struggles in the water with confused
flashbacks often interrupting the hero's attempts to prevent himself
from drowning. What is significant about this passage from a stylistic
point of view is that a pattern of transitivity emerges which is disconcer-
tingly similar to the 'Neanderthal' language identified by Halliday. A
great many of the clauses which describe Martin's struggle express,
quite predictably, material processes. However, a substantial proportion of these processes feature a human ACTOR which acts either on
itself or simply on nothing at all. Here is a selection of both types:

> He hunched his body . . . (p. 7)
> . . . his distant body stilled itself and relaxed (p. 9)
> He gathered himself . . . (p. 10)
> He crouched . . . (p. 31)

He slumped into the angle and his head fell. (p. 31)
He snored. (p. 31)

(Faber & Faber edn)

Even more striking is the proliferation of meronymic, as opposed to holonymic, agency in these material processes. The text, in fact, abounds in such 'body-part' ACTORS, a brief sample of which is:

. . . the lips came together and parted, the tongue arched, the brain lit a neon track. (p. 8)
His mouth stopped full . . . (p. 10)
His eyes returned to the pebbles and watched them idly . . . (p. 25)
His teeth came together and ground. (p. 27)
His hand let the knife go . . . (p. 38)

Again, the 'body-part' ACTOR was identified as one of the important features of Lok's Neanderthal language.

Another transitivity pattern which the two Golding texts share is the tendency for event processes featuring inanimate Agency to be used to depict activity which one would normally attribute to the Agency of human beings. So when, for example, the protagonist of *Pincher Martin* spits out water, the following pattern is used:

. . . sea water would burst out over his tongue. (p. 10).

Similarly, the following sequence is used to describe the action of swallowing sea water:

The lumps of hard water jerked in the gullet . . . (p. 8).

The stylistic similarity of the texts is not restricted to the system of transitivity. For instance, another characteristic of Halliday's Neanderthal language is the use of *general nouns*. This is a product of the imputed inability of the central character to lexicalize particular concepts into words. Thus, nouns with generalized reference – such as *stuff* and *thing* – are substituted for more specific terms. Yet this also is a feature of the *Pincher Martin* passage, where the general nouns presumably function to capture the drowning man's failure to comprehend clearly the normally familiar objects within his line of vision. Consequently, while one of Lok's opponents wears 'white bone *things*' on his face, so Pincher Martin has 'hard *things*' touching his face and chest. While Lok peers at the '*lump* of bone' which forms the point of an arrow, Martin feels the 'hard *lumps* of water' in his throat. And while Lok examines the 'sticky brown *stuff*' on an arrow, so Martin touches the 'hard *stuff*' of his oilskin and feels the 'soft, cold *stuff*' below him.

To summarize, then. We are confronted here with two texts which describe completely different characters and settings, but which display uncannily similar patterns of language. I cannot for a moment imagine that any critic would want to argue that the *Pincher Martin* text reflects the same Neanderthal consciousness which is portrayed in the extract from *The Inheritors*. Rather, it might be argued that the former highlights the fragmentation of the consciousness of a drowning man, his loss of physical self-control, his near exhaustion – anything *but* the limited intelligence of prehistoric man. Where the problem of interpretative positivism arises is where a *direct* connection is made between the world-view expounded by a text and its linguistic structure. Amongst other things, this step will commit an analyst to the untenable hypothesis that a particular linguistic feature, irrespective of its context of use, will always generate a particular meaning. As we have seen, equating a language form directly with a particular mind-style is problematic, especially when the *same* linguistic feature is used by the *same* author to develop a completely *different* fictive world.

But things are not really as bad as they might sound and avoiding interpretative positivism often requires no more than a modicum of caution. First of all, linguistic analysis, whether literary-stylistic or not, still remains an important, if not essential, means of explaining how texts mean. The question really is how far one goes in the interpretation which accompanies linguistic analysis. For instance, Fish criticizes Halliday for making an interpretative leap from the analysis of language to a 'Darwinian' reading of the linguistic impoverishment of Neanderthal man (1981: 63). Yet this is not the *only* interpretation which Halliday makes in the course of his analysis: as we have already noted, he suggests that the stylistic characteristics of Lok's language help to express 'a combination of activity and helplessness'. Now this is an interpretation which would be entirely compatible with the analysis of the *Pincher Martin* episode, where activity and helplessness epitomize the drowning man's struggles in the water. Isolating an interpretative 'lowest common denominator' in this way also highlights the fact that both texts, despite markedly divergent story-lines, are at one level of analysis stylistically very similar.

It would be difficult, indeed, to exorcize interpretative positivism completely from stylistic analysis. Throughout this and the previous chapter, I have tried to resist the temptation to extrapolate directly from observations of particular configurations of modality and transitivity to overgeneralized statements about literary genres. The discussion of the passage from *Blackwoods* in 4.3 was a case in point, where negatively shaded modality combined with a highly 'ergative' transitivity pattern to create the alienating effect which, I argued, typifies much of the 'Gothic' genre. However, not only can both of these linguistic features occur in contexts other than this, but they are only two of a host of linguistic layers which make up the structure of any utterance. Certainly, one would be hard put to develop an exclusively linguistic definition of the 'Gothic'. Yet if we look at the problem of interpretative positivism from another angle, a literary stylistic analysis which avoided *all* attempts at interpretation would appear strange and perhaps somewhat pointless. Even early studies such as those of Sinclair (1966) and Halliday (1966), which are purportedly concerned with analysis alone, still suggest that their linguistic findings may provide a basis of interpretation for other critics. One normally expects, then, some interpretation to develop from an analysis; it is the nature of this interpretation, or, more specifically, the way it is predicated upon observable features of language use, that has attracted criticism from critics like Fish.[4]

Critical linguistic applications of the transitivity model are prone to comparable problems of interpretation. Although the main aim of a critical linguistic analysis is to examine the ideologies which underlie texts, practitioners are none the less subject to making the interpretative leaps which characterize many stylistic analyses. A crude formulation of the problem as it relates to critical linguistics would be to say that linguistic analysis is invoked to support what an analyst already knows and that, rather than being able to decipher ideological bias, linguistics is therefore really only a supplement to the prior political reading the analyst has made. This criticism has been put most bluntly by Sharrock and Anderson, who argue that a stock technique of the critical linguists

> is to look in the wrong place for something, then complain that they can't find it, and suggest that it is being concealed from them.
>
> (Sharrock and Anderson 1981: 289)

One of the features of transitivity which is frequently presented as a reification of this ideological practice is the use of the passive with agent deleted. A clear example of such a pattern is the sequence 'Eleven Africans were shot dead', quoted during the discussion of Trew's work in section 4.4. Because this suppresses the agency of such unpleasant activity, it is suggested that such a strategy encodes ideological bias in favour, in this case, of the political right wing. As the individuals responsible are removed from the surface realization of the process, they are thus concealed from the readers of the text. But not all agentless passives are deployed so nefariously and so insidiously.

For instance, in the previous two sentences a total of three agentless passives were used – four if you include the one you have just read! Did any readers feel that things were being kept from them or that the suppression of agency which this technique engenders had any ideological significance? Assuredly, no duplicity was intended on my part. The point is simply that passives of this sort are employed in a wide variety of contexts. Certainly, they may carry ideological significance – as the analyses undertaken in 4.4 should have shown – but they may also be a requirement of a particular register, as in the writing of scientific reports, or simply an 'elegant variation' which breaks temporarily a dominant pattern of active constructions in a text. One needs to recognize, therefore, that a specific grammatical form may yield not one but a host of interpretative possibilities.

Another point about the interpretation of linguistic forms concerns the position of the analyst relative to the text. The purpose of much critical linguistic analysis is to lay bare the ideological structure of discourse and to expose the (invariably right-wing) political bias that is encoded therein. Such 'diagnostic' readings employ linguistic analysis to explain what is missing from texts, thus highlighting what is being concealed or kept from non-academic or 'lay readers'.[5] What is needed is explicit recognition that these diagnostic readings may themselves be ideologically motivated and that the analyst has a political stance which informs their particular interpretation. In other words, writing *about* ideology does not automatically mean release *from* ideology. Engaging in a polemic against right-wing bias in language can hardly be considered neutral and objective and the assumption that such linguistic analysis is somehow free from ideological motivation is absurd. Readers may care to test this thesis in the following way. In section 4.4, a transitivity analysis was provided of the BBC's account of the Shorthouse trial. This was preceded by my own version of the events surrounding the trial, a version which I felt was an appropriate contextualization of the analysis which followed. Now this account lends itself readily to an analysis of transitivity. In fact, a comparative analysis between my own account and that of the BBC could easily be developed, and the strikingly different patterns of transitivity that emerge could open the way for interpretation of the different ideological positions that are adopted in both texts. Indeed, readers may conclude, on the basis of a transitivity analysis, that my own discourse privileges the political left, or that it is hostile to the institutional discourse of the BBC, or that it is simply unsubtle, stark or too direct in its portrayal of the grim events surrounding the trial.

In short, interpretations are not value-free. Writing about the politicization of language is in itself politicized. However, by the same token, being a participant in the discourse does not prevent scrutiny of that discourse and the machinery of linguistics can help foreground the ways in which ideology is expressed in language. This is an entirely viable means of exploring language as a form of cultural expression, provided, of course, that the element of subjectivity in such exploration is recognized. It is noticeable that more recent critical linguistic scholarship, such as Fairclough (1989), includes an explicit statement of the analyst's own political and cultural predisposition.

In this chapter, the model of transitivity was proposed as one means of analysing a text's meaning. Although no single model of language will yield an exhaustive account of textual meaning, it would be hard, as Montgomery points out, to imagine what an exhaustive account of the meaning of a text would look like if it *ignored* patterns of transitivity (1986b: 55). Still further ways of examining textual meaning will be presented in the chapter which follows, where special attention will be given to the role of addressees and readers in message construction.

4.6 SUMMARY

This chapter began with an introduction to the system of transitivity in language, a system which forms an important component of the analytic toolkit which is being assembled progressively in the course of this book. It was argued that transitivity helps account for the 'ideational' aspects of point of view by showing how our experiences of events and activities are encoded in grammatical configurations of the clause. This is intended to supplement the 'interpersonal' dimension of point of view which is realized chiefly through the system of modality. However, the transitivity model also constitutes a framework of analysis in its own right and, to this effect, it was developed in two different ways in the central sections of the chapter. First, in section 4.3, it was deployed stylistically, in that it provided a further means of analysing point of view in narrative fiction. In section 4.4, on the other hand, its potential as a critical linguistic technique was demonstrated through the analysis of a variety of short media texts. This critical linguistic application signalled our first foray into the analysis of what was defined as 'ideological' point of view in chapter 1. The chapter concluded with a collection of cautionary remarks stressing the complexity of the relationship between analysis and interpretation. Special attention was given to the problem of making explicit and direct connections between features of language and aspects of world-view.

Textual meaning, it was argued, is not rigidly fixed and a particular linguistic form may have a number of functions, depending on its context of use. It is these parallel notions of 'functions' and 'context of use' which will form the bridge with the next chapter, where a pragmatic dimension will be built onto our developing analytic package.

NOTES AND FURTHER READING

1 Frameworks for the analysis of transitivity are many and varied. Indeed, almost every linguist working within the systemic tradition will have his or her own version of a transitivity model. The main sources for the composite model assembled here are: Halliday (1970, 1971 and particularly 1985), Berry (1975) and Simpson (1988). A more simplified version of the system of transitivity can be found in Montgomery (1986a), which also includes an illuminating analysis of British media coverage of the 1984/5 miners' strike. Some systemicists may be alarmed at the lack of theoretical purity of this model, but as is the case with all the stylistic machinery constructed in my book, the need for applicability and manageability overrides some of the finer points of linguistic theory.
2 Readers may be interested to know that le Carré's style has been compared to that of Joseph Conrad, especially that which Conrad employs in many sections of his novel *The Secret Agent* (see Barley 1986 for a full account). Le Carré himself has apparently acknowledged this influence and it might be worth undertaking a comparative analysis of both writers within the dual frameworks of modality and transitivity. It is significant, for instance, that Kennedy's (1982) analysis of a scene from *The Secret Agent* sought to account for the effects of distancing and suppression created through patterns of transitivity.
3 Consider, for example, how *The Times* carried a report of the trial on the same day:

> The officer, who shot the boy through the heart from nine inches range during a police raid on the Shorthouse home in Birmingham, had to wait two and a half hours for the jury of seven women and five men to reach its unanimous verdict.

(p. 1)

4 One article which takes a very strong anti-stylistic line is that of Barry (1988). Barry declares that the insights offered by stylistic analysis are seldom beyond those obtained by intelligent 'close reading'. The criticisms levelled by Fish in his article 'What is stylistics and why are they saying such terrible things about it?' (1981) have been addressed by stylisticians in a number of places. Two good recent responses are Shen (1988) and Toolan (1990: 15–23). The second of these, entitled 'Getting off the Fish hook', constitutes a useful rejoinder from the stylistic camp and also proves that stylisticians too are capable of inventing witty titles!
5 The terms 'diagnostic reading' and 'lay reader' are taken from Richardson (1987). Richardson suggests that critical linguists have not paid enough attention to the intuitive responses of lay readers of texts, relying instead on

the informed critical competence of the researchers themselves. Her study provides a generally more sophisticated review of the methods of critical linguistics than can be undertaken in this chapter, and also contains a bibliography which will be of interest to anyone who wishes to explore this branch of linguistics further. With regard to the validity of the transitivity model in critical linguistic analysis, Montgomery (1986b) and Thompson (1986) develop a useful debate, commenting directly on each other's work, while Pateman (1981) provides a general critical survey of developments within the critical linguistic tradition.

5 Pragmatics and point of view

I know you believe you understand what you think I said, but I'm not sure you realize what you heard is not what . . . I meant!
(inscription on novelty mug from bric-à-brac shop, Blackpool, England)

5.1 INTRODUCTION

On an advertising hoarding in the London Underground, there appears, in bold capitals on a white background and with no accompanying text, the following injunction:

IF YOUR ASSISTANT READS *THE ECONOMIST*, THEN DON'T PLAY TOO MUCH GOLF.

What exactly does this text mean? Or, perhaps more significantly, *how* does this text mean? By what methods, for example, can one arrive at a satisfactory interpretation of so cryptic a message? What steps need to be taken in order to decode its meaning? And through what set of inferences do we come to deduce that this text advertises a particular newspaper?

Providing answers to these questions will be one of the main aims of this chapter. Where the previous two chapters have concentrated on, respectively, the ways in which attitudes are conveyed through language and the ways in which experience is organized in language, this chapter will explore the mechanisms by which meanings are transmitted and negotiated. It will, in other words, be preoccupied with the *process* of communication. The chapter should also form a bridge between the work of previous chapters and the study of gender and ideology which will be undertaken in the next chapter. It will enrich this work by drawing attention to the different linguistic strategies that are available for communicating meanings and in doing so will add another component to the linguistic machinery which is being developed progressively through the book.

The section which follows will offer a basic account of some of the ways in which producers of texts encode meanings in language. It will also provide an explanation of the mechanisms by which we arrive at interpretations of those texts. To this effect, ideas will be developed from relevant research in the parallel disciplines of *semantics* and *pragmatics*. The first of these two branches of linguistics is broadly concerned with the study of meaning in language. Practitioners of semantics ('semanticists') are interested in explaining the meaning potential of linguistic units of various sizes, ranging from the meanings of single words or even parts of words to the logical structures that pertain between whole sentences. The second of the two disciplines, pragmatics, seeks to expand semantics by examining the meaning of language when it is produced in a *context of use*. Pragmaticians, therefore, seek to explain 'meaning in context': what happens to language when it is deployed in real interactions between people. A simple way of formulating the relationship between the two disciplines would be through an equation like the following:

pragmatics = semantics + context

Where semantics focusses on the abstract underlying propositions of the contextless *sentence*, pragmatics (in theory, if not always in practice) concentrates on the *utterance*. The utterance is what happens when a sentence, or even bits of a sentence, are transformed into real chunks of language in a real context of use. In other words, utterances are what make up actual spoken or written *texts*. In the next section, the terms *sentence* and *utterance* will be used with this distinction in mind.

Despite the professed aims of its practitioners, work in pragmatics still devotes a lot of energy to the study of contrived, contextless sentences. Theories about language use are developed from sentences which are invented by the linguist and then discussed in terms of what they *would* mean if they occurred in some idealized interaction between imaginary speakers and hearers. In fact, this method is similar to that practised in semantic analysis, and while the insights offered by both disciplines are extremely important, there remains little engagement with attested examples of language use. The 'real' world of language thus tends to be much messier than is suggested by many semantic and pragmatic theories and the particular form an utterance takes is often conditioned by the non-linguistic assumptions, beliefs and ideologies which a speaker holds. This makes analysis more complex, to be sure, but if a proper understanding of the mechanisms of language use is to be reached, then there must be some engagement with its public domain, even when that public domain includes ambiguities, misunderstandings and communicative breakdowns. Wherever possible in the following section, attested examples will provide illustrations of analytic categories and will show how elements of a theoretical model of language can be aligned with their naturally occurring counterparts. The theoretical model proposed has been simplified to include just four meaning components and these components are drawn eclectically from a range of work in pragmatics and semantics. By blending research in this way, a pragmatically orientated model emerges which is designed to account for contextual properties of language, thus facilitating the analyses of different types of text which follow.

It has become a commonplace in linguistics to design models of language which are based on 'face-to-face' interaction. This discourse type is normally privileged in favour of, say, the more 'displaced' type of interaction which is characteristic of media discourse. Thus, interaction between speakers and hearers who share the same physical context provides the norm from which general theories are projected. By contrast, less attention is given to discourse types where communication takes place between participants who are separated in space and time. Media language, advertising language – indeed, written language generally – all exhibit this 'staggered' type of discourse situation where producers of texts are removed from consumers of texts both spatially and temporally. Furthermore, messages are projected by producers towards an invisible, ideal consumer who represents the many real consumers who process the text. With reference to media language, Fairclough makes the following useful remarks:

> since all discourse producers must produce with *some* interpreter in mind, what media producers do is address an *ideal subject*, be it viewer, or listener, or reader. Media discourse has built into it a subject position for an ideal subject, and actual viewers or listeners or readers have to negotiate a relationship with the ideal subject.
>
> (1989: 49)

This 'displaced' communicative situation is none the less amenable to analysis within the parameters of a linguistic model designed largely on face-to-face interaction. Although the direct 'feedback' which characterizes everyday conversation will be missing, media and advertising language still relies on a kind of interaction between producers and interpreters. This is a heavily one-sided interaction in many respects, but it is none the less one where meanings need to be negotiated between sender and receiver. The 'dialogic' principle in non-face-to-face interaction is widely recognized by many theorists, one of whom is Voloshinov, who comments:

> Dialogue can be understood in the broader sense, meaning not only direct, face-to-face vocalized verbal communication between persons, but also verbal communication of any type whatsoever.
>
> (1973: 4)

The remainder of this chapter should illustrate how different types of written discourse contain at least some interactive element, even though this element may be characterized as heavily one-sided. To this effect, the two sections which follow will introduce and review a model of meaning transmission. Both of these sections illustrate each category of the model with examples drawn from a range of discourse types. The chapter concludes with a section devoted specifically to the analysis of newspaper and advertising language.

5.2 A PRAGMATIC MODEL OF MEANING

Over the last few decades, the question of how speakers transmit meanings through sentences has been explored in great detail both by linguists and by philosophers.[1] One consequence of this research is that there now exists an enormous body of literature offering an at times bewildering array of theories about meaning. Moreover, this work is informed by a wide range of theoretical perspectives, incorporating linguistics, natural-language philosophy and artificial intelligence (AI). Many of these studies provide painstakingly intricate accounts of the ways in which sentences can be broken down into constituent propositions, or conversely, the ways in which abstract underlying propositions combine to form sentences. One concept which underpins much of this type of analysis is the notion of *entailment* in language. In fact the question of what this or that sentence entails has become arguably one of the most important issues in semantics in recent years. At the most basic level, the entailments of a sentence can be regarded as those propositions that can be inferred from it in any context. Put another way, an entailment is the most 'literal' component of a sentence's meaning as it expresses a core proposition which remains stable whatever the context in which the sentence occurs. To take a much-used example from the literature, the sentence

(1) The cat is on the mat.

will entail the following basic proposition *p*, indicated by the italicized sequence:

p: *the cat is on the mat*

Of course, this proposition only holds if the sentence by which it is entailed expresses a true claim; if, for instance, it is not the case that the cat happens to be on the mat, then the entailment will consequently evaporate.

The concept of entailment also extends to sentences which contain more than one basic proposition. For example, the following sentence

(2) Mary ate an apple and John an orange.

will entail two propositions. These may be expressed as *p* and *q* in the following way:

p: *Mary ate an apple*
q: *John ate an orange*

Assuming that sentence (2) expresses a true claim, it follows that *p* and *q* must also be true. In the light of this then, a more rigorous definition of entailment might be proposed as follows:

A sentence *S* entails a proposition *p* if and only if in every possible circumstance where *S* is true, *p* is true.

So far this account of entailment has proceeded largely on the basis of common-sense reasoning: if someone says to you that the cat is on the mat, then you would quite naturally expect that person to be committed to the truth of the entailment which follows. However, the concept of 'truth' is both abstract and complex and the search for an adequate definition of truth has exercised linguists and philosophers considerably. A great deal of effort has been devoted to explaining the conditions under which a particular sentence may be regarded as true or false. These 'truth-conditions' form the bedrock of semantic description by specifying the components of meaning which give a sentence an overall truth-value. For instance, consider the conditions which must be satisfied if the following sentence is to express a true claim:

(3) Martha is a woman.

Clearly, for (3) to be true, Martha must be (a) female, (b) adult and (c) human. These three characteristics are necessary and sufficient conditions, therefore, for the truth of (3). And if any of these truth conditions are not satisfied (if, say, Martha happens to be a goldfish) then (3) no longer expresses a true claim.

Although establishing sets of truth-conditions for most sentences often requires little more than a modicum of intuitive reasoning, there are some sentences to which truth-values are more difficult to assign. One particular example, which has been trundled out regularly ever since it was first coined by Bertrand Russell, is the following:

(4) The present king of France is bald.

This poses problems for a truth-conditional analysis in that for (4) to be true, there must exist a king of France. And as no such monarch exists, then sentence (4) is said to lack a truth-value.

The inordinate amount of attention which has been devoted to problematic sentences like example (4) has, in my opinion, been more of a hindrance than a help in the development of a comprehensive theory of meaning. For one thing, it shows how many linguists and philosophers can become enmeshed in debates over highly contrived sentences which are unlikely ever to be uttered in any actual context of use. Not only does this have little to say about real speakers involved in real-time interactions, but it takes no account of the many other ways by which meaning may be communicated. Moreover, there is no recognition of the role of the reader/listener in the communicative process and of the complex inferencing work they often undertake in the development of meaning. So let us move on from the Gallic monarchy, bald or otherwise, and begin to examine some of the other components which go to make up a composite model of communication.

While the concept of entailment, as presented above, is an important aspect of sentence meaning, it still only provides a partial description of what that sentence means in a real situation of use. To give a clearer picture of how this works, I propose to develop an analysis of the following short sentence. The context in which this sentence was uttered will be withheld for the moment so that each of its meaning components can be dealt with in an orderly sequence. Despite its superficial simplicity, the sentence should none the less provide a good illustration of the multilayered nature of meaning.

(5) Well darling . . . the dog has . . . erm . . . stopped sleeping in its kennel.

In a strictly literal sense, what this sentence 'means' should be clear and we can derive from it an entailment of the sort:

(5a) *the dog does not sleep in its kennel*

In other words, if the sentence as a whole expresses a true claim, then its entailment must also be true. But (5a) is not the only proposition that is derivable from sentence (5). Inside the sentence lurks a number of other propositions which do not behave in quite the same way as its entailment. These other propositions, to which the speaker of (5) would be expected to be committed, are known as *presuppositions*. Presuppositions normally fall into two types: *existential* presuppositions and *logical* presuppositions. Existential presuppositions, as the label suggests, are propositions which state the existence of certain referents in the sentence. For instance, the referring expression *the dog* will naturally presuppose the existence of a particular dog; indeed, noun phrases containing the definite article *the* are generally strong indicators of existential presuppositions. Moreover, the possessive phrase *its kennel* presupposes that the dog referred to has a kennel – genitive constructions like this function as even stronger presupposition signals than constructions which just contain *the*. In short, then, the existence of the dog and its kennel is presupposed by certain phrases within sentence (5).

It was noted also that in sentence (5) there resides a second type of presupposition. This *logical* presupposition, which is brought into play primarily through the use of the verb *stop*, might be formulated thus:

(5)b. *the dog has previously slept in its kennel*

Because change-of-state verbs like *stop* activate presuppositions in this way, they are often referred to as *triggers*. A range of other devices exists which trigger logical presuppositions in a way similar to change-of-state verbs. The so-called 'factive' verbs of English are one example. This is a collection of verbs like *regret*, *realize* and *discover* which presuppose their grammatical complements, thereby representing them as 'facts'. Here are a few examples:

(6) Martha regrets drinking Mike's beer.
    (presupposes that Martha has drunk Mike's beer)
(7) John realizes that Russell is dead.
    (presupposes that Russell is dead)
(8) Mary discovered that sparrows are monogamous.
    (presupposes that sparrows are monogamous)

Although there are numerous other types of logical presupposition trigger in English, the following three are particularly common:

(9) It was Bill who stole the camera.   (cleft sentence)
    (presupposes that someone has stolen the camera)

(10) You can't buy Bay City Rollers records anymore.   (iterative)
(presupposes that you could once buy Bay City Rollers
records)
(11) Joe is as sexist as Billy.   (comparator)
(presupposes that Billy is sexist)

Now, the point about presuppositions – whether they be existential or
logical – is that they are normally distinguished from the entailments of
a sentence. Basically, where the truth-value of entailments rests on
whether the sentence as a whole is true or false, presuppositions
operate under no such constraint. Consider what would happen if
sentence (5) were altered to the following negative form:

(5) c. . . . the dog hasn't stopped sleeping in its kennel.

While the entailed proposition *The dog does not sleep in its kennel* is no
longer valid, all the presuppositions remain intact. In other words, the
dog still exists, it has a kennel and it has slept in this kennel prior to the
time referred to in (5c). The same type of negation test may be carried
out on the other examples of logical presuppositions presented above.
For example, if, in the case of sentence (6), it happens that Martha *does
not regret drinking Mike's beer*, the fact remains that she has drunk the
beer in the first place. Similarly, in (8), even if Mary is not acquainted
with sparrows' mating habits, the facts of their mating habits are not
affected by her ignorance. Or, even if Bill does not steal the camera in
(9), the camera still gets stolen. A particularly clear illustration of this
basic difference between entailment and presupposition is provided by
Levinson (1983: 178) with the following example.

(12) John managed to stop in time.

The following two basic propositions may be derived from this sentence, the first of which is entailed and the second presupposed:

(12) a. *John stopped in time*
b. *John tried to stop in time*

Whereas (12a) would no longer be valid if John *did not* manage to stop
in time, the presupposition that he had at least tried would remain
intact.

The presuppositions of a sentence combine with its entailments to
form what might be referred to as a *semantic base*. This cluster of
meanings yields the most 'literal' sense of a sentence; they are those
meanings which may be inferred from it in any context. While the
semantic base is clearly necessary in a description of meaning, the
question of whether it is a *sufficient* definition in its own terms is

entirely another matter. In fact, over the past few years, linguists have demonstrated convincingly that a great deal of importance is to be attached to the context in which a sentence is uttered. As interest in this socially situated aspect of communication developed, so did the availability of models which explain the contextual information required for the processing and communication of meaning. This work allows us then to bolt a 'pragmatic' dimension onto our semantic base, a dimension which will help account for what language is doing in a specific context of use and the shared assumptions that pertain between speakers as abstract sentences are transformed into real utterances.

Returning to example (5), it will probably not have escaped attention that there are additional elements in this sentence which have so far received no explanation. These extra features are highlighted as follows:

(5) *Well, darling* . . . the dog has . . . *erm* . . . stopped sleeping in its kennel.

Although they may look like innocuous appendages to the sentence proper, these italicized items none the less constitute important components of its overall meaning. For instance, the use of a term of endearment marker like 'darling' will conventionally indicate that some relationship of intimacy pertains between speaker and hearer. While such information is not relevant to the truth-conditions of (5), it still forms part of the general 'message' which (5) transmits. In one respect, as the term of endearment operates to encode information about speaker and hearer it could be said to function as a presupposition, but in no way does it resemble the type of semantic presuppositions which were discussed above. Similarly, the particles *Well* and *erm*, which also lie outside the truth-conditional component of the sentence, still have an important function in terms of the way the sentence is used. Here, they function as 'hedges' by softening the impact of the message on the addressee. The pragmatic significance of these little hedging words has been well documented, not least because of their use as a politeness strategy. Yet such markers of mitigation, while highly relevant to the way a message is shaped and delivered by a speaker, are not accountable within a truth-conditional analysis.

In the light of this discussion, the non-truth-conditional inferences which the use of the term of endearment and the hedges would generate might be termed *pragmatic presuppositions*.[2] These are the meanings that attach conventionally to particular items or constructions which derive from their normal contexts of use. Crucial to this definition is the fact that pragmatic presuppositions are mediated in utterances through the contexts of speech and writing; they are not derivable from the context-free semantic base of a sentence. Thus, pragmatic presuppositions reside in the shared conventions of language use, rather than in the more formal patterns of its logical structure. A good illustration of how a strictly semantic analysis would fail to account for pragmatic presuppositions can be obtained by considering the following pair of examples:

(13) It's windy and it's raining.
(14) John got sick and he spent two weeks at a spa-town.

Each of these sentences entail two propositions apiece: example (13) entails both that *it is windy* and that *it is raining*, whereas (14) entails both that *John got sick* and *John spent two weeks at a spa-town*. In semantic terms, therefore, both (13) and (14) are equivalent formulae: they each express two conjuncts linked by the logical connector *and* and have an underlying structure which can be represented as $p \& q$. Yet this is only a partial description of what the second of the two examples would communicate if uttered in the course of interaction. In such a context, it would normally be assumed that the event described by the first conjunct of (14) precedes the event described by the second. In short, a temporal relationship between the two conjuncts would be pragmatically presupposed. For instance, if the two conjuncts of (13) were reversed, no significant change in interpretation would occur. Yet performing such an operation on (14) would suggest a parallel reversal in the chronology of the events described. It is difficult to specify exhaustively the criteria which lead to the sequence in (14) being interpreted temporally and that in (13) not, but a generally strong clue is whether the sentence is uttered as part of a narrative. Narrative clauses often express material action processes (see chapter 4.2) within a simple past-tense framework. It would be expected, then, that a story-teller would present such 'actional' clauses in a sequence which preserves the chronology of the original story-line. Thus, a pragmatic presupposition develops through speakers' shared assumptions about the way narratives are structured. But the point to be borne in mind here is that the connective *and*, arguably the most basic conjunction of English, performs a variety of pragmatic functions, not all of which are handled systematically by a semantic description alone.

The notion of pragmatic presupposition will be developed more fully in later sections as we discuss examples of newspaper language and advertising language. There remains, however, quite a bit more to be said about sample sentence (5). Up to now this example has been examined in isolation, with little attention being paid to the linguistic and extralinguistic context in which it occurred. Such contextual detail, as was suggested earlier, plays an important part in interpretation. So here, first of all, is the actual linguistic environment in which (5) occurred:

A: What are all these hairs doing on the sofa?

B. Well, darling . . . the dog has . . . erm . . . stopped sleeping in its kennel.

An important feature of the non-linguistic context of this exchange is that the dog referred to, although a family pet, is primarily the responsibility of speaker A. The exchange also occurs after A had given instructions to all other members of the household that the dog should be prevented from sleeping on furniture. In A's absence, however, these strictures tended to be relaxed somewhat.

How does this contextualization affect our original interpretation of (5)? Would the meanings proposed so far for (5) adequately account for what speaker B is trying to convey? I imagine not. If anything, the main import of B's utterance is that the dog is responsible for the hairs on the sofa, not that it has stopped sleeping in its kennel. Yet this interpretation can only be reached by a subtle process of inferencing on the part of B's co-conversationalist. Such a process of inferencing would be triggered by the indirectness of B's answer to A's question. Thus, if speaker A assumes that B is still being a co-operative interactant and not, say, producing totally irrelevant remarks, then A will need to expend some effort on reaching a satisfactory interpretation of B's remark. The meaning which the exchange as a whole generates is derived then from a combination of B's indirectness and A's inferencing work. Such jointly produced meanings may be termed *implicatures* or, more precisely, *conversational implicatures*. Implicatures are therefore those meanings which unfold when it is clear that the semantic content of an utterance is alone not a reliable guarantor of the meaning of that utterance in context. In this way, implicatures can be regarded as inferences that develop from a mutual understanding between speakers engaged in interaction. Recourse to a truth-conditional analysis alone, then, is not really a satisfactory means of explaining many of the linguistic routines characteristic of many types of interaction. Indeed, what an utterance implicates in a particular context may even be the opposite of its semantic entailments. In the following exchange, for example, speaker B's reply would be unlikely to be intended literally:

(15) A: You've just failed your philosophy exam.

B: Terrific.

Given the unlikelihood of an expression of joy at such news, B's remark would be taken to implicate the inverse of what it entails. And like ironic uses of language generally, this implicature rests on the speakers' mutual recognition that B's utterance is not to be interpreted literally.

Returning to the exchange in which example (5) was eventually located, the question still remains as to why B should choose a linguistic strategy which demands greater processing effort from an interlocutor. Why, for instance, could B not have answered more directly with something like sentence (16)?

(16) The hairs are there because I allowed the dog to sleep on the sofa.

While directness may lead to greater clarity in interaction, it is a strategy which is often evaluated as tactless or impolite. Politeness is not only an important behavioural system, it is a pan-human principle of social interaction. And one of the chief cross-cultural realizations of politeness is the use of indirectness in language. Amongst other things, indirectness tends to stagger the way in which information is presented and this is especially effective if that information is likely to impinge in any way upon an interlocutor. By this strategy, speakers can to some extent 'get off the hook' in a way not always possible through direct or unambiguous utterances. The actual utterance which B produces, through its very obliqueness to A's request for information, thus functions as an apology and excuse as well as a reply. Furthermore, the pragmatic presuppositions in the utterance supplement its indirectness: it was noted earlier how the term of endearment and the hedging particles had an interactive role to play.

The use of implicature as a politeness strategy also extends to requests as well as replies. A hypothetical scenario, much used in the literature on pragmatics, is one where a speaker wants to get an addressee to open a window. The speaker may select, at the least polite end of the spectrum, a direct and unambiguous approach like:

(17) Open the window.

At the other end of the spectrum, a strategy may be employed which is so indirect that it bears no obvious link to the service implicitly requested:

(18) It's hot in here.

Where strategy (17) gains in terms of its conciseness and efficiency, it loses in terms of the way directness of this sort conveys impoliteness. On the other hand, whereas (18) risks no such charge of impoliteness, more onus is placed on the addressee to decipher the implicature. So while the second scenario 'pays off' in terms of politeness, there is always the risk that the addressee may fail (or refuse) to access the intended meaning of (18). In this situation, (18) may simply receive a response like:

(19) Yeah, it *is* hot in here.

The use of implicature is not restricted to the strategies of politeness. A great deal of attention has been given to the part it plays in a host of linguistic devices, including metaphors, idioms and figures of speech. The type of linguistic 'conundrum' produced by the advertisement which opened section 5.1 is a case in point. Some of the questions which were raised in relation to this text may now be answered within the parameters of the pragmatic model developed in this section. Here again is the advertisement:

IF YOUR ASSISTANT READS *THE ECONOMIST*, THEN DON'T PLAY TOO MUCH GOLF.

In linguistic terms, solving the riddle which the advertisement presents amounts to decoding the implicature through which it operates. Although we may conclude that we are simply being persuaded to read *The Economist*, the inferences which lead to this conclusion are triggered by a subtle combination of linguistic and contextual cues. A suggested pattern for the sequence of inferences would be as follows. First of all, the text appears in a public space which is conventionally allocated to the marketing of products, a semiotic cue which orientates us towards a particular expectation about the text's ultimate goal. It consists of a single sentence comprising two propositions arranged in a conditional 'if p, then q' relationship. Although the immediate connection between the two propositions is not transparent, a guarantee of relevance still pertains. In other words, if we assume that what is asserted is relevant and is intended to yield information, then a search for a satisfactory interpretation is activated. This search may develop from the way the text projects its own 'universe of discourse'. For instance, the genitive construction 'your assistant' acts as an existential presupposition inviting readers to position themselves as participants in a specific occupational setting. This setting is the hierarchical system of the business world, and the reader occupies a position of superiority over an acknowledged inferior. The suggestion of power and class is strengthened further: you, the reader, are a boss who plays golf in your leisure time. However, if your putative assistant devotes his or her leisure time to reading a particular newspaper, *The Economist*, then you need to be careful. You can no longer sustain your own interests, because readers of *The Economist* are likely to be both capable and ambitious and they may even oust their superiors. The text thus projects a bivalent message: talented high-fliers read *The Economist* and reading *The Economist* is for talented high-fliers. Of course, the inferencing processes proposed here may not be true for all readers of the text: but part of the strategic motivation behind the use of implicatures is that the meanings projected are reliant on some input from those to whom the text is directed. Clearly, not everyone will arrive at precisely the same interpretation. Furthermore, different aspects of the text will appeal to different readers on the basis of their own social situation: real-life golf-playing bosses may feel flattered that they are addressed directly while the real-life assistants may be amused to learn about new ways of 'getting on'. Those who occupy other social situations may even enjoy the text as a parody of the treacherous machinations of the business community. One thing that the basic interpretation reveals is that even though the text is couched in the form of a linguistic conundrum, it still functions as a successful advertising gambit. Moreover, the processing effort required to solve it makes it a more effective communicative strategy than a simple directive like 'Read *The Economist*' or a bland assertion like '*The Economist* is worth reading.' And even when a text is not spoken in face-to-face interaction but is written on a billboard there may still be an interactive dimension to the decoding of its meaning.

Some further illustrations of implicatures will be discussed in the next section, but what the present analysis and the discussion preceding it has sought to explain is how a single expression may carry with it a complex mosaic of meaning. It has also attempted to explain how the meaning of an utterance in context is mediated through a number of different channels. These channels are: entailment, semantic presupposition (including the existential and logical subvarieties), pragmatic presupposition and conversational implicature. The interplay of levels illustrates how a strictly context-free interpretation of a sentence is not a sufficient explanation of how that sentence functions in interaction. Furthermore, the process of inferencing is also a significant stage in the development of meaning. A useful summary of this aspect of the communicative process is provided by Sperber and Wilson:

> Communication is successful not when hearers recognise the linguistic meaning of the utterance, but when they infer the speaker's 'meaning' from it.

(1986: 23)

It might be useful at this stage to draw together various strands of the discussion into a simple visual schema. Figure 5.1 is intended as a mnemonic for the different levels of meaning identified so far. Arranged as a series of concentric rings, it attempts to capture an utterance's multilevelled communicative components. Each ring encapsulates a particular layer, and the rings fan out radially from entailment through to implicature. As the rings develop outwards, greater importance is placed on context. So, while entailment is the most 'literal' context-free meaning, implicature rests on the jointly produced meaning between speaker and hearer. Of course, it is the case generally that linguistic categories tend to have fuzzier boundaries than those captured by visual representations of this sort.

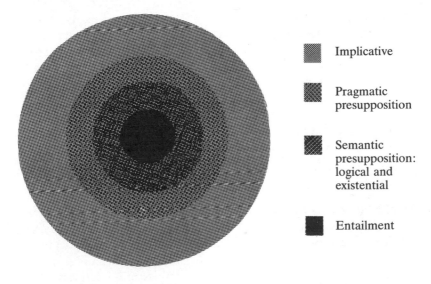

Implicative

Pragmatic presupposition

Semantic presupposition: logical and existential

Entailment

Fig. 5.1. Levels of utterance meaning

The next subsection will review the implications of this 'concentric' pragmatic model and will provide extra examples in order to clarify further its basic categories. This should further inform the analyses which will be undertaken both in the remainder of this chapter and in the chapter which follows.

5.3 IMPLICATIONS AND CONSEQUENCES

One important issue which has not been touched upon so far concerns the ways in which meanings may be cancelled, suspended or even contradicted by speakers without any loss to the coherence of the utterance. The blanket term normally reserved for such cancellation, suspension or contradiction is *defeasibility*.[3] Speakers may defease all aspects of the meaning mosaic, illustrating how none of the layers is inviolable, permanent or completely stable. Regarding the more contextually orientated outer layers of the model, it is easy to defease implicatures and pragmatic presuppositions by simply indicating that what an addressee may infer from an utterance does not actually pertain. For instance, if, in the case of example (18), an addressee responds by opening a window, the speaker may deny that an implicature was intended in the first place. They might point out:

(20) I was only remarking that it was hot, that's all.

Whether this is true or not is, of course, another matter, and it highlights the tactical possibility of withdrawal which the use of implicatures opens up. Pragmatic presuppositions may be defeased in a similar way. It was suggested, for example, that the two conjuncts of sentence (14) conventionally presuppose a chronological sequence:

(14) John got sick and he spent two weeks at a spa-town.

However, this chronological sequence is easily defeased through the addition of an extra premise:

(14) a. John got sick and he spent two weeks at a spa-town – although not necessarily in that order.

Defeasibility also extends to semantic presupposition even though many theorists consider these the 'safest' and most inviolable parts of an utterance's meaning. Although there are greater syntactic constraints on the ways in which this happens, both logical and existential presuppositions may be defeased without loss to an utterance's coherence. A good example of this is provided by the following exchange, which was overheard recently in a busy office:

(21) A: Have you posted the letter?
     B: I haven't posted the letter because I haven't typed it yet.

The definite referring expression *the letter*, which is used in A's question and the first half of B's reply, presupposes that the letter referred to actually exists. Yet the second conjunct of B's reply defeases this presupposition by indicating clearly that the letter has not come into existence. The point is, however, that defeasing presuppositions in this way does not result in meaningless or aberrant communication.

The principle of defeasibility also extends to other types of existential presupposition, including the normally strong genitive constructions. For instance, if we return briefly to example (5), the presupposition conveyed through the 'its kennel' construction may be defeased by appending a sequence like the following

(5) c. . . . the dog has stopped sleeping in its kennel because its kennel burnt down last night – it doesn't even have a kennel anymore.

Logical presuppositions, like those identified in example sentences (6)–(11) above, can be defeated in a way similar to that for existential presuppositions. However, this is normally restricted to situations where the main clause of the sentence has a negative polarity, as in the following examples:

(6) a. Martha doesn't regret drinking Mike's beer because she never drank it in the first place.
(9) a. It wasn't Bill who stole the camera – in fact, no-one stole the camera.

Adding extra premises onto *positive* main clauses will not have the same effect, however:

(6) b. ?Martha regrets drinking Mike's beer but she never drank it in the first place.
(9) b. ?It was Bill who stole the camera, although no-one actually stole the camera.

A consequence of this principle of defeasibility is that presuppositions can be regarded as much more fluid than many semantic theories would allow. Although this does not mean that the theory of semantic presuppositions should be abandoned *per se*, it does need to be acknowledged that presuppositions of this sort exhibit varying degrees of strength. In other words, not all presuppositions are susceptible to manipulation or cancellation in a context of use. One linguistic practice which hinges upon this feature of presuppositions is the use of the so-called 'leading question'. This is a question which is couched in such a way as to preserve its presuppositions irrespective of the polarity of the response it receives. To take a rather uncomfortable example from the literature, consider the following question asked of a married man:

(21) Have you stopped beating your wife?

If you are the addressee, then offering either a *yes* or *no* response will still endorse the presupposition that you had previously been beating your wife. Either way, your answer is an admission of guilt. Of course, this depends on your having highly restricted interactive rights, perhaps like those pertaining in a courtroom, where you can be forced into providing only a *yes* or *no* response. Otherwise, it is perfectly possible to defease your interlocutor's presupposition in the way discussed above:

> (23) I haven't stopped beating my wife because I never beat her in the first place.

So although leading questions provide a strategy whereby speakers can project their own point of view onto an interlocutor, the success of the strategy depends on the nature of the interlocutor's response. Nowhere, perhaps, is this tactic more widespread than in the political arena where presuppositionally 'loaded' questions are repeatedly directed by speakers at political opponents. Of course, responses to such questions will be determined by whether addressees accept the presuppositions encoded therein. As the first of three short illustrations of the political use of this strategy, consider the following exchange, which took place between former British prime minister, Margaret Thatcher, and a prominent and outspoken member of the opposition party. This occurred during a parliamentary debate on the government's rejection of the Single European Act on 30 April 1989:

> Dennis Skinner: Does the Prime Minister regret using a three-line whip as a guillotine on the Single European Act?
> Margaret Thatcher: No, I don't, Mr. Speaker, no, no, no.

Despite the accusation of belligerence in Skinner's question, Thatcher seems happy to accept the terms in which the question is phrased. Indeed, the repeated 'no' endorses strongly the presupposition which is triggered by the factive verb 'regret'. Bearing in mind the political context in which this occurred, the government's use of a 'three-line whip', if considered heavy-handed by many, was never contested as fact nor was it seized upon by the media as a controversial story. However, when the presuppositions in a question *are* contestable and politically controversial, then seldom is endorsement offered. A clear instance of rejection is provided by the next exchange which took place between political journalist, Jon Snow, and former Conservative Party chairman, Norman Tebbit. The reference in Snow's question is to one of Tebbit's colleagues, who had just begun a leadership challenge which was to result eventually in the resignation of Mrs Thatcher.

Jon Snow:	Did you know that during all these years you'd been sitting next to an interventionist Labour sympathizer?
Norman Tebbit:	Let me point out first of all that the Tory party does not necessarily exist for the business of being elected.
	(Channel 4 News, 19 November 1990)

This exchange underscores the point made earlier concerning the constraints which operate on interactants. In this exchange, the material which Snow embeds under the factive verb 'know' is clearly provocative and controversial, and his question as a whole is uttered in the context of a particularly turbulent political period. Yet there is no topical link whatsoever in the reply offered to this question – Tebbit, it seems, is having none of it. Instead, he simply opts out of the strictures imposed by the leading question and proceeds with what looks like a prepared statement about his own party's policies.

Much the same principle extends to our last illustration of the use of leading questions in a political context. This is taken from a parliamentary debate between Prime Minister John Major and the leader of the Labour opposition party, Neil Kinnock on 13 January 1991. The debate occurs in the context of the controversy created when John Major, in an interview in Africa, allegedly renounced his promise of tax reductions in the 1992 budget:

| Neil Kinnock: | Doesn't the prime minister recall saying in Zimbabwe last year that tax reductions in the March budget would be fool's gold? |
| John Major: | What I said in the interview in Harare that he quotes from was that the reduction in interest rates just to stimulate the economy would be fool's gold, as it would be. |

Notice here how Kinnock phrases his question with a negativized auxiliary ('doesn't') and a factive verb ('recall') in order to elicit a *yes/no* response from his interlocutor. But again we see an opting out of the presuppositional 'game' as Major refuses to be manipulated into endorsing the presupposition which Kinnock's question encodes. Major chooses instead to reshape the material he is alleged to have said.

Where presuppositions offer one strategy for projecting a speaker's point of view, the success of the strategy in the context of face-to-face interaction is, as we have seen, often reliant on confirmation by co-interactants. Of course, when the strategy is employed outside this context then conditions for confirmation or denial are problematic and we shall explore this further when we come to deal with newspaper and advertising discourse in the following sections.

Like those of presuppositions, the interactive consequences of defeasing entailments are also significant and they merit some brief discussion here. An especially important point concerns the ways in which speakers may blatantly contradict the entailments in a sentence, yet the utterance in which these contradictions occur remains meaningful at the level of what is implicated. In other words, straightforward contradictions often present a perfectly viable means of conveying meaning. However, as is the case generally with the outermost strategy on our meaning model (figure 5.1), the success of such a gambit will depend on the inferencing work which the addressee is prepared to undertake. In the following attested exchange, B's use of a straightforward contradiction is still a reasonable reply to A's question:

A: So is *Terminator 2* a good film then?
B: Mmm . . . it is and it isn't.

In terms of a strict entailment analysis, B's response communicates nothing: it simply asserts the truth and falsity of the same proposition. Yet if A assumes that this response carries with it a guarantee of relevance, then this will activate an inferencing process that will result in A decoding satisfactorily B's intended message. And even outside the original context of interaction, it is still possible to work out that B felt the film was uneven in quality and that not all of it appealed to him.

A similar principle extends to the use of *tautology* as an implicature-generating device. This is the situation where an entailment simply entails itself, so to speak, thus offering no new assertion. So, when in the course of a lecture on the First World War a historian remarks that 'War is war and a bullet is a bullet' then, strictly speaking, nothing has been said. However, while uninformative at the level of entailment, the tautology is still accessible at the level of implicature. In this respect, it may be interpreted as a comment on how in the harsh realities of war, death and destruction are inevitable.

Not all contradictions and tautologies are as easily accessed, however, and in many situations where such strategies are used implicatures may remain opaque or debatable. A stark illustration of this can be gained if we re-introduce very briefly some of the material discussed in chapter 3. In the course of the analysis of point of view in narrative fiction, one style was identified as being especially problematic in linguistic terms. This was the 'uncooperative' negatively shaded modal pattern employed by Beckett in novels like *Molloy*. What supplements this modal pattern is a widespread use of straightforward contradictions of the sort identified above. Amongst other things, this makes it even more difficult to get any cognitive purchase on whole sections of the narrative, with many events which are purported to have taken place being flatly denied at a later point in the story. Here are two brief samples, the second of which concludes the novel:

> But how could I press my legs together in the state they were? I pressed them together, that's all I can tell you . . . I didn't press them together. What can that possibly matter?
>
> (p. 78)
>
> It is midnight. The rain is beating on the windows. It was not midnight. It was not raining.
>
> (p. 162)

The literary-critical response to this type of language is intriguing, not least because of what it reveals about the inferencing effort which readers are prepared to devote to arguably nonsensical language. Unravelling literary implicatures in the face of stark contradictions requires a great deal of commitment to a text, and it shows how many readers are prepared to put up with an unreliable narrator who continually opts out of the narrative 'contract'.[4]

Outside the context of literary communication, the use of contradictions and tautologies carries with it a fair amount of calculated risk. If an interlocutor suspends the inferencing work necessary for the uptake of an implicature, then the utterance may simply look silly. Indeed, there is a thriving humorous publication which draws much of its material from what are arguably failed attempts by broadcasters to generate implicatures. The type of utterances which are prime candidates for the collection are the following, which are all contradictions and tautologies produced by luckless sports commentators:

> Lawrenson slipped the ball through to Williams, and he beat Shilton from 35 yards . . . and you don't beat Shilton from 35 yards.
>
> . . . saved by Bailey, son of Roy Bailey, once the Ipswich goalkeeper. He's no longer being called the son of Roy Bailey.
>
> The loss of a life is – well – the loss of a life . . .
>
> I think if you've got a safe pair of hands, you've got a safe pair of hands . . .
>
> (cited in Simpson, 1992)

Although it is still possible to see what these speakers are trying to say, when stripped of their original context of utterance, tautologies and contradictions of this sort can appear particularly nonsensical. This again highlights the contextual inferencing upon which this type of communicative strategy depends.

In summary, then. This section has sought to develop further an account of the various ways in which meanings are negotiated and transmitted. It has been argued that utterances realize a complex array of meaning potentials, and that different meaning components require different interpretative procedures. Although the four basic categories proposed here and in the previous section are not always easy to distinguish, they none the less provide useful broad reference points for a textual analysis. Thus, they should not only help enrich the subsequent analyses of this chapter but should also enable more sophisticated discussions of the issue of gender and point of view which will be developed in the next chapter.

5.4 ANALYSING TEXTS FROM A PRAGMATIC PERSPECTIVE

5.4.1 Newspaper language

The purpose of the two short analyses which conclude this chapter is to illustrate how aspects of the pragmatic model outlined in section 5.2 may be usefully employed in the examination of ideological point of view in texts. The first of the two analyses will concentrate on extracts from six different newspapers, all of which purportedly describe the same event. A study of linguistic structure should reveal how, despite their shared topic, each text presents a different 'angle of telling'. While those different representations of reality can be to some extent aligned with the respective political orientations of each paper, four of the six papers share broadly similar political outlooks, so not all of the variations in point of view correlate directly with differing ideologies. In fact, each of the papers has some measure of originality in the way it chooses to treat its subject matter.

It would be possible to undertake a full-blown analysis of the transitivity patterns of these extracts along the lines suggested in the previous chapter. However, as the point of the present discussion is to highlight additional linguistic strategies, and as transitivity received ample treatment in chapter 4, comments within this framework will be informal and general. By contrast, components of the meaning model introduced in this chapter will be used to help identify how ideological positions are shaped in each text. The concept of pragmatic presupposition, particularly, will provide a means of investigating the type of naming practices employed in each text. In the relevant discussion in section 5.2, it was pointed out that terms of address conventionally provide clues about the social relationships that pertain between interactants. In face-to-face interaction, they function as indices of power, formality and social distance. A similar principle extends to naming strategies in written texts, where a choice of one type of name over another can encode important informaton about the writer's attitude to the individual referred to in a text. But first, to the texts themselves.

In 1984, the ruling Conservative Party of Great Britain launched its controversial 'rate-capping' Bill. This Bill was designed to place a fixed upper limit on the amount of money that a council could demand of its ratepayers. The anger which this Bill generated led to a break in Conservative Party ranks, with former British prime minister, Edward Heath, leading a group of party colleagues in a vote against the government's Bill.

Reproduced below are the headlines and opening texts of six newspapers reporting the event on 16 January 1984. The first four are 'popular' tabloids of which only one, the *Daily Mirror*, represents the political left. The remaining two are so-called 'quality' broadsheets: the *Telegraph* is a strongly pro-Conservative publication whereas the the *Guardian* is left of centre politically. Of all the papers, then, the *Mirror* and the *Guardian* would be expected to adopt an anti-Government stance.

1 HEATH'S 'TREACHERY'
Edward Heath finally and openly walked the plank of party dis-loyalty last night when he led a Tory revolt against Mrs. Thatcher over plans to curb high rates. After years of sniping and back-biting since he was overthrown, the former Party leader kicked over all the rules and conventions to vote against his own Prime Minister in the Commons.

Daily Mail

2 TED LEADS 33 REBELS
Former Prime Minister Ted Heath led a Dad's Army meeting of Tory Troops in the Commons last night. In an old-stagers' revolt . . .

Daily Express

3 HEATH LEADS 34 IN REVOLT
Former Premier Ted Heath last night led a major Tory rebellion against Margaret Thatcher's 'curb-the-rates-Bill'. Mr. Heath was among 14 Tory MPs who voted against plans to clamp down on big-spending councils . . .

Sun

4 HEATH LEADS A RATES REVOLT
Former Tory Premier Edward Heath led a major revolt against Mrs.
Thatcher's Government last night. He was joined by 12 other rebel
Tory MPs . . .

Daily Mirror

5 TORY MPS REVOLT ON RATES
The Government's controversial Rates Bill was given its expected
second reading in the Commons despite a rebellion by Mr.
Heath . . .

Daily Telegraph

6 HEATH HEADS 40 TORY RATE REBELS
The former Conservative Prime Minister, Mr. Edward Heath, last
night led a revolt of at least 40 Tories in the Commons . . .

Guardian

If ever there was a good case for urging someone not to believe all they
read in newspapers, this must be it! There is no agreement at all on the
number of supporters Heath can muster, with the highest estimate at
forty (the *Guardian*) and the lowest at twelve (the *Daily Mirror*). The
Sun takes no chances and proposes two figures: thirty-four in the
headline dropping alarmingly to fourteen in the opening text. A brief
glance down the headlines, however, should reveal that all of the texts
convey roughly the same message; that is, that Edward Heath is the
instigator of a 'revolt' within his political party. Of course, the attitudes
to Heath's actions vary from paper to paper, with each paper representing the 'reality' of the event through different linguistic strategies. The
best way to proceed on this is to deal with each extract in turn
commenting on relevant linguistic features in the light of the model
outlined in this chapter.

Although the *Daily Mail*'s headline is the only one which does *not*
use an explicit verb, strong condemnation of Heath's actions is none
the less conveyed through the noun 'treachery'. This accusation of
treachery, which is not made in the other five texts, is carefully
mitigated by the inclusion of the noun within *scare quotes*. This pushes
responsibility for what is an extremely serious accusation away from
the paper and towards some unspecified source. However, rather than
dissociating itself from the content of the word included within the
quotes – which is one of the main functions of the use of scare quotes –
the paper, judging by the remainder of the text, actually endorses it. In
effect, the choice of 'TREACHERY' as opposed to TREACHERY helps the
paper to avoid the legal consequences which a direct accusation might
bring. The opening text develops the story in a number of directions.
Firstly, Heath is portrayed as a lone aggressor who is locked in a direct

confrontation with Thatcher. Despite the reference to his leading a 'revolt', no numerical indication of the amount of Heath's support is made. He is, moreover, the instigator of a highly personalized attack on the prime minister: his revolt is not directed at the government nor even at a particular parliamentary Bill but at 'Mrs. Thatcher' and '*his own* Prime Minister'. In other words, Mrs Thatcher alone is the participant affected by the actions attributed to Heath. The attitude which the paper takes to Heath's personal and vindictive attack is also encoded in the naming practices[5] for each of the antagonists. Heath is represented initially by his first name (FN) and last name (LN) ('Edward Heath'). This designation contrasts with the more respectful term of address used for Thatcher, which comprises title (T) and last name ('Mrs. Thatcher'). The second paragraph underscores this differential naming system in the way it represents the two in terms of status and achievement. Heath, who was once a prime minister remember, is referred to only as a 'former Party leader' whereas Thatcher's full status is signalled by 'his own Prime Minister'. This asymmetrical naming practice has a pragmatic function as it encodes asymmetrical deference towards the two individuals. Heath is designated by FN + LN and a partial description of status; Thatcher, by contrast, receives T + LN and a full description of status. These subtle variations in address forms and the division in loyalty which they reflect are developed further by the use of implicature in the text. Consider, for example, how Heath is reported to have 'walked the plank'. This non-literal description activates a framework of associations to do with a general theme of 'piracy',[6] a theme which is also supplemented with a suggestion of 'suicide' as Heath chooses to walk the plank and is not forced into it by others. Heath's piracy and political suicide are aligned with his other insidious and treasonous actions ('sniping'; 'back-biting'), yet when he himself is the victim of such actions ('he was overthrown') no mention is made of those responsible. This cluster of linguistic strategies serve to intensify the *Mail's* outrage at Heath's behaviour.

Although a different set of strategies is employed in the second extract, there is none the less a comparable level of condemnation. In the headline of the *Daily Express* account, Heath is referred to as 'Ted', a diminutive form of 'Edward'. Diminutives provide a means of encoding social attitudes into linguistic structure and in this instance its use suggests greater familiarity and less formality. The weakening of the social differential is continued by the repetition of the diminutive in the opening text, though here it is surrounded with LN and a full status description ('Former Prime Minister Ted Heath'). Noticeably, Heath's anti-government vote is non-personalized and the activities in which he is involved are primarily those of leading his supporters. The efficacy of this political move is questioned by the type of implicatures which the text projects, however. A parallel is made, for instance, between Heath's actions and those of a popular British comedy series set during the Second World War. The eponymous 'Dad's Army' of the series is a platoon of ageing and feckless Home Guard volunteers. In the context of Heath's activities, this Dad's Army meeting is parodied further by other militaristic yet comic clues ('Tory Troops'; 'an old-stagers' revolt'). By implication, then, the potential political power of the gathering is dismissed by association; and Heath and his followers are portrayed as comic, ageing and impotent.

The *Sun*'s account of the incident, extract 3, is interesting in terms of the way it projects a somewhat ambiguous representation of Heath's actions. The numerical discrepancy between headline and opening text has been mentioned earlier and other aspects of the text make it difficult to pinpoint the level of sympathy offered for Heath's political move. Clearly though, Heath's move is taken seriously, with lexical clues signalling this in the form of a transition from 'Revolt' to 'rebellion' and the introduction of the modifier 'major' ('a major Tory rebellion'). Compare this construction to the 'Tory revolt' and 'old-stagers' revolt' of extracts 1 and 2 respectively. Regarding naming strategies, while the opening text employs a diminutive + LN construction ('Ted Heath'), this is prefixed with a description of status and achievement ('Former Premier'), although the use of the term 'Premier' is often reserved for leaders of countries other than the United Kingdom. In contrast with the representation of Heath, Thatcher receives a straightforward FN + LN designation in which neither title nor status is included. This strategy is markedly different from that adopted in the *Daily Mail*'s account (extract 1) where such information is provided on Thatcher whilst it is Heath who receives the FN + LN designation only. The disparity between the two versions is further underscored by the way in which the focus of Heath's revolt is depicted. Whereas in extract 1 it is Mrs Thatcher alone who is the target, in the *Sun*'s account the attack is non-personalized, with Heath simply directing his actions towards the 'curb the rates Bill'. The scare quotes here are used diplomatically to capture the public's perception of what the Bill was about, although noticeably, responsibility for the Bill is attributed directly to 'Margaret Thatcher' and not, for example, to 'the Cabinet' or 'the Government'. The second sentence of the *Sun*'s version re-inforces the non-personal nature of Heath's revolt when, as before, Heath directs his actions towards 'plans' and not, as is the case in the first extract, towards 'his own Prime Minister'. This type of textual strategy is not quite what one might expect from a paper like the *Sun* which is normally strongly pro-Tory in terms of the ideological position it adopts. The account which it offers is far from alarmist or mocking; rather, it is relatively informative, giving credence to Heath's actions and arguably enlisting a little support for them. Perhaps significantly, of the three right-wing tabloids examined so far the *Sun*'s readership has the largest proportion of working-class Labour voters – 44 per cent at a recent estimate[7] – and this is in spite of the pro-Tory opinions it espouses. Thus, disarray in the ranks of a Tory government is perhaps less likely to inspire the same sense of alarm and condemnation amongst readers as it would in the case of the *Daily Mail* and the *Daily Express*.

A comparable measure of credence is given to the 'revolt' in the *Daily Mirror*, the only ostensibly left-wing tabloid of the four. Despite the low numerical estimate of support, the activity inspired by Heath is accorded the status, as it is in the *Sun*, of a 'major' revolt. And also like the *Sun*, the reference to Heath through LN in the headlines is elaborated upon in the opening text. The pattern develops in the following way:

Former Tory Premier Edward Heath . . .

Here, a titleless FN + LN construction is preceded by an ambiguous status description. The selection of 'Premier' instead of 'Prime Minister' (along with the connotations mentioned above) allows for two readings in this case: Heath is either a former premier of the United Kingdom or simply a former premier of the Tory Party. Like the extract from the *Sun*, Heath's revolt is non-personal in orientation, although, interestingly, the object of the attack is not a specific Bill but the government. Heath, one may recall, is a member of this same governing party. Moreover, his 'coup' is directed at a government which is not portrayed collectively, but rather as the property of one individual ('Mrs. Thatcher's Government'). So, while the *Mirror* removes any directly personal element from Heath's action, there is still the sense that his revolt is directed towards a somewhat dictatorial or autocratic system.

The account offered in the *Telegraph*, the right-wing broadsheet, employs a set of strategies which are different from anything we have seen so far. First, it is the only one of the six which does not refer directly to Heath in its headline, declaring instead that some collective group is responsible ('TORY MPS REVOLT ON RATES'). However, no numerical index is provided either in the headline or in the opening text. Another significant difference between this and the other texts is the way in which an agentless passive ('was given') constitutes the first verbal process in the opening text. All of the other texts place Heath in a prominent initial position as instigator and leader of the revolt, yet here, even when Heath is mentioned directly through T + LN, his actions are not encoded in an explicit verbal process ('despite a rebellion by Mr. Heath'). The phrase which details his participation in the incident is thus shunted into the 'circumstantial' slot and could even be deleted from the sentence without affecting its grammaticality. Curiously, the 'rebellion' which Heath instigates is represented as an entirely individual enterprise, and any support which he musters has to be calculated by inference from the headline. Although developed more subtly than that of the outraged *Mail* or the cajoling *Express*, this set of linguistic strategies is just about as damning in its version of the story. No acknowledgement of Heath's involvement is provided in the headline, nor are his activities encoded lexically as a full verbal process in the opening text. Instead, this minor altercation becomes subordinate to the government's strong and purposeful reading of an albeit 'controversial' Bill. The phrase which eventually describes Heath's involvement simply dismisses it as the personal (and irrational?) intervention of a single person. It is often said that insulting someone is not as bad as ignoring them: the second of the two tactics is the one which it seems is favoured by the *Telegraph*.

Our sixth and final extract, from the left-of-centre *Guardian*, provides a useful comparison with its 'quality' counterpart, the *Telegraph*. In the *Guardian*, Heath is re-instated as instigator and leader in the headline ('HEATH HEADS 40 TORY RATE REBELS'). He returns to a prominent position in the opening text and, moreover, is accorded a fuller designation than in any of the other texts:

The former Conservative Prime Minister, Mr. Edward Heath . . .

Here, a full description of status and achievement prefixes a T + FN + LN designation. The lexical selection of 'Conservative', as opposed to the less formal 'Tory', is also the only example of its kind in all six texts. So, far from ignoring Heath in the manner of the pro-right *Telegraph*, this paper suggests that Heath's actions are to be taken seriously. This is further supplemented with the highest numerical estimate of all: '*at least* 40 Tories'. Here, then, the event is portrayed in a manner not unlike that of the *Sun* and the *Mirror* in so far as the political gravity of Heath's 'revolt' is emphasized.

Although the six extracts examined in this subsection are quite short, and the analyses conducted upon them have been kept informal and cursory, there should none the less be some picture of how each paper develops a particular set of linguistic strategies to deal with the incident. The ways in which the chief antagonists in the dispute are named, for example, was identified as one means of conveying distance, respect or even contempt towards the individuals concerned. The point about such pragmatic presupposition triggers is that although they lie outside the formal truth-conditional range of each text, they nevertheless constitute an important dimension of the point of view projected by that text. In all of the extracts, an 'angle of telling' was constructed through specific linguistic devices, resulting in some aspects of the story becoming foregrounded and others de-emphasized. Just imagine confronting each extract from a position where you know absolutely nothing about the politicians involved in the incident and the reasons behind the incident itself. What would you learn from the headlines and opening texts? How, for instance, is the personality of Heath constructed in each of the extracts? While the *Sun* is actually quite informative regarding Heath's political background, a very different picture of Heath's background emerges in the *Mail* and the *Express*. The sort of pragmatically informed analysis proposed here can help explain how these various positions are developed in the texts. It can also provide the formal metalanguage required for exploring the ways in which different ideological viewpoints are projected through language.

5.4.2 Advertising language

In the second of the two brief analyses which conclude this chapter, the concept of *modality*, which received extensive treatment in chapter 3, will be aligned with the meaning model proposed in this chapter. One of the reasons for doing this is to show how a particular linguistic category may enrich a second category, offering extra insights into language structure and function; another is to highlight the ways in which a specific concept like modality can be used productively not only in the analysis of narrative fiction but in a range of discourse types. Before proceeding any further with this, however, readers may care to re-acquaint themselves with the concept of modality by glancing back over the second section of chapter 3.

Modality intersects with our four-tiered pragmatic model in a rather subtle way. The best way of conceptualizing this intersection is to imagine the layers of the schema represented by figure 5.1 being permeated radially with a series of lines. Each line represents a different modal category (epistemic, deontic and so on) which cuts through all four of the meaning layers. This signals how each layer of meaning is capable of being 'modalized', whether it be a basic entailment or a more complex, contextually dependent implicature. A few illustrations should help clarify this before we move on to our analysis. First of all, a good example of how a straightforward entailment might be modalized comes from the very public domain of government health warnings on cigarette packets. Until recently, the normal form for such warnings was the following:

SMOKING CAN SERIOUSLY DAMAGE YOUR HEALTH

The epistemic (knowledge) modal *can* weakens the commitment to the basic entailment *p*, which can be expressed as:

p: *smoking seriously damages your health*

With modalization, the overall formula for the warning becomes: 'it is possible that *p*'. More recently, however, such warnings are becoming 'de-modalized' in the light of indisputable medical evidence. Here are two recent examples:

SMOKING CAUSES CANCER
TOBACCO SERIOUSLY DAMAGES HEALTH

Another public manifestation of modality occurs in the high-profile advertising campaign for Carlsberg lager. On billboards all over Britain, the product is presented in the following way:

Carlsberg. Probably the best lager in the world.

If the basic entailment *p* is *Carlsberg is the best lager in the world*, then the addition of the modal adverb *probably* develops the following more cautious formula:

it is probable that *p*

Although this modalization makes the claims of the Carlsberg company much weaker, it has nevertheless become the stock-in-trade of the advertising campaign with a range of imaginative gambits developed around the use of this simple modal adverb.

Moving towards the outer layers of the meaning modal, the pragmatic potential of modal constructions in politeness strategies is considerable. The principle of 'indirection' has already been touched upon in section 5.2, and modal auxiliaries in particular provide an important means of developing this type of politeness strategy. For instance, an unmodalized imperative like *Close the door* will conventionally be interpreted as less polite than a modalized interrogative like

Will you close the door. This in turn would be considered less polite than a form like *Could you close the door* which contains an epistemically weaker modal auxiliary. Thus the degree of modality affects the *force* of the three versions of the request. In some cases, the interactive context will shape the way in which a modalized construction is to be interpreted. If uttered in the course of a posh dinner party, for instance, the deontic construction *You must have some cake* would normally be interpreted as an offer; yet the same construction uttered by a mother to a recalcitrant child would be likely to function as a command. So, as is the case with the outer layers of the model generally, context will often shape the way in which modalized utterances are to be understood.

The advertisement which lends itself well to a bipolar modal–pragmatic analysis is taken from the *Daily Telegraph* of Thursday 4 January 1990. It advertises Newton's 'Herbal Remedies'. The total space occupied by the advertisement is 13cm. across and 23cm. deep – slightly smaller than a standard A4 sheet – and it is broken down into a collection of smaller blocks. In addition to blocks containing an introductory script and an order form, there are four blocks which detail the specific remedies on offer, from the hot pepper catarrh remedy to the free slimming remedy. These four blocks also each include a picture of two bottles of tablets, one of which presumably comes free with a regular purchase. Although too cumbersome to reproduce in its entirety, a substantial proportion of the text appears below, enough to represent its particular linguistic 'flavour'. Lines have been numbered and blocks have been assigned letters for ease of reference. As readers progress through it, they may care to consider three interrelated questions: what attitude does the company, via the copywriter, convey to the product? What claims are being made about the effectiveness of the product? And what are the linguistic strategies which project these claims?

Block A FREE HERBAL MEDICINES

    Hardly a week goes by without national and local newspapers, TV or radio comment about alternative medicines. You must be aware of the tremendous worldwide interest in these natural 'green' medicines and of the wide ranging claims being made for
5   their beneficial effects and the highly publicised research being carried out by teams of eminent scientists into the biochemistry of many of these wonderful plants and herbs.

    Why has this tremendous upsurge of interest come about? Could it be because more and more people are discovering for

10 themselves that these traditional herbal medicines really can
work for the individual even when other treatments may have
had little effect.

Because we want you to experience for yourself the wide
ranging benefits of this tried and tested method of self help
15 medicine, we are offering you the opportunity to purchase the
remedy of your choice at a special offer price. Pick any medicine
you need and we will send you double the quantity . . . that is
one remedy free for every one paid for. . . . We think you will be
absolutely delighted with the way these natural medicines could
20 improve your life.

Block B FREE SPECIAL 'HOT PEPPER' CATARRH REMEDY

Special 'hot pepper' catarrh tablets. They are intended to allevi-
ate stubborn catarrh and catarrhal problems like discharge of
mucus, discomfort, difficult breathing, nose blockage, disturbed
sleep, coughing, sinus pain, headache, etc. They contain a
5 superb combination of herbs including hot peppers. They work
swiftly, through the bloodstream to bring relief by helping expel
your catarrh from the system. Our regular customers 'swear' by
them. Like all Newtons brand tablets we only sell by mail order.
We have no retail shops. Don't miss this chance to experience
10 what could possibly be the 'ultimate' in catarrh breaking power.

'I had to write to thank you for your catarrh tablets. They have
made the world of difference to me. I honestly feel a new
woman. I can get about a lot easier, not so breathless, able to go
upstairs easier.'

E.F., Berks.

Block C FREE ANTI-RHEUMATIC PAIN REMEDY

We believe that this herbal rheumatic pain tablet could delight
and amaze sufferers of rheumatic pain. It could possibly be the
most effective treatment you may have tried. Why endure
rheumatic pain in shoulders, neck, arms, hands, legs, toes, etc.
5 when this valued and highly acclaimed remedy could bring you
positive relief. It has worked for many people when other
treatments had had little effect.

Block D FREE NERVOUS TENSION REMEDY

Are you feeling under pressure? Things getting on top of you?
Unable to relax and recharge your batteries? Tense, nervous,
jittery, irritable, difficult to live with? Making life a misery for
yourself and those around you? That's when you should try the

5 calming effects of this superb formula. Safe, non-addictive and
available without prescription. These tablets really could be of
great help to you. They relax the body so that you start to feel the
tenseness ease away, thus helping you feel more tranquil and
mellow, less jumpy and less irritable. Nervous exhaustion starts
10 to recede. You'll feel so much better. Easier to live with too!

Block E FREE SLIMMING REMEDY

Here is a herbal remedy that every overweight person should
seriously think about trying. However many slimming products
you may have tried over the years with little effect, you should
treat yourself to a course of these fabulous herbal aid to slim-
5 ming tablets. We have thousands of letters from delighted
customers. This slimming remedy really could help you to lose
all the weight you desire. The multi herbs in every tablet
combine to give you the effect you want. The one month supply
of tablets come with our own very special simple diet advice to
10 ensure that you lose weight right from the start. Money back
guarantee if you are not delighted.

'I have gone from 14st 1lb to 12st 12lb in ten weeks. My friends
are delighted as I am much better in myself.'

Miss C.T., Leicester.

A noticeable characteristic of the advertisement is the way in which
it exploits the interactive potential of written language. In the introduction to this chapter, some explanations were offered of the way a
written text may be designed to engage with an *idealized* reader, and it
is through this idealized reader that real readers come to mediate with
the text. This particular text is peppered with interactive signals,
including direct address in the form of offers and advice, and explicit
first- and second-person pronouns which delineate clearly the positions of both producer and consumer of the text. Built into this dialogic
framework are the commentaries of 'satisfied customers', those who
have apparently once occupied the position of reader/consumer but
whose language has now been appropriated into the advertisement by
the text's producer(s).

A facet of the text's overall message is the caution it displays on the
claims made for the product. There is a tension between the constraint
to tell the 'truth' and the desire to make extremely positive claims
about the efficacy of what is on offer. In the course of his own study of
this aspect of advertising, Fairclough cites the first article from the
British Code of Advertising Practice, which states that

All advertisements should be legal, decent, honest and truthful.

(Fairclough 1989: 201)

The 'honest and truthful' condition requires claims of 'fact' to be amenable to objective verification, although claims of 'opinion' need no such substantiation. As far as the legal implications of the Code of Practice are concerned, copywriters are expected to differentiate clearly between matters of fact and matters of opinion. In the case of the 'Herbal Remedies' advertisement, this distinction is not always particularly clear-cut and a little linguistic unpacking should help reveal the strategies which blur it.

As far as 'opinions' about the product go, the text is packed with evaluative adjectives and adverbs which present the product in very positive terms. The plants and herbs used for the remedies are 'wonderful', interest in their properties is 'tremendous' and the formulae used are simply 'superb'. In short, your herbal remedies look like a panacea capable of dealing with every conceivable ailment.

This may be the 'angle' which the text develops, but to what extent can we say that it is committed to the truth of the claims it makes? In other words, to what degree are the powers of the remedies presented as 'fact'? A closer look at the language will reveal that a subtle blend of modal and presuppositional strategies are brought into play at key points in the text. Particularly common in this regard is the use of straightforward epistemic modalization. Instead of expressing claims unequivocally in the form of categorical assertions, the entailments of sentences are often modified through epistemic modal auxiliaries like *could* and *can*. This effectively converts a proposition p into the more complex formula: 'it is possible that p'. So, in preference to an unmodalized assertion like 'these natural medicines improve your life', the realized form is 'these natural medicines *could* improve your life' (block A, lines 19–20). Similarly, instead of a herbal remedy which 'brings you positive relief', it '*could* bring you positive relief' (block C, lines 5–6). This strategy often multiplies the number of epistemic operators within particular sentences, so it is common to find not one but *two* qualifiers of epistemic commitment. When two modal devices are used to convey the same degree of commitment in this way they are said to operate in *harmonic combination*. Here are two examples from the text:

Don't miss this chance to experience what *could possibly* be the 'ultimate' in catarrh breaking power. (B, lines 9–10)
It *could possibly* be the most effective treatment. (C, lines 2–3)

Here the double modal configuration of auxiliary and adverb consolidates the level of commitment to the truth of the proposition expressed. This is why they function harmonically, in so far as they clarify the specific degree of confidence which the producer has towards the claims made in the text. However, not all multiple modal patterns are so used. A common tactic is the use of the *non-harmonic* combination. This is where modal operators exhibiting conflicting degrees of commitment are combined, and this practice is significant in terms of the way the product is presented at certain points in the text. Here are two examples:

> these traditional herbal medicines *really can* work for the individual (A, lines 10–11)
> These tablets *really could* be of great help to you. (D, lines 6–7)

In both cases, weaker particles 'can' and 'could' are combined with the stronger term 'really'. This promotes an interesting and perhaps insidious linguistic *trompe d'œil*. By using a strong term in the environment of claims about a product, it suggests that the claims can be expressed with more confidence than one might feel is warranted. Yet closer scrutiny reveals that the stronger terms really only modify the weaker ones and cannot be extended to cover the proposition as a whole. A breakdown of the first example should help clarify this process. In this sentence, there is a basic proposition p, which might be formulated thus:

> *these herbal medicines work for the individual*

However, the inclusion of 'can' alters the writer's commitment to the truth of p, resulting in a non-basic formula like the following:

> it is possible that p

The introduction of 'really' makes the formula more complex again, but it primarily affects the modal part in the following way:

> it is really the case that it is possible that p

In short, the only thing that is now certain is the possibility! The use of non-harmonic combination assists the copywriter's efforts by making the text 'feel' more confident in the effectiveness of the product than is actually stated. This modal technique gathers extra momentum from the way linguistic presupposition is employed. One common practice is to use both factive and non-factive verbs to introduce long and detailed expositions of the benefits of herbal remedies. Factive verbs, it may be recalled, are those which presuppose the truth of their complements and a good example occurs early on in tandem with a modal auxiliary:

> You must be aware of the tremendous worldwide interest in these natural 'green' medicines (A, lines 2–4).

More will be said of the function of the modal shortly, but what the factive verb ('aware of') does is effectively to encode as truth the remainder of the entire paragraph. Noticeably, however, what is presupposed is not the *content* of the claims of researchers, but simply the *existence* of the claims in the first place. The principle even extends to the opening of the second paragraph, where a '*wh*-question' – another form of presupposition trigger – is used to endorse the truth of the presupposition that a tremendous upsurge in the product has come about. Yet as the text progresses, factive verbs and other types of presupposition trigger tend to drop out and are replaced by non-factive verbs. Non-factive verbs are those which do *not* presuppose the truth of what they govern.[8] A good example occurs at the end of block A:

> *We think* you will be absolutely delighted

Because the proposition *you will be absolutely delighted* is embedded under 'We think' its truth is no longer vouchsafed: in other words, your anticipated delight at the remedies is now a matter of the producers' subjective opinion rather than of verifiable fact. A similar technique is used to open block C:

> *We believe* that this herbal rheumatic pain tablet could delight and amaze sufferers

Again, a non-factive verb avoids commitment to the truth of a complement which in any case is further mitigated by the inclusion of a modal auxiliary ('could delight'). However, the principle of non-factivity still allows controversial propositions to be *asserted* in a text; it is just that by incorporating them in a framework of non-factivity, complete commitment to the truth of the proposition can be avoided.

Woven around the strands of epistemic modality and presupposition in the text is a strand of deontic ('obligation') modality. Noticeably, as the text progresses, it gradually becomes more 'coercive' in terms of the way the product is presented to the idealized reader. Early on there are few explicit deontic markers, but by the time we reach the 'Slimming Remedy' the text is rich in these modal operators. In fact, in block A, the modal auxiliary which precedes the factive ('You *must* be aware . . .') permits a dual reading; it may be interpreted as a statement of belief about your state of knowledge or as a statement of your obligation to become 'aware'. (Where dual interpretations of this sort are possible, the two compatible epistemic and deontic readings are said to undergo a *merger*.) Other early examples of deontic modality include the letter from 'E.F.' in block B which goes:

I had to write to thank you

Interesting here is the way in which deontic obligation is directed towards a third party outside the immediate interactive situation.

By the time we reach blocks D and E, advice is much more explicitly mediated through overt deontic strategies and the claims made for the product are noticeably stronger. In block D (line 10), the strongest claim for the product is made, although it still retains a contracted form of the modal *will*:

You'll feel so much better.

In the 'Free Slimming Remedy' block, persuasive strategies are intensified and are now pointedly directed at the 'overweight' person's responsibility for finding a 'cure' for obesity. This advice is couched in the following deontic constructions:

Here is a herbal remedy that every overweight person *should* seriously think about trying. (E, lines 1–2)

you *should* treat yourself to a course of these fabulous herbal aid to slimming tablets. (E, lines 3–5)

This progressively coercive section exploits what Fairclough refers to as *implicit assumptions* in advertising (1989: 202). These are assumptions about the sets of beliefs readers are expected to hold. In this case, the concept 'overweight' is assumed to be socially stigmatized, something for which a 'remedy' is required. The text then locks onto a subject position for readers who feel they need to lose weight. This desire to lose weight is naturalized, and the text re-inforces this assumption by continual reminders about what readers need ('. . . lose all the weight *you desire*.'; '. . . combine to give you the effect *you want*'). Thus, in offering a 'remedy', the text re-inforces the very insecurity of those to whom it is addressed.

What this short analysis has sought to highlight is how a network of linguistic strategies is used to create a specific 'angle' on a particular consumer product. By personalizing the relationship between producer and audience through direct address, the text then draws upon epistemic modality and presupposition in making its claims for the product. Particularly effective use was made of non-harmonic modal combination to give these claims a 'look' and 'feel' of greater confidence than is strictly asserted. Factive and non-factive verbs are deployed strategically, with non-factives offering a 'get-out' device in the environment of controversial or untenable claims. Yet this strategy still allows the claims to be stated in the first place; it simply brings them under the control of a verb which is not an explicit guarantor of truth. The deontic modal system comes into play as the text progresses. Later sections of the advertisement construct subject positions for the 'stress sufferer' and the 'overweight person', and numerous deontic statements are targeted to meet the projected desires of these idealized readers. As we have seen throughout this chapter, pragmatic aspects of language use provide yet another means of developing a 'point of view', an 'angle of telling'. In this advertisement, the bipolar linguistic devices of modality and presupposition are the mechanisms by which this possibility is exploited.

5.5 SUMMARY

The main concern of this chapter has been to develop a simple model of pragmatics, thereby enabling a more contextualized dimension to be bolted onto our developing analytic framework. To this effect, sections 5.2 and 5.3 were largely theoretical in orientation, introducing, illustrating and reviewing the basic features of meaning construction. The mechanisms by which meanings are transmitted and negotiated were proposed as: entailment, semantic presupposition, pragmatic presupposition and implicature. Each was discussed with, wherever possible, attested examples of language usage. This included advertisements and political language, and the aim of the analysis was to show not only how speakers project their point of view, but how certain accessing procedures are necessary for the interpretation of these texts. Some aspects of the pragmatic model informed the final section of the chapter where two short studies of newspaper language and advertising language were undertaken. I hope this will have highlighted the interactive nature of both types of language and the way in which communication operates as a two-way process between producers and interpreters of texts.

The next stage in the programme will be to direct the various techniques in linguistics assembled over the course of the book towards one important issue: the question of gender bias in language. The chapter which follows will employ the strands of linguistic analysis opened up in this and the previous three chapters to investigate what has now become a central concern in feminist-stylistic criticism.

NOTES AND FURTHER READING

1 The analytic model proposed in this section draws on an extremely broad range of research in semantics and pragmatics. It does not restrict itself to a single theory of meaning, nor does it adhere exclusively to any specific 'tradition' of thought. Among the seminal publications which are subsumed in the present account are J.L. Austin's theory of *speech acts* and *illocutionary force* (Austin 1962) and H.P. Grice's work on *conversational maxims* and the *co-operative principle* in interaction (Grice 1975). The basic tenets of Austin's and Grice's research have been refined and extended by a number of scholars, and particularly important and influential adaptations of this work can be found in Brown and Levinson (1986) and Sperber and Wilson (1986). Other books on pragmatics include Gazdar (1979) and Leech (1983), although Levinson's (1983) textbook remains the most substantial and accessible introduction to this complex field of linguistic enquiry. A collection which purportedly seeks to integrate pragmatics with the study of style is Hickey (1989). However, the papers in this volume tend to focus either on pragmatics or stylistics, but not on both. Articles which provide useful accounts of the potential of pragmatic models in textual analysis include: Porter (1986), Spolsky (1988) and Pateman (1989). Finally, a book which is specifically devoted to the pragmatic analysis of political language is J. Wilson (1990). Wilson's concerns echo many of those in this chapter, particularly his emphasis on using pragmatic models to deal with attested, non-contrived examples of language usage. He also devotes an entire chapter of his book to a subject which receives some attention in the main body of this chapter: the strategy of the *leading question* and the tactics which politicians use to evade them. Wilson provides a more detailed account of this topic than is possible here and readers interested in exploring it further will find his exposition illuminating.

2 Readers may notice that the term *pragmatic presupposition* is intended to cover both 'pragmatic presupposition' in the sense proposed by Levinson (1983) and D. Wilson (1975) as well as Grice's concept of *conventional implicature*. Although Grice's term is notoriously underillustrated, there seem to be sufficient grounds for incorporating it into a general category which accounts for the conventional (yet non-truth-conditional) meanings which attach to particular expressions. Levinson (1983: *passim*) explains in more detail why Grice's term can be subsumed within the broader category in this way.

3 The property of defeasibility has stimulated a great deal of argument about the theoretical validity of the concept of linguistic presupposition. D. Wilson, in fact, uses defeasibility as a formula for rejecting the concept of presupposition outright (Wilson 1975). Certainly, defeasibility shows how presuppositions are not the stable meaning-category which many linguists and philosophers have believed, and Wilson's monograph is a challenging and thorough exploration of this issue. In this chapter, defeasibility is extended to cover *all* layers of meaning. This does not mean that we need to abandon specific layers such as semantic presupposition because of this; we just need to recognize instead that all of the layers are in some sense 'malleable' and are thus susceptible to retraction and contradiction. In order to maintain the highly specific technical sense of the concept of defeasibility, the verb 'defease' will be employed. This is in preference to the more

standard derivation 'defeat' which tends to carry wider non-linguistic reference.

4 The use of implicature in narrative fiction has received a great deal of attention over the years, with the first book-length treatment of the subject published by M.L. Pratt in 1977. Numerous articles have appeared since then, of which the following are especially useful: Weber (1986), Henkel (1988), Nair *et al.* (1988), Pilkington (1990). All of these analyses offer a specifically pragmatic perspective on literary communication.

5 An extremely influential account of the interactional significance of naming strategies is Ervin-Tripp (1972). Some of the methods used in the present analysis are adapted from Ervin-Tripp's article. J. Wilson (1990: 77–103) assesses the pragmatic implications of *self-referential* naming strategies. Where the present analysis concentrates on the third-person naming techniques characteristic of newspaper accounts of political events, Wilson focusses, for the most part, on the ways in which politicians refer to themselves in the course of parliamentary debates.

6 The 'piratical' subtext developed here could be productively analysed within the terms of models developed in artificial intelligence. Many AI models seek to account for the 'knowledge store' which is activated when discourse processors are confronted with texts. For instance, in the extract under scrutiny, the reference to 'walking the plank' can be said to trigger a *frame*. A frame is a fixed representation of knowledge about the world, and in this case a frame of 'piracy' is activated which may include additional concepts such as the Jolly Roger, eye-patches, stolen treasure and so on. Thus, extra density of meaning may be created by mapping frames onto a text in this way. Unfortunately, a more detailed AI approach is beyond the remit of this chapter. However, a useful survey of frames and related categories can be found in Brown and Yule (1983: 236–56), while an extensive application of these categories to advertising language can be found in Cook (forthcoming).

7 These figures are provided by a poll on tabloid readership patterns commissioned by BBC television's *The Late Show*.

8 If the distinction between factive and non-factive verbs is not clear, reconsider, first of all, an earlier example containing a presupposition-carrying factive verb:

(7) John realizes that Russell is dead.

Now alter the verb to a non-factive counterpart like *believe* or *think*:

(7) a. John believes/thinks that Russell is dead.

This sentence no longer contains a presupposition trigger, and the sequence *Russell is dead* is therefore no longer presupposed.

6 Gender, ideology and point of view

Cats possess so many of the same qualities as some people (expensive girlfriends for instance) that it's often hard to tell the people and the cats apart.

(P.J. Rourke, *Modern Manners*)

6.1 INTRODUCTION

A weekly television magazine recently included a conversation with Brian Walden, a well-known British political interviewer and commentator. Walden, popularly regarded as an astute and tenacious interviewer, provided an assortment of opinions about his *métier*, politicians and the British political climate in general. The insights offered included the following theory about why politicians cannot always be trusted:

> Anybody who wishes to have power over his fellows should be regarded with some suspicion. It's unusual. Most people don't feel like that. They want a good job, a nice wife, pleasant children, friends and a bit of fun.

(*TV Times*, 29 September 1990, p. 9)

As this little discourse unfolds, it seems that the generality suggested by 'Anybody' is not quite intended, and that Walden has a rather exclusive view of who exactly make up 'people'. The point of view which is projected in the text is one where men appear to constitute a centre of being around which other more sundry items, like fun and wives, revolve like satellites. The response of most of the women to whom I have presented this piece has been a mixture of anger, incredulity and resigned amusement. Female readers in particular may care to reflect on their own immediate reactions as they were reading through the piece.

The type of language-use which the Walden quotation epitomizes will be the central concern of this chapter. It seems fair to say that the world-view projected by the quotation is not untypical of that represented by many everyday discourses. But what are the implications and consequences of these discursive practices? Do they forge sexist divisions into the structure of society, actually determining gender-biased behaviour, or are they simply innocuous 'off-the-cuff' remarks which merit no serious scrutiny? Certainly, the question of 'sexist language' and the world-view it reflects now occupies a central place in feminist linguistics. As we shall see shortly, some exponents have argued that sexist language is directly responsible for the way we see the world. Others, more guardedly, see it as an important means of reinforcing sexist assumptions. Cameron sets the agenda for the 'reinforcement' theorists:

> our linguistic habits often reflect and perpetuate ideas about things which are no longer embodied in law, but which continue to have covert significance in the culture. This is one reason why feminists have often paid detailed attention to language and discourse: our ways of talking about things reveal attitudes and assumptions we might consciously disown, thus testifying to the deep-rootedness of sexism.

(1990: 16)

The ideological implications of this 'linguistic habit' will be explored in detail in the next two sections. Although this chapter, unlike the previous four, does not introduce an explicit linguistic framework, it draws on many elements of the models developed throughout the book. Moreover, the section which follows will provide an opportunity to discuss more general questions concerning the interrelationship between language, thought and reality. This largely theoretical section will be complemented by section 6.3 which, by contrast, offers a selection of analyses intended to illustrate how the critical linguistic analysis of gender, ideology and point of view in language might be undertaken. This section also provides an appropriate place at which to re-assess the quotation which opened this section. First, however, we need to define more precisely the nature of the topic which is being investigated.

6.2 SEXISM *IN* LANGUAGE OR SEXISM *THROUGH* LANGUAGE?

This section reviews an important controversy which has developed over the relationship between language and gender.[1] The controversy hinges on the degree to which one can say that the system of language projects sexist bias. One side of the debate views sexism in language as inherent to the system itself, and considers that by using a system which is intrinsically biased speakers and writers actively construct the inequality that exists between men and women in society. The other side proposes that sexism is encoded into language, either consciously or unconsciously, by users of language. In this way, linguistic practices will tend to re-inforce and naturalize sexist divisions in society. An underlying premise which is shared by both sides of the debate is the valid assumption that Western society is organized in terms of a *patriarchal order*. This is a symbolic order into which we are all born; a behavioural system in which men simply have power over women. Thus, patriarchy is endemic to all types of social interaction and organization, and as language is crucial to the way society is organized, it is not surprising that language has been identified as a site of struggle by many feminist linguists.

Foregrounding and demystifying the ways in which language is used to bolster the patriarchal order has now become a major concern of such work. Closely related to this concept of patriarchy is the notion of *androcentrism* (Coates 1986: 15). Androcentrism describes a male-centred word-view wherein male activities are evaluated positively and female activities negatively. The principle extends even to explanations of language itself, so that usages which are attributed to men are regarded more favourably than those attributed to women. For instance, when language change was generally stigmatized by scholars of the eighteenth century, blame for the introduction of new constructions into the language was assigned to women. By the turn of the twentieth century, when it had become clear that linguistic change was not only inevitable but a valid object of scholarly study, the chief innovators of language were, it may come as no surprise, believed to be men. This type of asymmetry prompts Coates to formulate an 'androcentric rule' which states roughly that men's linguistic behaviour fits the view of what is admirable or desirable, whilst women will be blamed for whatever is considered negative or reprehensible (Coates 1986: 15). Even feminist critiques of language have unconsciously embraced this pervasive androcentric rule. In her famous account of 'women's language' (1975), Lakoff contends that women have a tendency to use 'empty' adjectives like *adorable*, *divine* and *cute*. Whether they actually do or not is debatable, but what is not made clear is why these adjectives are considered 'empty' in the first place. After all, greater elaboration of vocabulary is surely a positive achievement and one wonders how these words would be evaluated if they were identified as a specifically *male* usage.

One of the most influential contributions to the debate on sexism in language in recent years has been Dale Spender's book *Man Made Language* (1980). In addition to the extensive media coverage which it has received, the book continues to be adopted on both language courses and literature courses in university departments. Perhaps more importantly, as Cameron points out (1985: 3), it has put the subject of women and language on the map for many people outside the women's movement. The provocative title of Spender's book captures the spirit and essence of her argument. She contends that by a straightforward act of linguistic appropriation men have constructed a supremacist social position, a position which oppresses and excludes women. Men, she argues, have literally 'made' the English language and have never relinquished control of it. Through their control of language, men are able to exercise their control over women. An especially trenchant statement of this theory of control is the following:

> it has been the dominant group – in this case, males – who have created the world, invented the categories, constructed sexism and its justification and developed a language trap which is in their interest.

> (1980: 142)

Spender makes a direct connection between this type of linguistic domination and the existence of the patriarchical order. The chain of reasoning involved in her argument might be set out as follows:

1 Men made language.
2 Language controls reality.
3 Men control reality.
4 Men control women.

The examples used to support this argument are, if selective, none the less interesting. Spender contends that many everyday words reflect a kind of 'trapped' expression because their meanings have been 'fixed' by men. One item that receives extensive discussion is the word *motherhood*. Because men have appropriated the meaning of the word to signify things like 'replete with joy' and 'the epitome of feminine fulfilment', women are effectively denied an experience which for many is both painful and traumatic. The same principle governs the use of the word 'frigidity'. This has become codified in dictionaries as 'failing' to become sexually aroused. However, this negative evaluation is not carried over into the male equivalent, *impotence*, which, Spender argues, is defined as not a failure but an 'inability' to become aroused. In standard androcentric terms, women 'fail' where men, through no fault of their own, are simply unable. By foregrounding linguistic asymmetries of this sort, Spender calls for a wholesale re-invention and rejuvenation of the English language.[2] Only through this type of linguistic overhaul will sexism be tackled head on.

A key to understanding the theoretical foundation of Spender's argument lies in the view it takes of the relationship between language, thought and reality. Half-way through the book, the following concise statement of her theoretical position is provided:

> It is language which *determines* the limits of our world, which *constructs* our reality.
>
> (p. 139; my emphasis)

This determinist view of language is one which can be traced directly to a specific tradition of anthropological linguistics. Before going any further with our discussion of Spender we will need to digress for a moment and consider some of the basic tenets of this tradition of linguistics.

The theory of *linguistic determinism* is attributable largely to the work of anthropologists Edward Sapir and Benjamin Lee Whorf. Their ideas on language are collectively known as the 'Sapir–Whorf hypothesis' or more recently 'Whorfianism'. The basic principle of Whorfianism is that linguistic differences determine differences in world-view. Thus, our language delineates the boundaries of our understanding; or, put another way, the way we 'see' the world is constructed by the language we use. Taken a little further, the Sapir–Whorf hypothesis specifies that the linguistic system is the 'shaper of ideas, the programme and guide for the individual's mental activity' (Whorf, quoted in Carroll 1956: 212); consequently, speakers are therefore 'very much at the mercy of the particular language which has become the medium of expression for their society' (Sapir 1929: 207). In this view, words precede concepts, so if you have few words, your perception of the world around you will be seriously impoverished.

The degree of linguistic determinism which the Sapir–Whorf hypothesis espouses has never been easy to pinpoint exactly, but in its raw form – the form outlined here – the hypothesis is very difficult to sustain. Words simply do *not* precede concepts. An 'anteater', as Lakoff (1975: 46) astutely points out, is so named because of what it does; it is not some animal which obligingly eats ants in order to satisfy a lexical entry in the language system. Similarly, the term *skyscraper* has been coined to account for a specific modern achitectural phenomenon and it is manifest nonsense to claim that people were only able to notice this phenomenon once equipped with the word. In fact, if followed through, a Whorfian solution to the problem of urban decay would not be to demolish tall ugly buildings, but simply to remove, Orwellian style, the words that refer to them. In this way, the concepts associated with them would cease to exist, and environmentalists could turn to other issues.

A more realistic alternative to Whorfianism is to propose that the language system is shaped by the functions which it serves. In this sense, language reflects and to some extent re-inforces the cultural and ideological practices which it describes. Concepts become *lexicalized* in language, and the system expands or contracts relative to the concepts it needs to express. This is the type of process by which *skyscraper* has entered English, or, for that matter, its calqued counterpart *gratte-ciel* has entered French. So when, in the course of their development, cultures are confronted with new concepts and objects, their respective languages make use of a range of available devices for introducing new words into the lexicon. The Spanish never had any trouble with 'hot-dogs' (*los perros calientes*), nor the Arabs with 'paracetamol' (*paraseetamool*) nor the Chinese with 'telephone' (*dyan-hwa-ji* (literally, 'electric speaker apparatus')). Furthermore, the more prominent a concept becomes in a particular culture, the more economical the linguistic means of describing it. Thus, in Colombian and Venezuelan Spanish the phrase *el traficante de drogas* ('trafficker of drugs') appears to be undergoing a rather telling change to a single lexical item *el narcotraficante*. By contrast, as long as ice-cream remains a relatively remote commodity in many southern African countries, its linguistic designation in Swahili is likely to remain *chakula kitamu kilichofanyizwa kwa maxiwa na vitu vingine na kugandishwa kwa baridi* – which can be translated roughly as 'delicious food made from milk and all sorts of things and kept cold'!

Although it is not difficult to adduce evidence which contradicts the basic tenets of Whorfianism, the principle of linguistic determinism has been used to underpin a great deal of language-related research. In some areas, it has been appropriated as a means of denigrating non-standard language, especially the systems used by working-class or ethnic groups. Honey (1983), for instance, argues that those who do not have standard English are intellectually trapped by the 'substandard' forms they do use. He cites the case of primitive tribespeoples who are unable to handle the complex constructs and 'delicate nuances' which are available to speakers of Standard English, adding that this cognitive impoverishment will become immediately apparent to

> anyone who has actually tried to translate a scholarly paper in physics, psychology or semantics from a major world language into the speech of a preliterate jungle tribe or into the local dialect of a remote province.

> (1983: 6)

For a start, standard languages do not have a monopoly on technical vocabulary, and if, by some malevolent quirk of fate, semantics did become culturally prioritized by these tribes, then their linguistic systems would be altered accordingly. The host of linguistic devices available for such alteration has already been illustrated. As far as the question of 'translation' is concerned, Honey may simply have forgotten to mention that many of the complex concepts which are lexicalized in the so-called preliterate jungle languages – such as terms for kinship, weather conditions, vegetation and types of religious ceremonies – are notoriously difficult to translate into standard English. Speakers, whatever their culture, enrich their language in order to cope with what they need to talk about; their language is not a monolithic grid through which a restricted set of concepts is filtered. Honey's position, like many other deterministic accounts of linguistic diversity,[3] is highly 'monocultural' in its outlook.

In the light of this short review of determinist approaches to language, we may re-assess Spender's theory of sexism in language. By proposing that male control of language facilitates male control of reality, Spender is clearly arguing within the parameters of an un-challenged Whorfian model. Despite its vehemence, her argument is difficult to sustain theoretically and in many respects highlights flaws in the very model of language it seeks to espouse. Moreover, parts of the argument, if looked at more closely, are actually patronizing and critical not of the behaviour of men but of women themselves.

First, the issue of 'trapped expression'. Spender argues that men have fixed the meaning of the word *motherhood*, thereby denying many women the more unpleasant aspects of the experience. Yet if men really had appropriated the terms, how would women know about the unpleasantness in the first place and, more importantly, how have they been able to articulate this experience so clearly? In other words, if it is the positive term which determines the reality, how can we explain negative experiences of that reality? This also raises the more general questions of the language system which Spender herself uses in the book. If men genuinely do have control over language, then she is forced into one of two possible positions: either she is writing with a form of language which is as trapped as any other form of female expression or she is writing in a liberated language outside male control. If the first position is occupied, then the book is a waste of time in so far as it is only another example of male-appropriated meaning; if the second is occupied, then all men and presumably most women would be unable to understand this 'new' language in which it is written.

The practice of making selective forays into the dictionary to elicit sexist usage is also highly problematic. This etymological method assumes that dictionaries are accurate repositories of what words mean in every context. Yet we have already seen in chapter 5 how context shapes the interpretation of much everyday language. If there is to be an objection about asymmetrical definitions of *impotence* and *frigidity*, then it should be directed towards the dictionary makers. This 'etymological fallacy'[4] has important consequences for other parts of the argument. Spender claims as a feminist victory the now widespread use of the expressions *chauvinism* and *sexual harassment*. It is, she says, a case of women, not men, 'naming the world'. But within the terms of her position on language this is surely the last thing women should do. After all, if the word constructs the reality, women, by introducing these terms, are actively bringing about their own repression. What they should be doing is exorcising these words from the system, not introducing them into it. A more realistic explanation for this, of course, is that women have sufficiently alerted society in general to endemic sexist practices. Thus, 'sexual harassment' has come into everyday parlance, and specific manifestations of it, such as harassment in the workplace, have now been placed firmly on the agenda. Similarly, the word *chauvinism* has entered common usage and has become associated specifically with male sexism – that is, in its common usage and not its dictionary usage!

Finally, there remains the question of how exactly men made language. At what notional point in prehistory did this linguistic schism occur, this schism which was to have such far-reaching implications for gender relations in society? And what was one half of the population doing when the other half was busy making language? These questions have a serious side. Disenfranchised groups who have been excluded from dominant or mainstream cultures encounter no problems in developing languages of their own, whether they be market-traders in seventeenth-century England or members of the underworld of present-day Calcutta. These specialized languages, or 'anti-languages',[5] are complex, rule-governed systems entirely suited to the needs of their users. Spender is asking us to believe, then, that women, as a disenfranchised group, have been both excluded from language, but been perversely incapable of developing even the most simple system of their own. At the very least, this is a facile interpretation of the evolution of English.

There are clearly problems, then, with a strictly determinist approach to sexism in language. Trying to remove sexual bias from society by altering the lexicon is like trying to cure a patient of measles by painting over their spots. We need to replace determinism with a more *functional* view of language; a view which explains the structure of language in terms of the functions which language serves. This does not mean that the analysis of sexism in language becomes any less radical. On the contrary, sexist assumptions and biases are reflected, perpetuated and naturalized in language use and critical linguistic analysis can bring these discursive practices into sharper focus. The point is simply that it is not the language code but the way in which the code is used that is significant – and this has been the guiding principle behind all of the critical linguistic analyses of previous chapters. It may be that the angle of telling adopted in a text represents the world in a sexist way. Linguistic analysis can unpack the 'angle of telling' and the representation which it produces, thereby 'denaturalizing' this type of discourse. Just how such analyses might be conducted is explained in the next section, where a variety of text types are examined from a functional linguistic perspective.

6.3 ANALYSING GENDER BIAS IN LANGUAGE

Part of the concern of feminist critical linguistic analysis has been to uncover asymmetries and inconsistencies in the way language is used. These discursive practices, as Cameron argues, represent historically evolved ways of defining the limits of femininity and masculinity. She adds:

> One attacks these discourses primarily by becoming aware of them and by developing rival discourses (ways of representing) that people will eventually incorporate into their own method of dealing with reality.

> (1985: 69)

One discursive practice which has received much attention is the use of so-called 'he/man' language and the related category of 'common gender'. The first of these describes the institutionally sanctioned adoption of words like *he* and *man* to refer generically to male and female. However, evidence suggests that, despite being prescribed as 'correct' usage, the practice does represent a male-centred view of things. If it did not, then there would be nothing odd about the following oft-quoted example:

> Man is a mammal which breastfeeds his young and experiences difficulty in giving birth.

Common-gender words encode a similar asymmetry, even though we are led to believe that they are non-sex-marked. Nouns like *people*, *teacher* and *linguist* (or the *boss* at the beginning of chapter 4) can in principle have either feminine or masculine reference, yet in actual usage they often assume male reference. And when the terms are used to refer explicitly to women, specific female markers are tacked on to the basic noun (*female linguist*, *woman teacher*). To give a clearer picture of how this works, let us return briefly to the Walden quotation which opened the chapter:

> Anybody who wishes to have power over his fellows should be regarded with some suspicion. It's unusual. Most people don't feel like that. They want a good job, a nice wife, pleasant children, friends and a bit of fun.

The text is littered with he/man language and common-gender nouns, but as it progresses it becomes clear that Walden is using what are supposed to be non-sex-marked generics to refer exclusively to men and to exclude women. The *coup-de-grâce* is delivered with the sequence which stipulates that 'most people' want 'a nice wife' in addition to their other sundry requisites like children and a bit of fun. Throughout, Walden appropriates the terms for humanity in general ('Anybody'; 'people') and attaches them exclusively to male desires. Women are delineated as somehow contingent to this middle-class male heterosexual order, in other words, the patriarchal order. The mild-mannered smugness with which this world-view is projected is alarming: society can be arranged into a natural pattern where people (men) are defined in terms of a set of needs. These needs can then be identified as commodities like employment, leisure and, of course, women.

Where the isolation of linguistic asymmetries of this sort is one approach to the study of sexism in language, another is to undertake more systematic and sustained analyses of texts within a feminist-linguistic perspective. The analytic models developed in the course of this book all lend themselves to this type of critical linguistic approach. The model of transitivity, in particular, has proved insightful in its application to a range of discourse types. One notable example of this is Burton's (1982) analysis of a passage from Sylvia Plath's auto-biographical novel *The Bell Jar*. Burton examines the transitivity patterns used in a disturbing sequence detailing the narrator's experi-ence of electric shock therapy. This examination highlights the ways in which, on the one hand, the narrator is affected by the actions of others, yet, on the other, is herself unable to exert any influence on the people and objects around her. Adopting the principle that 'the personal is political' (201), Burton extrapolates from her analysis to a more general critique of the male-dominated power relations that pertain in society. The correlation of the situation of a woman under-going shock therapy with the societal alienation of women is a bold interpretative move, though it is one which arguably manifests a strong degree of the type of *positivism* which was discussed towards the end of chapter 4. For instance, a description of the treatment from a male perspective, with the subject literally strapped in and with little physical control over his environment, would be likely to yield similar patterns of transitivity. Nevertheless, the polemic in which Burton engages still illustrates how linguistic analysis can be used in a product-ive and radical way.[6]

One of the most incisive applications of the transitivity model to non-fiction is Clark's (1992) study of newspaper reports of male violence towards women. Clark examines the *Sun*'s coverage of John Steed, the notorious 'M4 Killer' who was sentenced to four life sentences for killing one woman and raping three others. (Ironically, the verdict delivered on the killing was *man*slaughter.) Unlike other British newspapers which covered the event, the *Sun* devoted most of its coverage to Steed's girlfriend and the part she played in shielding his crimes. In fact, the bulk of the space allocated to the story was filled with pictures of this woman in the 'sexy' poses which have become the hallmark of the *Sun*'s soft-core pornography policy. Again, unlike other papers, the *Sun* devoted little space to the actual crimes Steed committed, and when it did, the choices it made from the system of transitivity were highly significant. Here is an example of the pattern which the paper adopted:

(1) Two of Steed's rape-victims – aged 20 and 29 – had a screwdriver held at their throats as they were forced to submit.

(the *Sun*, 11 November 1986, p. 4)

This is an odd configuration in that Steed's victims, although positioned at the head of the sentence, are represented only obliquely to their attack. The first process with which they are associated is a relational–possessive one displaying a 'X *had* Y' pattern. What they 'have', in fact, is encoded as a separate process with the following transitivity structure:

GOAL	PROCESS	CIRCUMSTANCES
a screwdriver	held	at their throats

This is the classic 'agentless passive', with the holder of the screwdriver having been removed totally from the process. The final clause of the sentence exhibits a similar format:

GOAL	PROCESS
they	were forced to submit

Again, an agentless passive is used where the 'doer' of the process remains completely unspecified.

Other parts of this news report are equally significant. Here is another example:

(2) His third victim, a 39-year-old mother of three, was attacked at gunpoint after Steed had forced her car off the M4.

Here, there is an absence of any agency from the process expressed by the first clause, although the GOAL element receives considerable elaboration:

GOAL	PROCESS	CIRCUMSTANCES
His third victim . . . mother of three	was attacked	at gunpoint

In fact, the agency involved in this process has to be inferred by implication from the process expressed by the second clause where Steed does now feature in the role of ACTOR/AGENT:

ACTOR/AGENT	PROCESS	GOAL	CIRCUMSTANCES
Steed	had forced	her car	off the M4

The message is constructed in such a way as to obscure the relationship between Steed and the attack. The only entity upon which Steed acts as AGENT is 'her car', whilst the victim of the attack, although prominent in the information structure of the report, is acted upon only by an implicit and unspecified agency. Indeed, so obscured is the relationship between attacker and victim that it allows a possible reading wherein someone else attacks the woman at gunpoint while Steed only forces her car off the road.

Like many of the examples encountered in chapter 4, we see a wilful refusal to 'tell it like it is'. What, for instance, is so difficult about presenting the details of the story in the following way, where the relationship between attacker and victim is not obfuscated:

(1) a. Steed held a screwdriver at the throats of two of his victims as he forced them to submit.
(2) a. Steed attacked at gunpoint his third victim, a 39-year-old mother of three, after he had forced her car off the M4.

Of course, these 'rewrites' are no more ideologically neutral than the original version – notice, for instance, how the victim in (2a) is still referred to as a 'mother' and not simply a woman – but at least they do not use language to shield the perpetrator of the crimes. It is not the objective 'truth' of the *Sun*'s account which is at issue; rather, it is the way the 'angle of telling' is predicated upon an underlying dominant political ideology. Playing down these crimes, Clark suggests, helps to avoid awkward questions like why such acts of violence are committed against women at all. In this case, the *Sun* is unable to shift the blame for the attack onto the women themselves – a practice traditionally reserved for the murder of female prostitutes who are considered somehow 'responsible' for their own demise. Furthermore, the position of the killer and rapist cannot be rationalized by casting him in the role of the 'monster', 'beast' or 'fiend'; in other words, in the role of a social outcast which distances him from 'normal' men. The 'mystification' which this social and psychological distancing offers is elaborated upon by Cameron and Frazer, who comment:

> the archaic formulas of tabloid journalism have just this mystifying effect: the pages of *The Sun* and *The News of the World* are apparently still stalked by motiveless 'fiends' whose 'brutal lusts' remain for ever unspecified, their connection with masculinity somehow obvious, yet unexplained.
>
> (1987: 44)

And finally, there remains the entertainment value which is to be gained from the story. This report is different from the paper's normal strategy of reporting violence against women in that prurient blood lust is overridden by the 'exclusive' which the paper secures by getting the killer's partner to pose in leather underwear. So sensational a 'scoop' will presumably grab more attention than more peripheral and prosaic matters such as murder and rape.

We can supplement the analytic procedure adopted in this section with some of the material introduced in the previous chapter. The strategies of naming and referring constitute another important facet of the discursive practices examined here. The way in which referring expressions are deployed asymmetrically to designate men and women is another index of a symbolic order in which 'male' constitutes the norm and 'female' a deviation from that norm. To illustrate this, we will concentrate initially on a short report which appeared in the *Daily Mirror* of 17 November 1983. As important as patterns of transitivity are the expressions used to refer to the participants within the story.

CRAZED DOG BITES OFF A WIFE'S EAR
A crazed bull terrier attacked a 36-year-old wife without warning and bit off half her right ear.

Ambulancemen called to [Dora Smith's] home in Denby Dale Way, Royton, nr. Oldham, found it.

It was packed in ice and rushed to Withington Hospital, Manchester, where it was stitched back.[7]

There is no need for a detailed breakdown of the transitivity structure of the headline of the story; suffice it to say, the key participant roles involved in the material process of 'biting off' are the 'dog' (ACTOR) and perversely, not the woman, but her 'ear' as the GOAL element. In the opening text the dog is further defined ('bull terrier') while the affected participant now becomes 'a 36-year-old-wife'. It becomes clear, as the report progresses, that the key players in the drama are to be the dog and the ear, resulting in an almost comic denouement where it is the ear, and not the woman, that is rushed to hospital for emergency surgery. The way the woman is referred to in the text is also significant. It hinges on an important pragmatic principle concerning the degree of *specificity* which attaches to words. Lexical specificity, as it is known,[8] is a way of conveying pragmatic, non-truth-conditional meanings. It describes the practice of selecting a term which exhibits a greater degree of either precision or generality than would be expected in a particular context of use. For instance, if you are on your way out to the shops and are asked where you are going, you might reply *Out!*. By being less specific than the exchange would require, you are implicating perhaps that your interlocutor should mind her own business. Similarly, an injunction on a recalcitrant family pet couched in underspecific terms like *Take that animal away* may implicate distance or dislike, if only momentary. Overspecificity may carry similar pragmatic significance. If, in response to a question like *What have you got in the case?*, you reply *A Fender Stratocaster* instead of, say, *A guitar*, you may be attempting to convey expertise, superiorioty or in-group knowledge. The point is that the interpretations deriving from the degree of lexical specificity employed are contextually driven, so greater or lesser specificity will not always generate the same type of meaning in every situation. Returning to our report, the term 'wife' forms part of a lexical scale which might be postulated thus:

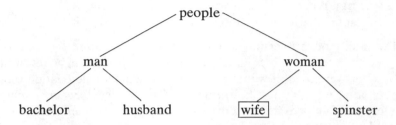

In this 'consists-of' configuration, items lower down are always instances of those immediately above. Thus, all wives are women and all women people. Put another way, the term *wife* can be said to be a *hyponym* of *woman*, and the term *woman* a *superordinate* of *wife*. This 'consists-of' relationship does not, of course, operate downwards on the scale; not all women are wives, and not all people are women. What this highlights in relation to the *Mirror* story, is the way in which the woman is identified through a more specific term taken from a lower level on the lexical scale. The same 'markedness' would surely not apply if the victim were a married man. Would we really expect a headline to read: *Crazed dog bites off husband's ear*? What further entrenches this markedness is that the woman's identity is mediated through her relationship to a man, through the fact of her being married. (Indeed, even the marriage ceremony itself encodes this asymmetry with its dictum 'I now pronounce you *man* and *wife*.') It is only by the time we reach the second paragraph of the text that a name, in the form of FN + LN, is provided and only then is any independent status accorded to her. Finding similar examples of asymmetrical lexical specificity in public discourse is not difficult. Here is an example from *The Liverpool Echo* of 1989:

MURDER POLICE IN BEDSIDE VIGIL ON SPINSTER, 78
A woman police officer was last night keeping a constant vigil at the hospital bedside of battered spinster, [Ethel Braithwaite].

(9 November, p. 3)

Lexical specificity in this example extends not only to the victims of the attack but to the 'woman police officer', where a common-gender phrase has been prefixed with an explicit gender marker. Regarding the use of 'spinster', we now have a woman defined through the *absence* of her relationship with a man, a tactic presumably designed to make her plight appear all the more pathetic. If the victim were an unmarried man, a transposition of relevant parts of the text to reflect a comparable degree of lexical specificity would look very strange:

MURDER POLICE IN BEDSIDE VIGIL ON BACHELOR, 78
. . . at the bedside of battered bachelor . . .

The oddity of this version reveals just how naturalized the type of language used in the original has become. Interestingly, even if *bachelor* were used, it would not carry the semantic derogation that often attaches to terms like *spinster* which designate specific female reference. Compare also the positive and negative evaluations that are ascribed to other relational opposites such as the following: master/mistress; patron/matron; governor/governess.

It might be objected that too much attention is being directed here towards trivial, inconsequential texts and that, furthermore, as journalists are often hard-pressed to meet publishing deadlines they cannot be held responsible for the odd 'sexist' slip here and there. Well, for a start, such commonplace 'trivial' texts are what characterize everyday discursive practices, the very practices which reflect in language gender differentation in society. Moreover, the fact that rushed or ill-prepared reports result in this type of asymmetry highlights the basic assumptions which are first brought into play in the construction of these reports. In fact, analysing a text which is constructed on the basis of 'the first thing that comes to mind' can often be more insightful than analysing one which has been carefully preplanned and revised.

Other principles of pragmatics can be employed productively in the explanation of language and gender. The concepts of semantic presupposition and implicature, which were discussed extensively in the previous chapter, provide useful instruments for investigating the gender-related assumptions which underlie texts. As a brief illustration only, consider the following extract from an advertisement which appeared in an edition of *Exchange Contracts*, a magazine produced by lawyers which purportedly offers advice to potential home-buyers. The advertisement is for 'booster showers' and the heading and opening text are reproduced below. The written text which makes up the advertisement is arranged in a columnar format against a background of squares resembling bathroom tiles:

GIVE

YOUR

WIFE

A HARD

TIME

IN THE

BATHROOM

Turn on a little excitement. Choose your shower pressure. The
Stuart Monsoon booster pump range makes it easy.

(November 1985, p. 28)

This certainly takes the concept of phallocentrism in language to a new
extreme! At the level of implicature, there is the crass play on the image
of male sexual arousal and the 'hardness' of the booster pump on offer.
This is not to mention the sinister connotations which accompany the
expression *to give someone a hard time*. In addition to this 'suggestive'
layer of the text's meaning, which hardly merits further discussion,
there are other, more insidious devices operating in the advertisement.
One way of tackling these is to consider, first of all, what preconditions
need to be met for the heading to function as an appropriate speech
act. In other words, to what type of idealized reader is the text
addressed? An examination of the presupposition-carrying items will
reveal that the text places this reader in a specific gendered and socio-
economic role. Existential presuppositions create a specific discourse
situation, operating very much in the manner of the advertisement
which was examined at the beginning of the previous chapter. For
example, the phrase 'your wife' constructs a subject position which is
to be occupied by a married man, one who, moreover, needs 'a little
excitement'. The specific targeting of a notional 'bread-winning head-
of-the-family' unfolds towards the end of the advertisement, which
runs:

Show this ad to your plumber. He'll know just what you're after.

The idealized reader is now one who is *au fait* with a plumber (common
gender again[9]) and who, by implication, has the responsibility and
wherewithal for maintenance of the home. The text thus presupposes
its own interactive context, establishing a subject position through
which real readers come to mediate. In this case, the subject position is
constructed as that of a married male, and, remembering that the
magazine targets potential house-buyers, as one who has financial
means and responsibility for decision making. Women as a group
occupy, by contrast, only an oblique relationship to the text and,

moreover, only a sexual relationship to men. Again, language use functions to reflect and support an ideological system.

The short analyses undertaken in this section have only been a few of a range of possible suggestions as to how the critical-linguistic analysis of gender bias in language might be undertaken. Aspects of the linguistic model not touched upon here, such as *modality*, can be equally productively applied to the issue. Indeed, some investigation into the gender-related use of modal constructions has already been undertaken (Coates 1987). The general thrust of the present critical linguistic analysis is to illustrate how language use functions as an index of a particular social order. By examining linguistic practice, we gain a point of entry into a societal system, a system, which feminists argue, is influenced if not controlled by a patriarchal order. The package of analytic procedures proposed in this section provides one means of denaturalizing these endemic and everyday discursive practices.

6.4 SUMMARY

After a brief introduction which broached the issue of gender and language, the chapter began a more extensive survey of the different strands of feminist-linguistic research on language. One particularly influential strand was identified as the 'determinist' approach of Dale Spender. Spender's view of language, heavily influenced by Whorfianism, proposes that the language system delineates the limits of our understanding, our perception of reality. Thus, sexist language creates a sexist world. However, in the light of linguistic evidence presented it was argued that this theoretical perspective is largely untenable and that if an adequate account was to be developed then a more theoretically sound model was required. The alternative model proposed was a 'functional' one, which postulates that the shape of a language is conditioned by the functions which it serves. This functional framework governed the analyses which were undertaken in section 6.3, where a range of texts were examined from a critical linguistic perspective. In keeping with the later chapters of this book generally, newspaper language and advertising language occupied a central position, although brief attention was also given to feminist-stylistic approaches to narrative fiction.

An underlying premise not only of this chapter but of all the chapters of the book has been that language use cannot be regarded as neutral, value-free or exempt from at least some 'angle of telling'. Rather, it is shaped by a mosaic of cultural assumptions, political beliefs and institutional practices – in other words, ideologies. The concern of this chapter has been to target the ideology of *gender* and to explore the mechanisms by which it is mediated and transmitted between producers and interpreters of texts. It is to be hoped that this discussion will have highlighted some of the ways in which linguistic habits can reflect and perpetuate deep-rooted sexist attitudes and assumptions.

NOTES AND FURTHER READING

1 The discussion here is not to be confused with that branch of sociolinguistics which is concerned with the study of 'sex differences in language use'. Although there is some overlap with the issues covered in this chapter, this type of sociolinguistic analysis is normally directed towards sex-related accent and dialect variation. The goals of such analyses, moreover, are often descriptions of the phonological and syntactic changes which influence particular linguistic systems. Patterns of sex differentiation in language use are thus viewed as important determinants of linguistic change. A useful collection of essays on this topic is Coates and Cameron (1988).

  The term gender is used in this chapter to refer to the socially determined distinction between male and female. Gender thus encompasses the various social, cultural and psychological meanings that attach to sexual identity. The term sex, on the other hand, is reserved for the straightforward biological distinction between women and men. The use of these terms is consonant with the way it is used in the body of research covered in this chapter. Although the term gender is also used elsewhere by linguists to refer to a particular grammatical category, no confusion between these uses should arise in the context of this chapter.

2 Spender is not alone in her call for a 're-invented' language. Feminists like Irigaray, Cixous and Kristeva, whose influences include Lacanian psycho-analysis, have attempted to write with explicitly 'female' voices. Their work is characterized by complex puns and word-play, interpretation of which often requires detailed knowledge of psychoanalysis, philosophy and major world languages. Specifically female innovations include 'Gyn/Ecology', 'The M(other) Tongue' and 'Herstory' (for 'History'). Not surprisingly, such coinages have been criticized for being elitist and obscure as well as being inaccurate linguistically. An excellent review of the 'female language' issue can be found in Ryder (1989).

3 A similar deterministic principle is evident in many educational-linguistic theories about non-standard language. Perhaps the most notorious of these is Bereiter and Engelmann's 'language-deficit' hypothesis. This hypothesis seeks to explain the relative academic underachievement of American black children in terms of the language they use. Bereiter and Engelmann contend that not only is Black English Vernacular (BEV) an unsuitable medium for education but it hinders the intellectual development of its users. Seen from this perspective, BEV is a 'basically nonlogical mode of expressive be-haviour' (Bereiter and Engelmann 1966: 112–3). The model of language which unfolds in the course of section 6.2 and the arguments presented against a strongly determinist view of language should demonstrate how ill-founded this language-deficit hypothesis actually is. An extremely influen-tial and convincing book which challenges the deficit theory head-on is

Labov (1972; *passim*, but especially pp.201–40). Reviews of the debate can be found in Trudgill (1983) and Wardhaugh (1986).

4 The term, attributed to Crystal, derives from the assumption that dictionaries always store single, correct and exhaustive meanings for individual words. Wilson (1990: 17–18) surveys the implications which the 'etymological fallacy' has for linguistic analysis.

5 The term 'antilanguage', which is used to refer to the specialized and often secret languages of alienated social groups, is introduced and discussed in Halliday (1978: 164–82). For an illuminating stylistic application of the concept, see Fowler's analysis of the use of antilanguages in Anthony Burgess's *A Clockwork Orange* and William Burroughs's *The Naked Lunch* (Fowler 1981: 142–61).

6 Another feminist-stylistic analysis which examines narrative fiction from the point of view of transitivity is Wareing (1990), which concentrates specifically on romance fiction, investigating the extent to which the passivity of the female protagonist is a characteristic of the genre. More general surveys of women's language within a stylistic perspective include Attridge (1989) and Milesi (1989). Attridge undertakes an analysis of the 'Penelope' episode from Joyce's *Ulysses*, supplementing this with a critique of some gender-biased literary criticism (including ostensibly 'feminist' criticism) on the episode. Milesi provides a rather erudite study of aspects of the language of Joyce's *Finnegan's Wake*, arguing that the novel 'covertly elaborates a grammar of sexual positions in male dominant society' (1989: 574). As Milesi writes the article very much in the manner of the novel he examines, his argument is less than transparent in places!

7 For obvious reasons, the name of the victim of the attack, which appears in the second paragraph of the opening text, has been altered. However, the FN + LN naming configuration has been preserved. The same principle extends to the extract from *The Liverpool Echo* which is discussed later.

8 The concept of *lexical specificity* and its pragmatic significance is explored in Cruse (1977).

9 It might reasonably be pointed out that it 'makes sense' to assume male reference in the case of a term like 'plumber' as the profession is almost exclusively a male preserve. Furthermore, if women are not treated as special cases, then there is a risk of ambiguity. Consider what reading would be made if the following headline did not contain gender specification:

WOMAN POACHER CONVICTED AT BUNCRANA COURT
(*The Derry Journal*, 21 June 1992, p. 23)

Had the noun 'poacher' not been so marked, then the 'natural' tendency is to assume male reference. This would be borne out by the fact that this is the first case of female poaching reported by this paper – indeed, part of the newsworthiness of the story rests on this aspect of the text. Yet this type of common-sense assumption is far removed from assumptions which are made without this type of warrant, such as the assumption, for example, that the reader of this book is male. The appropriation of common-gender terms which have no clear demographic or occupational differentiation is the real issue here and I have attempted to argue that such appropriation serves to reinforce the 'unmarked-male, marked-female' dichotomy which forms a substratum of meaning in many of the texts examined in this chapter.

7 Afterword

It's the way I tell 'em!
(catchphrase of standup comic, Frank Carson)

As part of their ongoing publicity campaign, the Australian Tourist Commission recently produced a poster displaying a map of the world headed by the slogan 'Australia: No Longer Down Under'. What is striking about the poster is that the map is inverted, so that the familiar layout of the continents and oceans is, literally, turned upside-down. The Antipodean countries, no longer 'down under', now preside over the globe from their commanding position in the north-west. On the other side of the Northern Hemisphere, South America becomes a formidable iceberg-shaped mass which rises from the equator, while Southern Africa moves to the central position that was once occupied by Europe. Europe itself becomes a minor cluster of states over-shadowed by what was originally North Africa and the Near East. Canada and the United States are marginalized to the extreme south east of the globe, a position initially allocated, of course, to the Antipodes. The Tourist Commission make their point in an extremely interesting way. By inverting a highly conventional representation of the earth, they invert our framework of perception. We are encouraged to see the earth in a way that is not 'normal', but in a way that has as much validity as the format through which it is conventionally presented. In more theoretical terms, it might be said that the standard presentation of the globe has become 'naturalized' as an everyday discursive practice. Yet, as the action of the Australian Tourist Commission shows, this practice can be 'denaturalized' by a simple act of inversion. Why, indeed, must Australia be viewed as 'down under' and not 'up over' – it is, after all, only a cartographical convention which dictates that we see the world in this way.

The 'linguistic map', and the way it is shaped by conventional discursive practices, has been one of the primary areas of investigation of this book. In every chapter, there has been a concerted effort to explain what has gone into a text, what creates its 'angle of telling' and what types of interpretative procedures are invoked in order to understand it. The models of language which have been used to explore this linguistic map have helped foreground the ways in which writers and speakers employ particular choices from the system of language, choices which, on the surface, often appear insignificant and unproblematic. Throughout the book, transpositions and rewrites have been used as a means of inverting the viewpoint adopted by a text. Whether this involves a transposition between narrative viewpoints in the manner outlined in chapter 3 or the kind of non-sexist rewrites developed in the previous chapter, both types of exercise provide a way of assessing how a text represents a set of choices from a pool of available options. This comparative activity throws into sharper relief the very features of language which might otherwise remain below the level of awareness and by denaturalizing language in this manner, we are able to develop a mechanism 'through which the strangeness of an obstinately familiar world can be detected' (Garfinkel 1967: 38).

As is the case with all stylistic and critical linguistic work, the programme outlined here is only a partial description of the ways in which texts mean. Many other linguistic models can be used productively in this type of investigation and the analysis can be extended to texts beyond the corpus examined over the course of this book. Regarding linguistic models, one line of enquiry that merits greater elaboration is the concept of *lexical specificity*. In the previous chapter, this concept was introduced simply as a means of highlighting some gender-related asymmetries in language use. It was able to explain systematically the 'markedness' which results from the practice of referring to women with terms taken from the lower points on lexical scales. The concepts of over- and underspecificity in lexis could easily be applied to narrative fiction, adding yet another dimension to our understanding of psychological point of view. In this way, it could supplement existing work on lexicalization and point of view such as that of Fowler (1986: 151–2).

With regard to the corpus of data, the models assembled over the course of the book can be usefully employed in the analysis of other sorts of discourse with the focus on other sorts of political issues. In the forefront of some recent critical linguistic analyses has been the discourse of racism (Seidel 1987; Threadgold 1988) while the media's representation of the AIDS pandemic has also been coming under scrutiny (Chuter and Seidel 1987). In keeping with the general critical linguistic rationale, this work engages with particular discourses not only with the aim of changing them but with a view to developing rival discourses which no longer encode and reflect the same ideologies.

The relationship between ideology and the process of communication also deserves closer inspection. In chapter 5, a pragmatic model of communication was developed in order to account for the manner in which meanings are organized and transmitted. It was stressed that communication functions as a two-way process built around a combination of 'core' meanings and non-truth-conditional inferences. Other branches of critical linguistic enquiry – especially those influenced by developments in deconstruction – place much greater emphasis on the role of the reader/hearer in the process of communication. Birch, for example, argues that 'meanings aren't simply "put into" a text by a writer/speaker, but are constructed by the reader/hearer' (1989: 21). He continues: You cannot make a statement about a particular idea *in* a text. What you can do is to make a statement about a particular idea that you have constructed *for* the text. (*ibid.*)

This strongly reader-centred view does problematize other critical linguistic tenets. In particular, it has implications for the practice whereby the analyst attempts to expose and resolve the ideologies which lurk insidiously within discourses. Birch himself upholds this 'crusading' spirit, arguing elsewhere that language is a form of social control and that textual analysis is the 'analysis of ideologically loaded structures and meanings, not of innocent, arbitrary, random structures' (1989: 167). If it is true that language can function in this ideologically repressive way and it is true that the reader has primary responsibility for the construction of meaning, then we are led to the problematic conclusion that readers actively construct their own repression. In other words, it does not matter what you put into a text, it is what is taken out that is important. So the social control which language exercises is really a product of reader predisposition, and is not anything that was 'meant' by the producer of the text. The stance adopted throughout this book has been that producers of texts *do* mean things when they say things, but that the negotiation of meanings is, in the words of Bakhtin (1981), a *dialogic* process. Communication is a necessarily two-sided act, where meaning is not under the exclusive control of any one side of the interaction. Writers, as Carter and Nash point out, have 'designs' on readers, and these designs, whether conscious or not, are manifested in stylistic choices (Carter and Nash 1990: 22). Certain kinds of readings may be encouraged and facilitated, while others may be suppressed or played down. What linguistic analysis can do is explore the ways in which these stylistic choices have been made. All this brings us on to the question of the position of the analyst relative to the interaction between producers and consumers of a text. A study of point of view in language must accommodate a point of view of its own. Moreover, writing *about* ideology does not carry immunity *from* ideology. Even the 'scientific' linguistic models which form the backbone of most of the chapters of the book have been developed within schools and traditions of linguistics which have their own cherished cultural and political preconceptions. Recognizing the subjectivity of the analyst in critical enquiry means that linguistic analyses themselves may be deconstructed within their own terms of reference. For example, in the fourth chapter I suggested how my own introduction to and interpretation of a news story might be analysed using the very model of language with which the chapter was concerned. Readers wishing to develop this 'meta-analysis' further may care to examine the ways in which *I* name the two antagonists in the study of naming practices in section 5.4.1, or the modal devices which *I* use in the analysis of modality in advertising carried out in section 5.4.2. Through this, a clearer picture of the ideological bias underlying this book may emerge and this will have been accomplished using the same analytic models and critical procedures which the book itself proposes.

And from here, what next? For a start, naturally occurring language forms a vast and heterogeneous field upon which the materials of this book can be tested. On the basis of this fieldwork, readers may decide that the linguistic 'toolkit' assembled here needs to be revised, or even replaced, but whatever the outcome, the analysis should have proved productive as a study in linguistic structure and an exercise in critical awareness. I hope it will have offered one means of seeing what writers get up to when they use language, whether they be an *avant-garde* novelist, a copywriter for a glossy magazine or a journalist for a local newspaper. If there is to be a clarion call, it is to look for the 'angle of telling', to explore the point of view in a text and, ultimately, to go forth and analyse!

References

Attridge, D. (1989) 'The writing of "Penelope" and the question of women's language', *Modern Fiction Studies* 35, 3: 543–64.

Austin, J. L. (1962) *How to do Things with Words*, Oxford: Clarendon Press.

Bakhtin, M. (1981) *The Dialogic Imagination* (ed. M. Holquist and C. Emerson), Austin: University of Texas Press.

Bal, M. (1977) *Narratologie: essais sur la signification narrative dans quatre romans modernes*, Paris: Klincksieck.

—— (1985) *Narratology: Introduction to the Theory of Narrative*, Toronto: University of Toronto Press.

Banfield, A. (1982) *Unspeakable Sentences*, New York: Routledge & Kegan Paul.

Barley, A. (1986) *Taking Sides: the Fiction of John le Carré*, Milton Keynes: Open University Press.

Barry, P. (1988) 'The limitations of stylistics', *Essays in Criticism* 38, 3: 175–89.

Barthes, R. (1975) 'An introduction to the structural analysis of narrative', *New Literary History* 4, 2: 237–72.

Bereiter, C. and S. Engellmann (1966) *Teaching Disadvantaged Children in the Pre-school*, Englewood Cliffs, NJ: Prentice Hall.

Berry, M. (1975) *Introduction to Systemic Linguistics: Structures and Systems*, vol. 1, London: Batsford.

Birch, D. (1989) *Language, Literature and Critical Practice: Ways of Analysing Text*, London: Routledge.

Birch, D. and M. O'Toole (eds), (1988) *Functions of Style*, London: Pinter.

Booth, W. (1961) *Rhetoric of Fiction*, Chicago: University of Chicago Press.

Brown, G and G. Yule (1983) *Discourse Analysis*, Cambridge: Cambridge University Press.

Brown, P. and S. Levinson (1986) *Politeness: Some Universals in Language Usage*, Cambridge: Cambridge University Press.

Brumfit, C. and R. Carter (eds) (1986) *Literature and Language Teaching*, Oxford: Oxford University Press.

Burton, D. (1982) 'Through glass darkly: through dark glasses', in R. Carter (ed.), *Language and Literature: an Introductory Reader in Stylistics*, London: Allen & Unwin, 194–214.

Cameron, D. (1985) *Feminism and Linguistic Theory*, London: Macmillan.

—— (1990) *The Feminist Critique of Language: a Reader*, London: Routledge.

Cameron, D. and E. Frazer (1987) *The Lust to Kill*, Cambridge: Polity Press.
Carroll, J.B. (ed.) (1956) *Language, Thought and Reality: Selected Writings of Benjamin Lee Whorf*, Cambridge MA: MIT Press.
Carter, R. (ed.) (1982) *Language and Literature: an Introductory Reader in Stylistics*, London: Allen & Unwin.
Carter, R. and W. Nash (1990) *Seeing Through Language*, Oxford: Blackwell.
Chilton, P. (ed.) (1985) *Language and the Nuclear Arms Debate: Nukespeak Today*, London: Pinter.
Chuter, C. and G. Seidel (1987) 'The AIDS campaign in Britain: a heterosexist disease' *Text* 7, 4: 347–62.
Clark, K. (1992) 'The linguistics of blame', in M. Toolan (ed.) *Language, Text and Context*, London: Routledge, 208–24.
Coates, J. (1983) *The Semantics of the Modal Auxiliaries*, London: Longman.
—— (1986) *Women, Men and Language*, London: Longman.
—— (1987) 'Epistemic modality and spoken discourse', *Transactions of the Philological Society 1987*, 110–31.
Coates, J. and D. Cameron (1988) *Women in their Speech Communities*, London: Longman.
Cook, G. (1992) *The Discourse of Advertising*, London: Routledge.
Coupland, N. (ed.) (1988) *Styles of Discourse*, London: Croom Helm.
Cruse, D. A. (1977) 'The pragmatics of lexical specificity', *Journal of Linguistics* 13: 153–64.
Culler, J. (1980) Foreword to G. Genette, *Narrative Discourse*, New York: Cornell University Press, 1 13.
—— (1983) *On Deconstruction. Theory and Criticism after Structuralism*, London: Routledge & Kegan Paul.
Dolezel, L. (1976) 'Narrative modalities', *Journal of Literary Semantics* 5, 1: 5–14.
Edmiston, W. (1989) 'Focalization and the first-person narrator: a revision of the theory', *Poetics Today* 10, 4: 729–44.
Ehrlich, S. (1990) *Point of View: a Linguistic Analysis of Literary Style*, London: Routledge.
Ervin-Tripp, S. (1972) 'Sociolinguistic rules of address,' in J. B. Pride and J. Holmes, *Sociolinguistics*, Harmondsworth: Penguin, 225–40.
Fairclough, N. (1989) *Language and Power*, London: Longman.
Fish, S. (1981) 'What is stylistics and why are they saying such terrible things about it?' D. Freeman (ed.), *Essays in Modern Stylistics*, London: Methuen, 53–78.
Fowler, R. (1981) *Literature as Social Discourse*, London: Batsford.
—— (1986) *Linguistic Criticism*, Oxford: Oxford University Press.
Fowler, R., B. Hodge, G. Kress, and T. Trew (eds) (1979) *Language and Control*, London: Routledge & Kegan Paul.
Fowler, R. and G. Kress (1979a) 'Rules and regulations', in R. Fowler, B. Hodge, G. Kress and T. Trew (eds), *Language and Control*, London: Routledge & Kegan Paul, 26–45.
—— (1979b) 'Critical linguistics', in R. Fowler, B. Hodge, G. Kress and T. Trew (eds), *Language and Control*, London: Routledge & Kegan Paul, 185–213.
Freeman, D. (ed.) (1981) *Essays in Modern Stylistics*, London: Methuen.
Garfinkel, H. (1967) *Studies in Ethnomethodology*, Englewood Cliffs, NJ: Prentice Hall.

Gazdar, G. (1979) *Pragmatics: Implicature, Presupposition and Logical Form*, New York: Academic Press.

Genette, G. (1980) *Narrative Discourse*, New York: Cornell University Press.

—— (1988) *Narrative Discourse Revisited*, New York: Cornell University Press.

Grice, H.P. (1975) 'Logic and conversation', in P. Cole and J. L. Morgan (eds) *Syntax and Semantics* vol. 3: *Speech Acts*, New York: Academic Press, 41–58.

Halliday, M. A. K. (1966) 'Descriptive linguistics in literary studies', in A. McIntosh and M. A. K. Halliday (eds) *Patterns of Language: Papers in General, Descriptive and Applied Linguistics*, London: Longman, 56–69.

—— (1970) 'Language structure and language function', in J. Lyons (ed.), *New Horizons in Linguistics*, Harmondsworth: Penguin, 140–65.

—— (1971) 'Linguistic function and literary style: an inquiry into the language of William Golding's *The Inheritors*', in S. Chatman (ed.), *Literary Style: a Symposium*, New York: Oxford University Press, 330–68. Reprinted in D. Freeman (ed.), *Essays in Modern Stylistics*, London: Methuen, 1981, 325–60.

—— (1978) *Language as Social Semiotic*, London: Edward Arnold.

—— (1985) *An Introduction to Functional Grammar*, London: Edward Arnold.

Heller, E. (1974) *Kafka*, Glasgow: Fontana.

Henkel, J. (1988) 'Speech-act theory revisited: rule notions and reader oriented criticism', *Poetics* 17, 6: 505–30.

Hickey, L. (ed.) (1989) *Pragmatics and Style*, London: Routledge.

Hodge, R. and G. Kress (1988) *Social Semiotics*, Cambridge: Polity Press.

Hollander, J. (1987) 'Dallying nicely with words', in N. Fabb, D. Attridge, A. Durant and C. MacCabe (eds) *The Linguistics of Writing: Arguments between Language and Literature*, Manchester: Manchester University Press, 123–34.

Honey, J. (1983) *The Language Trap* (Kay-Shuttleworth Papers on Education, 3), Middlesex: Council for National Academic Standards.

Kennedy, C. (1982). 'Systemic grammar and its use in literary analysis', in R. Carter (ed.), *Language and Literature: an Introductory Reader in Stylistics*, London: Allen & Unwin, 82–99.

Kress, G. (1989) 'History and language: towards a social account of linguistic change', *Journal of Pragmatics* 13, 3: 445–66.

Kress, G. and R. Hodge (1979) *Language as Ideology*, London: Routledge & Kegan Paul.

Labov, W. (1972) *Language in the Inner City*, Philadelphia: University of Pennsylvania Press.

Lakoff, R. (1975) *Language and Woman's Place*, New York: Harper & Row.

Leech, G. (1983) *Principles of Pragmatics*, London: Longman.

Leech, G. and M. Short (1981) *Style in Fiction*, London: Longman.

Levin, H. (1972) 'Observations on the style of Ernest Hemingway', in H. Babb (ed.), *Essays in Stylistic Analysis*, New York: Harcourt Brace Jovanovich, 321–37.

Levinson, S. (1983) *Pragmatics*, Cambridge: Cambridge University Press.

Lyons, J. (1977) *Semantics*, 2 vols, Cambridge: Cambridge University Press.

McHale, B. (1983) 'Linguistics and poetics revisited', *Poetics Today* 4, 1: 17–45.

McKenzie, M. (1987) 'Free indirect speech in a fettered insecure society', *Language and Communication* 7, 2: 153–9.

Milesi, L. (1989) 'Toward a female grammar of sexuality: the de/recomposition of "Storiella as she is syung"', *Modern Fiction Studies* 35, 3: 569–86.

Montgomery, M. (1986a) *An Introduction to Language and Society,* London: Methuen.

—— (1986b) 'Language as power: a critical review of *Studies in the Theory of Ideology* by J. B. Thompson', *Media, Culture and Society* 8: 41–64.

Nair, R.B., R. Carter and M. Toolan (1988) 'Clines of metaphoricity, and creative metaphors as situated risk-taking', *Journal of Literary Semantics* 17, 1: 20–40.

Nash, W. (1990) *Language in Popular Fiction,* London: Routledge.

Nelles, W. (1990) 'Getting focalization into focus', *Poetics Today* 11, 2: 365–82.

Page, N. (1973) *Speech in the English Novel,* London: Longman.

Palmer, F. (1986) *Mood and Modality,* Cambridge: Cambridge University Press.

Pascal, R. (1977) *The Dual Voice,* Manchester: Manchester University Press.

Pateman, T. (1981) 'Linguistics as a branch of critical theory', *UEA Papers in Linguistics* 14–15: 1–29.

—— (1989) 'Pragmatics in semiotics: Bakhtin/Voloshinov', *Journal of Literary Semantics* 18, 3: 203–16.

Perkins, M. (1983) *Modal Expressions in English,* London: Frances Pinter.

Peterson, R. K. (1974) *Hemingway Direct and Oblique,* The Hague: Mouton.

Pilkington, A. (1990) 'A relevance theoretic view of metaphor', *Parlance* 2, 2: 102–17.

Porter, J. A. (1986) 'Pragmatics for criticism', *Poetics,* 15, 3: 243–57.

Pound, E. (1960) *ABC of Reading,* London: Faber.

Pratt, M.L. (1977) *Toward a Speech Act Theory of Literary Discourse,* Bloomington: Indiana University Press.

Richardson, K. (1987) 'Critical linguistics and textual diagnosis', *Text* 7: 145–63.

Rimmon-Kenan, S. (1983) *Narrative Fiction: Contemporary Poetics,* London: Methuen.

Roeh, I. and R. Nir (1990) 'Speech presentation in the Israel radio news: ideological constraints and rhetorical strategies', *Text* 10, 3: 225–44.

Ryder, M. (1989) 'Feminism and style: still looking for the quick fix', *Style* 23, 4: 530–44.

Sapir, E. (1929) 'The status of linguistics as a science', *Language* 5: 207–14.

Scholes, R. and R. Kellogg (1966) *The Nature of Narrative,* New York: Oxford University Press.

Seidel, G. (1987) 'The white discursive order: the British New Right's discourse on cultural racism with particular reference to the Salisbury Review', in I. Zavala, M. Diaz-Diocaretz and T. Van Dijk (eds) *Approaches to Discourse, Poetics and Psychiatry,* Amsterdam: John Benjamins, 39–66.

Sharrock, W. and D. Anderson (1981) 'Language, thought and reality, again', *Sociology* 15: 287–93.

Shen, D. (1988) 'Stylistics, objectivity and convention', *Poetics* 17, 3: 221–38.

Short, M. (1988) 'Speech presentation, the novel and the press', in W. Van Peer (ed.), *The Taming of the Text: Explorations in Language, Literature and Culture,* London: Routledge, 61–81.

—— (ed.) (1989) *Reading, Analysing and Teaching Literature*, London: Longman.

Simpson, P. (1987) 'The narrative structure of Hemingway's *The Old Man and the Sea*', *Belfast Working Papers in Language and Linguistics* 9: 167–227.

—— (1988) 'The transitivity model', *Critical Studies in Mass Communication* 5, 2: 166–72.

—— (1990) 'Modality in literary-critical discourse', in W. Nash (ed.) *The Writing Scholar*, Newbury Park: Sage, 63–94.

—— (1992) 'The pragmatics of nonsense: towards a stylistics of *Private Eye's* Colemanballs', in M. Toolan (ed.), *Language, Text and Context: Essays in Stylistics*, London: Routledge, 281–305.

Sinclair, J. McH. (1966) 'Taking a poem to pieces', in R. Fowler (ed.) *Essays on Style and Language*, London: Routledge & Kegan Paul, 68-81.

Spender D. (1980) *Man Made Language*, London: Routledge.

Sperber, D. and D. Wilson (1986) *Relevance: Communication and Cognition*, Oxford: Blackwell.

Spolsky, E. (1988) 'The limits of literal meaning', *New Literary History* 19, 2: 419–40.

Stubbs, M. (1983) *Discourse Analysis: the Sociolinguistic Analysis of Natural Language*, Oxford: Blackwell.

—— (1986) '"A matter of prolonged fieldwork": notes towards a modal grammar of English', *Applied Linguistics* 7, 1: 1–25.

Thompson, J. B. (1984) *Studies in the Theory of Ideology*, Cambridge: Polity Press.

—— (1986) 'Language, ideology and the media: a response to Martin Montgomery', *Media, Culture and Society* 8: 65–79.

Threadgold, T. (1988) 'Stories of race and gender: an unbounded discourse', in D. Birch and M. O'Toole (eds), *Functions of Style*, London: Pinter, 169–204.

Toolan, M. (1988) *Narrative: a Critical Linguistic Introduction*, London: Routledge.

—— (1990) *The Stylistics of Fiction: a Literary-Linguistic Approach*, London: Routledge.

—— (ed.) (1992) *Language, Text and Context*, London: Routledge.

Trew, T. (1979). 'Theory and ideology at work', in R. Fowler, B. Hodge, G. Kress and T. Trew (eds), *Language and Control*, London: Routledge & Kegan Paul, 94–116.

Trudgill, P. (1983) *Sociolinguistics*, Harmondsworth: Penguin.

Uspensky, B. (1973) *A Poetics of Composition*, trans. V. Zavarin and S. Wittig, Berkeley: University of California Press.

Van Peer, W. (ed.) (1988) *The Taming of the Text: Explorations in Language, Literature and Culture*, London: Routledge.

Voloshinov, V. I. (1973) *Marxism and the Philosophy of Language*, trans. L. Matejka and I. R. Tutinik, New York: Seminar Press.

Wardhaugh, R. (1986) *An Introduction to Sociolinguistics*, Oxford: Blackwell.

Wareing, S. (1990) 'Women in fiction – stylistic modes of reclamation', *Parlance* 2, 2: 72–85.

Weber, J. J. (1984) 'Deontic, axiological and epistemic distance in Graham Greene's *The Honorary Consul*', *Nottingham Linguistic Circular*, 13: 146–56.

—— (1986) 'Inferential and evocational processing in literary texts', *Grazer Linguistische Studien* 26: 173–85.

—— (1989) 'Dickens's social semiotic', in R. Carter and P. Simpson (eds) *Language, Discourse and Literature: a Reader in Discourse Stylistics*, London: Unwin Hyman, 94–111.

Wilson, D. (1975) *Presuppositions and Non-Truth-Conditional Semantics*, New York: Academic Press.

Wilson, J. (1990) *Politically Speaking*, Oxford: Blackwell.

Index

active sentences 86
actor role, in material processes 89, 95, 97–8
additive conjunctions, and negative Narratorial modality 68
address, terms of 140–1
advertising language: and deontic modality 48; dialogic framework 151; and implicit assumptions 155; and linguistic conundrums 119, 131–2; pragmatic analysis 147–56; and pragmatic presupposition 128; as 'staggered' discourse 121; use of frames 158n
agency: inanimate 112; meronymic and holonymic 110, 112; in news reporting 105–9; removal of 114–15, 170; role in transitivity 92–5
alienation, and negative: Narratorial modality 65–6, 67; 'alteration' (Genette), and transition between modes 82
analyst, relation to text 115–16, 181–2
'and', pragmatic functions of 128
androcentrism 161–2
angle of telling see point of view
antilanguages 166, 177n
artificial intelligence (AI) 122, 158n
attribute role, in relational processes 92, 95
Attridge, D., on women's language 178n
Austin, J.L., theory of speech acts and illocutionary force 157n

Australian Tourist Commission, inversion of world map 179
author: distinction from narrator 64–5; and Free Direct modes 25, 27; and modality 41, 53; omniscience of 11–12, 53; point of view of 43; see also narrator

backshifted verbs 28–9, 35–6
Bakhtin, M., on dialogic process of meaning 181
Bal, M., on Genette 44n
Banfield, Ann, Unspeakable Sentences 21, 35–8
Banville, John, The Book of Evidence 29, 58–9, 60
Barley, A., on Conrad and le Carré 117n
Barry, P., anti-stylistic line 117n
Barthes, Roland, on narrative 31
BBC TV News, account of Shorthouse trial 106–8, 115
Beckett, Samuel 46, 83; Molloy 51–2, 58, 60, 75, 76–7, 138–9; Watt 77–8
Bennett, Arnold, Riceyman Steps 42–3, 65
Bereiter, C. and S. Engelmann, 'language-deficit' hypothesis 177n
Berry, M., on transitivity 117n
bias: gender see gender bias in language; political 106, 107–8, 114–16
Birch, D., on construction of meanings 181